# Infrastructural Lives

## Urban infrastructure in context

# Edited by Stephen Graham and Colin McFarlane

Routledge
Taylor & Francis Group

LONDON AND NEW YORK

from Routledge

PLYMOUTH UNIVERSITY
9009376865

First published 2015
by Routledge
2 Park Square, Milton Park, Abingdon, Oxon, OX14 4RN

and by Routledge
711 Third Avenue, New York, NY 10017

*Routledge is an imprint of the Taylor & Francis Group, an informa business*

*British Library Cataloguing in Publication Data*
A catalogue record for this book is available from the British Library

*Library of Congress Cataloging-in-Publication Data*
Infrastructural lives : urban infrastructure in context / edited by Stephen Graham and Colin McFarlane.
pages cm
Includes bibliographical references and index.
1. Sociology, Urban. 2. Urban economics. 3. Municipal services. 4. Infrastructure (Economics)—Social aspects. I. Graham, Stephen, 1965- II. McFarlane, Colin, 1979-
HT151.I536 2014
307.76—dc23
2013047618

ISBN13: 978-0-415-74851-3 (hbk)
ISBN13: 978-0-415-74853-7 (pbk)
ISBN13: 978-1-315-77509-8 (ebk)

Typeset in Goudy
by FiSH Books Ltd, Enfield

MIX
Paper from responsible sources
FSC
www.fsc.org    FSC® C013604

Printed and bound by CPI Group (UK) Ltd, Croydon, CR0 4YY

*Infrastructural Lives* is the first book to describe the everyday experience and politics of urban infrastructures. It focuses on a range of infrastructures in both the Global South and the Global North. The book examines how day-to-day experience and perception of infrastructure provide a new and powerful lens to view ͺecologies. An interdisciͺrchers examines critical ͺcontexts.

ͺitics in Mumbai, Kampala ͺispossession of Palestinian ͺin the run-up to the 2014 ͺectively operate as 'infraͺntative experiments with

by a shared sense of infraͺ?, but as a complex social ͺparticular kinds of action ͺr academics, researchers,

ͺat Newcastle University's School of Architecture, Planning and Landscape, UK. His research addresses the complex links between urban places and mobilities, infrastructures, militarization, surveillance, security and war. His books include *Telecommunications and the City*, *Splintering Urbanism* (both with Simon Marvin), *Disrupted Cities: When infrastructures fail* and *Cities Under Siege: The new military urbanism*. His next book, *Vertical: The politics of up and down*, is currently in preparation.

**Colin McFarlane** is Reader in Urban Geography at Durham University, UK. His research focuses on the experience and politics of urban infrastructure, especially in relation to informal settlements. His recent research has focused on the politics of sanitation in informal settlements in Mumbai, India. His books include *Learning the City: Knowledge and translocal assemblage*, *Urban Navigations: Politics, space and the city in South Asia* (with Jonathan Shapiro Anjaria) and *Urban Informalities: Reflections on the formal and informal* (with Michael Waibel).

# Contents

# Figures

# Contributors

**Harriet Bulkeley** is a Professor in the Department of Geography, Durham University, UK. Her research focuses on the processes and politics of environmental governance. Her recent books include *Cities and Climate Change* (Routledge, 2013), *Governing Climate Change* (Routledge, 2010), *Cities and Low Carbon Transitions* (Routledge, 2011), and *Transnational Climate Governance* (CUP, 2014). She is currently involved in researching the politics and practice of smart grids in the UK, low-carbon transitions in southern Africa, and continuing work on urban responses to climate change. She is a member of the DECC Defra Social Science Advisory Group and has undertaken commissioned research for the Joseph Rowntree Foundation, Friends of the Earth, UN-Habitat and the World Bank.

**Vanesa Castán Broto** is a lecturer at the Development Planning Unit, University College London, UK. Her research focuses on how sustainability aspirations are shaping modern societies, particularly in relation to climate change and energy transitions. She has developed comparative analyses of urbanisation, energy and innovation in different cities around the world, including Tuzla (Bosnia and Herzegovina), Bangalore (India), Monterrey (Mexico) and Maputo (Mozambique).

**Mariana Cavalcanti** (PhD in Social/Cultural Anthropology, University of Chicago, USA, 2007) is Associate Professor at the School of Social Sciences and History, Center for Research and Documentation for the Contemporary History of Brazil (CPDOC-FGV-RJ). She specializes in urban anthropology, and is interested in questions related to housing, urbanism and public policy, and recently co-directed the documentary film *Favela Fabril* (2012, 49'). She is also co-founder and board member of Casa Fluminense, a civil society association aimed at deepening democracy and reducing inequalities in the Metropolitan Area and the State of Rio de Janeiro.

**Renu Desai** is the Coordinator of the Centre for Urban Equity, CEPT University, Ahmedabad, India. Her research examines urban informality and urban transformation in Indian cities, with a focus on questions of equitable development and urban citizenship. She is co-editor of *Urbanizing Citizenship: Contested Spaces in Indian Cities* (New Delhi: Sage 2012).

**Stephen Graham** is Professor of Cities and Society at Newcastle University's School of Architecture, Planning and Landscape, UK. His research addresses the complex links between urban places and mobilities, infrastructures, militarization, surveillance, security and war. His books include *Telecommunications and the City, Splintering Urbanism* (both with Simon Marvin), *Disrupted Cities: When Infrastructures Fail* and *Cities Under Siege: The New Military Urbanism*. His next book, *Vertical: The Politics of Up and Down* is currently in preparation.

**Mike Hodson** is Research Fellow at the Sustainable Consumption Institute, University of Manchester, UK. Mike holds degrees from the University of Sheffield, UK; City University, London, UK; and the University of Salford, UK. His research interests focus on scale, geography and transitions to low-carbon economies. He has developed projects around this agenda funded by the European Commission, UK research councils and sub-national government. Mike has published and presented widely on various aspects of this agenda.

**Maria Kaika** holds a PhD from Oxford University, UK, and an MA in Architecture from the National Technical University of Athens, Greece. She is Professor at the University of Manchester, UK and co-Editor of the *International Journal of Urban and Regional Research*. Her research focuses on urban political ecology, land rent, land financialization, urban imaginaries, and iconic architecture. She is author of: *City of Flows: Modernity, Nature and the City* (Routledge, 2005) and co-editor (with N. Heynen and E. Swyngedouw) of *In the Nature of Cities: Urban Political Ecology and the Metabolism of Urban Environments* (Routledge, 2006).

**Simon Marvin** is Carillion Chair of Low Carbon Cities and Communities Department of Geography, University of Durham, UK. Simon obtained his degrees from the University of Hull, UK; the University of Sheffield, UK; and the Open University, UK. His research interests focus on the changing relations between cities, regions and infrastructure networks in a period of resource constraint, institutional restructuring and climate change. His research has been funded by the ESRC, the EPSRC, international research foundations, the European Commission, commercial funders, and many public agencies.

**Colin McFarlane** is Reader in Urban Geography at Durham University, UK. His research focuses on the experience and politics of urban infrastructure, especially in relation to informal settlements. His recent research has focused on the politics of sanitation in informal settlements in Mumbai. His books include *Learning the City: Knowledge and Translocal Assemblage, Urban Navigations: Politics, Space and the City in South Asia* (with Jonathan Shapiro Anjaria), and *Urban Informalities: Reflections on the Formal and Informal* (with Michael Waibel).

**Vyjayanthi Rao** is an anthropologist who works on cities after globalization, with particular attention to the intersection of art, design and planning. She has worked extensively in Mumbai, India, and has recently completed a book manuscript entitled *Speculative City: Infrastructure and Complexity in Global Mumbai*.

**Omar Jabary Salamanca** is an Urban Geographer and Research Fellow at the Middle East and North Africa Research Group (MENARG) at Ghent University, Belgium. His research lies at the intersection of urban studies, settler colonialism, political economy and Middle East studies.

**Rob Shaw** is a Teaching Fellow at Durham University, UK. His research explores how subjectivity emerges from the relationship between bodies and their environment, focusing on the urban night. He received his PhD in 2012. His 2014 publications explore topics such as assemblage, atmosphere, and subjectivity production under neoliberalism.

**AbdouMaliq Simone** is an urbanist with particular interest in emerging forms of collective life across cities of the so-called Global South. Simone is presently Research Professor at the University of South Australia and Visiting Professor of Urban Studies at the African Centre for Cities, University of Cape Town, South Africa. Key publications include: *In Whose Image?: Political Islam and Urban Practices in Sudan* (University of Chicago Press, 1994), *For the City Yet to Come: Urban Change in Four African Cities* (Duke University Press, 2004), and *City Life from Jakarta to Dakar: Movements at the Crossroads* (Routledge, 2009), and the forthcoming, *Drawing the City Near: Life and Relational Politics in Jakarta* (University of Minnesota Press).

**Stephanie Terreni Brown** is a Research Fellow at Edinburgh University, UK. Her recently submitted PhD explores the infrastructure of, and access to, sanitation in Kampala, Uganda. She is currently working on a comparative project that is looking at 'off grid' infrastructures in Scotland, India, Papua New Guinea, and Uganda.

# Foreword

This timely book is sure to become a definitive work on the now growing literature on urban infrastructure. It arrives at a moment when a variety of scholars, across a range of disciplines, have brought the topic of infrastructure out of the expert seclusion of policy, engineering and technology development into the more open daylight of anthropology, sociology, political science, and urban studies.

This rendering visible of a normally hidden reality is an interesting challenge in the case of infrastructure, which achieves its largest effects by being out of the way, taken for granted and sometimes deliberately hidden. Why is it normally a hidden part of the modern metropolis? Because the complex of pipes, wires, tubes, flows, fluids, gases, smells, energies and miasmas that constitute urban infrastructure is often dirty, dangerous and ugly. They enable everyday life but are also threats to it.

The development of invisible infrastructure may be claimed as the defining characteristic of the modern city, for infrastructure has always existed in cities, but it has usually been in the visible midst of the city, on its very surface, in the form of garbage pits, waste-filled waterways, gas-lit lamps, and other forms of energy management and disposal that hindered the life of the urban surface as much as they aided it. The hiding of this infrastructure, through technologies of excavation, burial, aerial transmission, offshore processes and subterranean technologies is the single biggest shared property of what we may call the urban civilizing process. The authors in this volume bring to the study of this new reality the rich tradition of interest in the technologies of everyday life that the historians of the French Annales School brought to agrarian and regional life in the first half of the twentieth century. And this volume thus has the same sensory excitement as the best work of those early French pioneers, for it connects the problems of everyday life to the tectonics of economy, power and class.

The historians of the Annales School may now be criticized for an uneven interest in the ways in which material life generated its own economies of class, caste and power. This criticism is not likely to be made by readers of the present volume who will recognize, in these numerous rich studies, that many urban populations negotiate the politics of the relationship between the visible and invisible properties of infrastructure through conflict, struggle and contention.

Indeed, urban politics is often incomprehensible without understanding the geography of infrastructure.

The analytical lens that gives this volume its originality is to make infrastructure more visible by tackling it not as a dimension of urban technology but as a dimension of urban everyday life. The interest in everyday life, which also entered the social sciences a few decades ago, is only now beginning to enter urban cities and this volume is a rich marker of this conjuncture. The editors and the authors recognize the challenge of this point of entry, for the most elusive quality of everyday life is that it appears unremarkable but is in fact the product of considerable effort, labor and investment. This aspect of everyday life has generally escaped the net of social theory that has tended to mistake the ordinariness of the everyday for some sort of naturalness or spontaneous social combustion. The truth is that the everyday is both practiced and produced. It takes a lot of work to turn the everyday into the taken for granted. And negotiations with infrastructure, with water, power, waste and transport, are major sites of the production of the everyday. And it is when these sites break down, tear or collapse that they reveal not only the weaknesses of technology but also the fragilities of those agreements and adjustments that constitute the fabric of predictability in social life.

Thus, to study infrastructure is, in truth, to study the technologies and techniques through which the visible and the invisible are separated, connected and managed in the social life of cities. Because cities are the sites of both technological and social density, this negotiation is highly prone to wear and tear, to entropy and to accidents. It is to these breakdowns that we owe our richest insights about the infrastructure of the everyday. And it is this fragility of the social that this volume so richly brings to light.

Arjun Appadurai
New York
October 2013

# Introduction

## Stephen Graham and Colin McFarlane

Urban infrastructure has become a major focus of recent debates on the rapid urbanisation of our planet. Few attempts, however, have been made to examine the nature, politics and experience of contemporary urban lives as everyday *infrastructural experience*. Much has been said about how complexes of communication, sanitation, energy, transport, and so on are built and maintained; how they are restructuring to become more 'splintered' in ways that sustain more socially polarised cities; how when infrastructure collapses it reveals the hidden materialities of cities; and how the infrastructure of cities works to imbricate technology, culture, nature and politics in subtle and important ways. Rather strangely, however, the people of the world's burgeoning cities, and the ways in which they experience urban lives that intermesh with, and are sustained by, the complexes of infrastructure, are often largely invisible in these accounts.

*Infrastructural Lives* seeks to help rectify this neglect. The book brings together a wide-ranging set of accounts of how complexes of infrastructure mediate everyday urban life. These are drawn from an influential group of leading urban scholars working in a wide variety of urban, national and disciplinary contexts. The perspectives which follow address water, sanitation, and waste politics in Mumbai, Kampala and Tyneside. They excavate the use of infrastructure to dispossess Palestinian communities. And they explore the pacification of Rio's favelas in the run-up to the 2014 World Cup, how people's bodies and lives effectively operate as 'infrastructure' in many major cities of the Global South, and the tentative experiments with low-carbon infrastructures. These diverse cases and perspectives are connected by a shared sense of infrastructure not just as a 'thing', a 'system', or an 'output', but as a complex social and technological *process* that enables – or disables – particular kinds of action in the city. It is this process, above all else, that a focus on everyday life reveals about infrastructure – its emergence as a set of achievements, operations, and platforms brought into being in particular ways at certain times, and always subject to different forms of (attempted) control, power and exclusion.

*Infrastructural Lives* thus examines how geographies, rhythms, politics, economies, cultures, natures and power relations constitute the everyday urban experience in the production and reproduction of urban infrastructures. A focus on the everyday is a powerful means of revealing the rhythms that in large part constitute urban life, inequality and change (see Graham and Thrift, 2007; Rigg, 2007). The everyday is both a key domain through which practices are regulated and normalised as well as an arena for negotiation, resistance and potential for difference.

There is, of course, a rich and varied literature on the importance of urban infrastructure to urban politics, economies, cultures, and ecologies, and much of this literature, of course, informs and inspires the book, as we will see. This includes: the emergence of privatised infrastructures (Graham and Marvin, 2001; Page, 2005; Shove et al., 2007; Guy et al., 2011); the role of large technical systems in urban and regional development; the growing importance of automated and 'smart' infrastructures that enable particular forms of mutual user–infrastructure relations (Thrift and French, 2002; Kitchen and Dodge, 2011; Furlong, 2011); urban ecological debates (Hodson and Marvin, 2009, 2010); the politics of what Keil et al. (2011) call the 'in-between city' that's neither city nor suburb; the removal of infrastructure through urban demolition or militarisation (Coward, 2008; Graham, 2010a); the mutual imbrications of technology and urban experience as manifestations of 'cyborg urbanization' (Gandy, 2005); or the metabolic transformation of urban life through changing alignments of bodies, physical networks, social systems, and commodification (Luke, 2003; Swyngedouw, 2004; Heynen et al., 2006; Loftus, 2007, 2012); for reviews, see Coutard (2008), Furlong (2011), and McFarlane and Rutherford (2008).

But across this multifaceted and critical set of debates, there has been relatively little explicit consideration of how a focus on the everyday might inform our conception of urban infrastructures and their role in urban production, negotiation and contestation. While infrastructure debates have made important contributions to how we understand the 'supply-side' dimensions of infrastructure, there has been surprisingly little about how people produce, live with, contest, and are subjugated to or facilitated by infrastructure.

## Motivating questions

The discussions that follow are concerned with four related questions. These focus, respectively, (1) on knowing infrastructure; (2) on being excluded from infrastructure; (3) on producing and managing infrastructure; and (4) on experimenting with infrastructure. First, how does a focus on the everyday help us to understand how urbanites know and use infrastructure? Second, how do processes of urban violence, pacification and dispossession through infrastructure impact everyday urban lives? Third, what everyday practices and discourses allow the production and management of urban waste infrastructure? And, finally, how do forms of everyday infrastructure adjustment and experimentation emerge from and reshape everyday urban life?

Why these four? First, and straightforwardly, these four areas represent key vectors of urban infrastructural research. They are not, of course, the only important questions that need to be asked about everyday urban infrastructures, but they do constitute concerns of serious significance. The question of how residents – or, indeed, researchers – come to know and experience infrastructure is one important challenge for our understanding of how infrastructures impact on and are shaped by urbanism. The question of how violence, pacification and dispossession affect everyday life is critical and one that has become increasingly important as infrastructures continue to be securitised, militarised, splintered and privatised globally (Graham and Marvin, 2001; Coward, 2008; Graham, 2010b). The question of waste production and management has been critical to understandings of infrastructures as metabolic processes (Swyngedouw, 2004; Gandy, 2005; Heynen et al., 2006), but there have been few attempts to interrogate the everyday dimensions of this. And the question of how infrastructures emerge through practices of experimentation and adjustment is becoming increasingly important, especially to accounts of emerging urban climate change initiatives (Hodson and Marvin, 2010), but here we ask how these practices operate in everyday life across a variety of contexts.

Second, and equally straightforwardly, the aim of this volume is to show that the relations between urban infrastructure and everyday life vary considerably across contexts. The chapters bring together cases that cut across the Global North–South divide, and which include cities as distinct as Bangalore, Jakarta, Kampala, Mumbai, Ramallah, Rio de Janeiro, and Newcastle in the UK; cases written by geographers, anthropologists and sociologists. In each context, the nature of the everyday under consideration is distinct, from extremely impoverished residents struggling to respond to urban infrastructure demolition in Mumbai, to discursive constructions of everyday sanitation normality in European or African urban contexts, and forms of elite maintenance in gated housing in Bangalore. Across the cases, the resources with which the everyday can be produced, or challenges responded to, or new formulations developed and politicised, vary considerably according to vectors of socio-economic and cultural position.

And third, and following this, a key aim with this book is to consider multiple different ways of posing the relations between infrastructure and the everyday. Some in the collection are interested in how infrastructures produce certain forms of everyday normality (e.g. Kaika in Chapter 6), others in how the politics of infrastructure can exclude and render a whole set of new responses in everyday life (e.g. Graham, Desai and McFarlane in Chapter 3; Cavalcanti in Chapter 4; Jabary Salamanca in Chapter 5; Hodson and Marvin in Chapter 10). Some are interested in how the everyday management of infrastructure is pieced together across a wide variety of often highly contingent actors (e.g. Shaw in Chapter 8; Castán Broto and Bulkeley in Chapter 9; Rao in Chapter 2), others by how everyday rhythms and connections reshape urban infrastructure for particular kinds of action (e.g. Simone in Chapter 1), and others still in the ways in which infrastructure coping strategies can be thought of as simultaneously political acts (e.g. Brown in Chapter 7).

The rest of this Introduction will set in context the chapters of the book according to these four themes.

## Part I Knowing infrastructure

How might we understand the relations between infrastructure and urban life? For AbdouMaliq Simone in Chapter 1, the main starting point is the social infrastructures that residents develop and use to make viable forms of inhabitation. He asks: how do the majority of urban residents in the postcolonial urban world put together ways of inhabiting the city? Drawing on a great deal of his work, especially his research, activism and community organisation in Jakarta, Simone identifies 'relational infrastructures' as critical here, i.e. the relations that constitute the constraints and possibilities of inhabitation. These relations enable movement, and are 'articulated in various forms in order to construct circulations of bodies, resources, affect and information' (p. 18). Simone uses the grammar of finance capital to describe the operation of relational infrastructures for urban residents. He writes:

> the 'devices' associated with the incursions and re-compositions engineered by global capital – such as speculative finance, cut-and-paste modularisation of spatial products, translocal configurations of production mechanisms, and the privileging of surface manoeuvres emptied of historical reference – also are appropriated by collective actors as a means to substantiate practices of creating space and opportunities that ensue from different logics and aspirations.

For example, people engage in speculative transactions through which they attempt to anticipate the actions of others (who in turn may be anticipating their actions), and they often try to steer transactions to develop new opportunities, for instance, a new contact, network or job opportunity. Or, to take a different example, residents will hedge their bets by becoming incrementally involved in multiple projects in the hope that some might work, whether a small enterprise or association to a political party, for instance. Infrastructure emerges here as a set of transactions that encounter one another in often unexpected ways. It is 'the materialisation of anticipation – that sense of timing of knowing how to make a "next move", of the incremental accretion of capacity and possibility'. For Simone, these are not simply resources for coping, adapting and improving circumstances, they are also 'the tools through which political imaginations and claims are exerted'. For instance, relational infrastructures are often subject to, and have to play carefully alongside, state regulations, eviction, and dispossession, while attempting to secure claims to space or activities in constricted and competitive environments.

Simone's emphasis on infrastructures as relational is not itself new – it is a position taken up in different ways by a range of work on infrastructure that emphasises the mutual imbrications of technology, nature, and city in the production, maintenance and contestation of infrastructure (e.g. Graham and Marvin, 2001; Gandy, 2005; Loftus, 2007, 2012). What is novel here is Simone's emphasis – building on his previous work (e.g. 2004, 2008, 2010) – on how everyday interactions render social infrastructures as anticipatory relations that involve forms of speculation and risk as people seek to consolidate or expand on opportunities. For the 'users' of these social infrastructures, what is important is not so much knowing the infrastructure, but knowing when to act and when not to act, and in what ways.

Chapter 2 closely connects to Simone's conceptualisation of infrastructure as a relational achievement. Vyjayanthi Rao's discussion of infrastructure experience in Mumbai shows how infrastructure, as entanglements of networks, materials and nature, emerges and becomes known as variously cooperative, conflictual, supportive, anticipatory and political. What's important here is not infrastructure as a thing, but infrastructure as *a set of operations*. Rao uses the concept of 'urban density' to think about ways of dealing with the large coexistence of people and things in Mumbai. She draws on experiences of travelling on commuter trains in the city, personal experiences through which she developed her own vocabulary for addressing urban density, and debates on Mumbai's streets, particularly following the 2005 monsoon floods. For example, she examines how people make space for each other on the train network as a form of adjustment, and considers how the floods led to a range of temporary social infrastructures through which different groups collaborated.

There are connections between Simone and Rao's approaches and other work on how everyday infrastructures are known and adjusted, speculated about and differently put to work. For example, Lisa Björkman's (2014) ethnography of the municipal housing colony of Shavajinagar-Bainganwadi in north-east Mumbai, where residents often pay both 'plumbers' (brokers) to 'transfer' their water connections to different parts of the pipes when the water quality or quantity suffers, and 'bhai charges' to local political parties to monitor the work of the water department in the area. A shifting set of infrastructures emerge. Tap owners, if there is enough water in their tap, may sell water to local residents. But circumstances here are often in flux as water timings vary, prices change, renting tenants move in and out, vertical home additions are added, pressures rise and fall, new connections appear while others dry up, or the police and municipality embark on 'raids' to remove illegal connections. All of which requires that residents have to keep on top of what's going on – to 'read the signs, interpret the rumors, and assess when and how to act, as well as when to wait' (Björkman, 2014). She argues:

> Water risk inhabits a landscape of rumor, stealth and speculation – on materialities such as pipe locations, water pressures, and the timings and operations of valves, as well as on networks of power and influence that might underpin the appearances and disappearances of water.
>
> (ibid.)

Björkman's account echoes other work in this area. For example, Karen Coelho's ethnography of water engineers in Chennai shows how the water distribution grid is actively shaped by geographies of power and influence as 'bypass connections were effected, valves were manipulated, furtive handpumps were installed, pipes were raised or lowered' (2006: 499) in response to the demands of local councillors and relations between engineers and the public. In these accounts, the water grid is an outcome of constant manipulation and compromise, trial and error, experimentation, rumour and risk as engineers react to political and economic interests. On a different register, Nikhil Anand (2011) uses the analytic lens of 'pressure' to disclose the ways in which politics, technology and physics interweave to configure Mumbai's water supply. Drawing on ethnographic work in informal settlements, he demonstrates the different ways in which 'pressure' in the water system is made and mobilised *technically*, via the work of engineers and the functioning of the water system, *politically*, via the influence of politicians, charismatic individuals and neighbourhood collectives, and *geophysically*, through the 'natural' terrain of the city. These literatures demonstrate the critical importance of thinking of infrastructure as an unequal, political and changing articulation of materials, bodies, politics, water, social relations, including class, gender and caste, and knowledge, that are remade through everyday activities. They build on existing debates on 'disrupted cities' (Graham, 2010b) by examining how disruption is perceived, experienced and normalised.

## Part II Infrastructural violence and dispossession

In Chapter 3, Steve Graham, Renu Desai and Colin McFarlane examine the 'raids' through which state and police actors destroy urban water connections in Mumbai's informal settlements. Drawing on an ethnography of experiences and perceptions of sanitation and water infrastructures in the city, they show how the state and the police – along with a concert of supportive voices in the media and among middle-class organisations – intensified the destruction of water connections in Mumbai following a relatively weak monsoon in 2009. They examine the consequences of this infrastructural violence for the everyday hydrological life of particular neighbourhoods in the city, and trace its connections to the nature of water provision across Mumbai, the city's political structure, and the economic aspirations of its elites.

The focus in this chapter is on the impact of the politicisation of metabolic infrastructures for different neighbourhoods in the city. In this sense – and this also connects with Chapter 7 by Brown (see below) – debates on infrastructures as metabolic processes are important points of departure. These debates have concentrated on how nature is metabolised through capitalist social relations, and have demonstrated how the metabolisation of water and waste through urban and rural space, bodies and materials is structured by the power relations and political economies that constitute the city (Swyngedouw, 2004). For example, Swyngedouw (2006), in his critical elucidation of urbanisation as the de-territorialisation and re-territorialisation of metabolic flows, argues that unequal relations of power allow particular actors to defend and create their own urban environments along the lines of class, ethnicity, race, and gender, a process that is reproduced through capitalism's translocal operations across the globe, which 'turn the city into a metabolic socio-environmental process that stretches from the immediate environment to the remotest corners of the globe' (ibid.: 106). The emphasis in Chapter 3 by Graham, Desai and McFarlane, as well as in Chapter 7 by Brown, is to examine how these processes emerge through and impact upon everyday urban lives.

The concern with how capitalist redevelopment impacts on everyday lives in marginal spaces is also at the heart of Chapter 4, Mariana Cavalcanti's study of the exclusionary, often violent and actively pacifying politics of informality in Rio in the run-up to the 2014 World Cup and 2016 Olympics. She shows how recent shifts in Brazil have acted to combine strategies of pacification and violence towards the shanty towns or favelas. In 2008, a major new favela development project was announced, the Growth Acceleration Program (PAC), designed to increase links with the 'formal city' (e.g. through roads and shared public spaces), improve urban aesthetics (e.g. through architect Jorge Mario Jauregui's designs), stimulate private investment, and improve the infrastructure (especially energy, transport, and social/urban development). A key difference from previous programmes is the emphasis on 'integration' with the 'formal city'. Alongside this programme is an attempt to destroy the city's infamous favela drug economies spearheaded by 'Pacifying Police Units' (UPPs), which also started in 2008, and the occupation of *favelas* by Police Elite forces. Taken together, both projects privilege improvements or control of areas around tourist sites. Cavalcanti demonstrates how a focus on how the impact of urban infrastructure projects on everyday life reveals informality 'as the ever-precarious accommodation of often contradictory organising forces, territorial logics, and modes of exercising sovereignty over particular stretches of urban space'.

Omar Jabary Salamanca's Chapter 5 also carefully unpacks how infrastructure is produced and experienced through contradictory forces that reflect unequal societal relations of power. He focuses on dispossession and segregation around the express route that runs through southern Ramallah, Road 443, built in the 1980s. A major connecting route between areas around Tel Aviv and Jerusalem, the construction of the road involved confiscating private land from a teachers cooperative, passing through several Palestinian villages while serving no Palestinian villages or towns, and – through a convoluted set of what Jabary Salamanca calls 'legal acrobatics' on the part of the Israeli High Court of Justice – and placing a ban excluding Palestinians from the route following the second intifada in 2000. Importantly, and in contrast to many accounts of infrastructure violence in Palestine, Jabary Salamanca locates these processes in the historical context of Israeli colonialism and the symbolic and material geographies of Zionism, where infrastructure has been central to the production of Jewish spatialities. The impacts on everyday Palestinian life have been dramatic, from the destruction of several Palestinian agricultural economies to the confining of Palestinian children walking to school to rainwater drain conduits under the road. Activists have mounted demonstrations and legal challenges, which led to the High Court ruling in 2009 that the road had to open to Palestinians. However, the army only opened a relatively small section of the road, and added a series of dehumanising checkpoints. Jabary Salamanca presents road infrastructure as both a tool of analysis of everyday urban life, and an 'archive' of Israel's settler colonial 'discourses, practices, actors, and experiences that justify, enable and characterise this infrastructure'.

Taken together, the chapters in this part of the book advance debates on urban infrastructure violence, militarisation and dispossession (e.g. Coward, 2008). They do so in that they focus not just on how violence and dispossession are produced through different logics – elite aspirations to build a 'world city', monopolising public resources, redevelopment to attract capital, or politicising access to infrastructure by identity – but by considering the implications of how people experience and perceive those infrastructures – in short, for how infrastructure is lived. In the process, they show how different neighbourhoods are often impacted in quite distinct ways, and how those impacts change over time. They also show how resistance emerges and might emerge in the future, for instance, through water-based social movements operating in informal settlements and objecting to the infringement of a human right, or residents pursuing legal claims in order to sustain their livelihoods and way of life.

## Part III Waste, process, infrastructure

We move in Part III of the book to consideration of how infrastructures become part of the constitution of what counts as the 'everyday', and do so in the context of urban waste. Maria Kaika's Chapter 6 presents an important discussion of the discursive separation of 'good' and 'bad' urban natures, such as clean water and metabolised waste, in the contemporary Western home, and reminds us of the mutually co-produced inside and outside of infrastructure spaces. She shows, for instance, that while the home and external water infrastructure are discursively separated in Western societies, the home in practice depends on water infrastructures for that very autonomy. The everyday experience of the metabolic infrastructures of the home are defined, argues Kaika, by a 'selective porosity' that welcomes certain things (e.g. clean water) and renders others invisible (e.g. the pipes and drains that remove waste water). These relations are cast asunder in moments of infrastructure disruption and crisis, producing a Freudian uncanny in the home as the 'guts' of a building are suddenly made visible. These can also be highly politicised moments, reflecting, for instance, the transformation of water supplies into commodities, or generating anxieties and new claims, or suggesting new forms of collectivity against the individualism of the atomised home.

In Chapter 7, Stephanie Terreni Brown focuses on metabolised waste in a context where the 'selective porosity' described by Kaika is not possible and in which a different set of discursive and material practices take precedence. Brown examines the everyday sanitation experiences of residents in informal settlements in Kampala, and considers how 'shit matters' in contestations over sanitation in the neighbourhood of Namuwongo. For Brown, the processes of acting without infrastructure can be about more than just necessary coping strategies, they can also be acts of anger played out as routine sanitary practices that serve to defy the city's socio-spatial hierarchies. For example, 'flying toilets' are for Brown an example of residents' discontent with state-sponsored pay-for-use latrines. She also shows that sanitation must be locally relevant by examining people's concerns about the new ecological toilets built by a non-governmental organisation that marginalised local building techniques, represented to residents an inferior kind of toilet, and left people suspicious about the idea of using human waste as a fertiliser. At the same time, the state often perceives neighbourhoods like Namawongo as 'not-quite city', as opposed to the modern city and undeserving of improved services, and reminds us of how particular normalisations of the 'everyday' are not neutral, but remain politically charged. Brown's discussion demonstrates the potential of a focus on the everyday to reveal the entwinement of multiple forms of inequality, experience and perception.

Brown's chapter taps into a broader concern that also runs through other chapters in the book – especially those of Cavalcanti, and Graham, Desai and McFarlane – as well as in the wider literature on the experience of inadequate infrastructure (e.g. Anand, 2011; Truelove, 2011): how do we make sense of infrastructure practices that exceed the domain of formal citizenship? One conceptual resource that is useful here is focused less on infrastructure *per se*, and more on the contexts through which relations between infrastructure and everyday life take place: Partha Chatterjee's (2004) concept of 'political society'. Here, Chatterjee shows, we find a different normalisation of the 'everyday'. In *Politics of the Governed*, Chatterjee (2004) influentially argued that understanding politics in India depends on making sense of practices that exceed the domain of formal urban citizenship. His argument has important implications for how we think about the attainment and maintenance of everyday infrastructure in many parts of the Global South, especially in contexts where a 'vote-bank' politics predominates. For Chatterjee, these are practices that involve and give rise to populations rather than citizens, characterised by an uncertain terrain of negotiation and violence where political expediency sometimes meshes with the field of citizenship – for example, in the form of vote-bank regimes – but only as part of a strategic instrumental moment. Here, people seek rights, but the state cannot view these rights as citizenship rights because to do so would threaten the apparatus of property and civic law.

Political society is a domain in which individuals become part of population groupings through recognition as a governmental category – including households, labourers, landless people, and people below-the-poverty-line, all official state categories. This involves a moral construction of a community tied by often nothing other than common occupation of land under threat. These categories can in turn be used by state officials to expand or secure their political base. But what is important about Brown's account here – and this echoes the chapters by Cavalcanti and Graham, Desai and McFarlane – is that political society is often an option that is not available to many excluded groups of the urban poor, or instead is not seen to be particularly useful. Instead, people are restricted to finding politics in other ways, such as in the ways in which they discard flying toilets. Here, a focus on the everyday reveals a wider range of ways in which people cope with and politicise the absence or inadequacy of urban infrastructures.

In Chapter 8, Rob Shaw is similarly concerned with the everyday management of waste in urban space, but in a radically different context. Shaw shifts the focus from the everyday to the every*night* in his ethnography of street cleaning infrastructures in Newcastle upon Tyne in the UK. He shows how waste management is constituted through a wide variety of actors and practices and that it involves not just cleaning streets, but managing night-time urban subjectivities. For example, the night can be a time of more care-free behaviour that creates waste that then needs to be managed, whether in the form of moving traffic cones or urinating in public space. Shaw conducted his research with Newcastle's night-time 'neighbourhood services team', and found that people often interfere with the process of street cleaning and that the team has to learn to manage or ignore the behaviour of drunken people. Shaw examines how, in the process, materials – from cigarette butts and fast food packaging to leaflets and vomit – are qualitatively changed in new contexts as they become waste. In doing so, Shaw offers an important reminder of the different and often highly contingent rhythms through which socio-material infrastructures are made.

Taken together, the chapters in Part III of the book show how processes of urban metabolisation can produce particular normalisations of the 'everyday' that can be used to judge others, whether informal residents who are perceived by the powerful to be 'unmodern' or night-time revellers performing subjectivities that go against the norm. What is clear is the production of the everyday through infrastructure and its government, discursive construction and material configuration is far from a taken-for-granted category. Instead, it is a power-laden, exclusionary political domain that can itself be usefully revealed through attention to daily practices.

## Part IV Adjustment and experimentation

The final section of the book, Part IV focuses on infrastructure adjustment but instead through the more purposeful, planned domain of experimentation. Vanessa Castán Broto and Harriet Bulkeley use the idea of 'experimentation' in relation to urban climate change governance in order to consider both the nature of low-carbon initiatives in the city, and the impact of those initiatives on urban space. They examine a low-carbon gated community in Bangalore called T-Zed, and focus in particular on how the process of maintenance led to the adjustment of the experiment to the local urban fabric. In particular, non-human agencies unexpectedly challenged existing social and political arrangements in the city. For example, the use of local materials for exposed brick walls had to be abandoned because they proved difficult to use on site, and the consequence of using multiple different materials led in some cases to cracks and leaks. Or, to take a different example, there were multiple attempts to get the LED lighting to work before it was eventually installed, working through indoor and outdoor uses, cost and appearance. Castán Broto and Bulkeley tell a similar story about the design of the air conditioning system and the customised refrigerators, where success is the product of several experiments that had led to failure. It is these unexpected moments and the processes of maintenance that go on around them that constitute low-carbon urban infrastructures as they are made in the city.

Finally, in Chapter 10, Mike Hodson and Simon Marvin examine the impacts of a range of low-carbon urban experimentation on everyday life. They examine the dominant pathways of low-carbon initiatives designed to meet the thirst for energy in urban Britain, particularly off-shore wind farms, low-carbon vehicles, retrofitting buildings, and the redesign of the electricity grid, and find that they tend to be characterised by exclusive coalitions of profit-driven social interests. These are efforts, in short, to build markets through the assistance of the state, and they have been characterised by a disconnection to users and everyday life. Everyday life tends only to feature in the form of consumers who will enable these new markets, and in this context Hodson and Marvin call for greater democratic control over the production of low-carbon initiatives as part of a wider 'right to the city'.

These three chapters on adjustment and experimentation, then, collectively raise the question of how these practices might enter into a more progressive form of urban politics. This is a theme that has been taken up elsewhere in useful ways. For example, writing in a different context, particularly in relation to urban South Africa, Edgar Pieterse (2008) outlines one set of possibilities here by describing how incremental processes of 'stumbling across what works and what does not' can build a politics that he calls 'radical incrementalism': 'Surreptitious, sometimes overt, and multiple small revolutions that at unanticipated and unexpected moments galvanize into deeper ruptures that accelerate tectonic shifts of the underlying logics of domination and what is considered possible' (ibid.). For Pieterse, this process of galvanising depends on the work of civil society organisations built on strong internal democratic practices – movements that are alert to the 'numerous and ever-changing rhythms of the city' which generate cultural novelty and potential resources for renewing political strategies (ibid.: 174). For Pieterse, these practices are closely linked to processes of empowerment, and therefore work most successfully in cities where governance structures allow genuinely participatory collaboration. Without those conditions, as is the case in many cities, politics requires 'militant direct action that can lead to the institutionalization of participatory democratic systems' (ibid.: 143). Hodson and Marvin's call for a more democratic low-carbon urbanism that would inform a project of rights to the city raises importance questions, then, about how to formulate political strategy in ostensibly democratic contexts that are in practice radically curtailed by powerful capitalist interests.

## Conclusion

Infrastructures often appear obdurate and rigid, historical urban constants buried beneath streets and walls or ignored due to their very consistent familiarity (e.g. Joyce, 2003; Otter, 2004). But when we shift focus from broad historical shifts to everyday practices, we see infrastructure in a different light. In order to become taken-for-granted, a lot of work is needed to normalise, maintain, repair, and stabilise infrastructure (e.g. Graham and Thrift, 2007). In this book, we showcase a range of work that powerfully demonstrates how infrastructures are lived as contingent, power-laden, processes. There is clearly an agenda here that seeks to examine infrastructure not just from the starting point of political economic production and fracturing – as critical as those issues are – but also from the engagements and perceptions through which infrastructures are lived and known. In closing, we want to highlight just two additional questions that this volume has left us with.

First, the chapters in this book raise a straightforward but important question: what is infrastructure? There are at least two critical concerns here that the book has pointed out. The first concern is the need to consider how experience and perception condition how infrastructure is known and lived. For example, to the planners preparing for Rio's Olympics and World Cup, infrastructure is a necessary investment in the generation of new markets and urban aesthetics, but for marginalised residents in the favelas it can be an exclusionary imposition that reformulates their livelihoods and social lives. While to the Israelis using Road 443, the road may be no more than a route to work or to visit friends, but to the Palestinian villagers who have been displaced or excluded, the road is a geopolitical expression of a long history of militarisation and containment.

The second concern identified in the book is to resist viewing infrastructure as a straightforward thing. The chapters in this book insist on understanding infrastructure as a changing set of processes that are often lively, powerful, and uncertain. Whether in relation to the networks, rumours, and exchanges through which infrastructure comes to be known in Mumbai's informal settlements or Jakarta's markets, or in the experimentations with infrastructure in climate change initiatives, or in the often unpredictable uses of waste in cities as different as Kampala and Newcastle, infrastructure is a process that is made and remade and experienced in radically different ways within and between cities. An everyday focus on infrastructure lives is critical to developing understandings of how infrastructure does not simply exist, but occurs.

Following on from this, the book raises the second question of whether there is anything that holds constant in urban infrastructure across different cities and contexts. What, if anything, is held in common across infrastructures as different as waste, roads, and trains? And between urban contexts as different as Jakarta, Mumbai, Kampala, Newcastle, and Ramallah? The conclusion from this collection has to be that there is little held in common beyond infrastructure itself as a set of socio-material processes. There is a tendency for infrastructure studies to focus on particular infrastructures, and this book points to the need to think more carefully about comparisons between different infrastructures. We are lacking studies specifically examining the similarities and differences between water, power, waste, transport, and so on, in terms of the actors involved, the political economies, the cultures around them, and the everyday experience. This book has only begun to open this up and clearly a lot more work needs to be done to develop a comparative theory of urban infrastructure.

## Bibliography

Anand, N. (2011) 'PRESSURE: The PoliTechnics of Water Supply in Mumbai', *Cultural Anthropology*, 26(4): 542–564.

Bjorkman, L. (2014) *Pipe Politics: Mumbai's Contested Waters*. Durham, NC: Duke University Press.

Chatterjee, P. (2004) *The Politics of the Governed: Reflections on Popular Politics in Most of the World*. Delhi: Permanent Black.

Chatterjee, P. (2008) 'Democracy and Economic Transformation in India', *Economic and Political Weekly*, 19 April, pp. 53–62.

Coelho, K. (2006) 'Tapping In: Leaky Sovereignties and Engineered (Dis)Order in an Urban Water System', in *Sarai Reader 06: Turbulence*. Delhi: Sarai.

Coutard, O. (2008) 'Placing Splintering Urbanism: Introduction', *Geoforum*, 39(6): 1815–1820.

Coward, M. (2008) *Urbicide: The Politics of Urban Destruction*. London: Routledge.

Furlong, K. (2011) 'Small Technologies, Big Change: Rethinking Infrastructure through STS and Geography', *Progress in Human Geography*, 35(4): 460–482.

Gandy, M. (2005) 'Cyborg Urbanization: Complexity and Monstrosity in the Contemporary City', *International Journal of Urban and Regional Research*, 29(1): 26–49.

Graham, S. (2010) *Cities Under Siege: The New Military Urbanism*. London: Verso.

Graham, S. (ed.) (2010) *Disrupted Cities: When Infrastructure Fails*. New York: Routledge.

Graham, S. and Marvin, S. (2001) *Splintering Urbanism: Networked Infrastructures, Technological Mobilities and the Urban Condition*. London: Routledge.

Graham, S. and Thrift, N. (2007) 'Out of Order: Understanding Repair and Maintenance', *Theory, Culture & Society*, 24(3):1–25.

Guy, S., Marvin, S., Medd, W. and Moss, T. (2011) *Shaping Urban Infrastructures: Intermediaries and the Governance of Socio-technical Networks*. London: Earthscan.

Heynen, N., Kaika, M. and Swyngedouw, E. (eds) (2006) *In the Nature of Cities: Urban Political Ecology and the Politics of Urban Metabolism*. London: Routledge.

Hodson, M. and Marvin, S. (2009) '"Urban Ecological Security": A New Urban Paradigm?', *International Journal of Urban and Regional Research*, 33(1): 193–215.

Hodson, M. and Marvin, S. (2010) *World Cities and Climate Change: Producing Urban Ecological Security*. Glasgow: Open University Press.

Joyce, P. (2003) *The Rule of Freedom: Liberalism and the Modern City*. London: Verso.

Kaika, M. (2005) *City of Flows: Modernity, Nature and the City*. London: Routledge.

Keil, R., Young, D. and Wood, P.B. (eds) (2011) *In-Between Infrastructure: Urban Connectivity in an Age of Vulnerability*. Kelowna, British Columbia: Praxis (e) Press.

Kitchen, R. and Dodge, M. (2011) *Code/Space: Software, Society and Space*. Cambridge, MA: MIT Press.

Loftus, A. (2007) 'Working the Socio-Natural Relations of the Urban Waterscape in South Africa', *International Journal of Urban and Regional Research*, 31(1): 41–59.

Loftus, A. (2012) *Everyday Environmentalism: Creating an Urban Political Ecology*. Minneapolis: University of Minnesota Press.

Luke, T. W. (2003) 'Global Cities vs. "Global Cities"', *Studies in Political Economy*, 7(1): 11–22.

McFarlane, C. and Rutherford, J. (2008) 'Guest Editorial: Political Infrastructures – Governing and Experiencing the Fabric of the City', *International Journal of Urban and Regional Research*, 32(2): 363–374.

Otter, C. (2004) 'Cleansing and Clarifying: Technology and Perception in Nineteenth-Century London', *Journal of British Studies*, 43: 40–64.

Page, B. (2005) 'Paying for Water and the Geography of Commodities', *Transactions of the Institute of British Geographers*, 30(3): 293–306.

Pieterse, E. (2008) *City Futures: Confronting the Crisis of Urban Development*. London: Zed Books.

Rigg, J. (2007) *An Everyday Geography of the Global South*. London: Routledge.

Shove, E., Watson, M., Hand, M., and Ingram, J. (2007) *The Design of Everyday Life*. Oxford: Berg.

Simone, A. (2004) 'People as Infrastructure: Intersecting Fragments in Johannesburg', *Public Culture*, 16(3): 407–429.

Simone, A. (2008) 'Emergency Democracy and the "Governing Composite"', *Social Text*, 95(26): 13–33.

Simone, A. (2010) *City Life from Jakarta to Dakar: Movements at the Crossroads*. New York: Routledge.

Swyngedouw, E. (2004) *Social Power and the Urbanization of Water: Flows of Power*. Oxford: Oxford University Press.

Swyngedouw, E. (2006) 'Circulations and Metabolisms: (Hybrid) Natures and (Cyborg) Cities', *Science as Culture*, 15(2): 105–121.

Thrift, N. and French, S. (2002) 'The Automatic Production of Space', *Transactions of the Institute of British Geographers*, 27: 309–335.

Truelove, J. (2011) '(Re-)Conceptualising Water Inequality in Delhi, India through a Feminist Political Ecology Framework', *Geoforum*, 42: 143–152.

Young, D. and Keil, R. (2010) 'Reconnecting the Disconnected: The Politics of Infrastructure in the In-between City', *Cities*, 27(2): 87–95.

# Part I

# Knowing infrastructure

Chapter 1

# Relational infrastructures in postcolonial urban worlds

*AbdouMaliq Simone*

## Introduction: relational infrastructures

In the so-called majority urban world of today, the trajectories of change sometimes seem univocal, at others, all over the place. Memories of national
imaginaries – of slights and wounds, power grabs and nagging liberations – both
harden and fade away. Speeds of transformation are deceptive in their manifestations. The seeming hegemonies behind the logics of mega-development appear
to chew up everything in their path. But in their production of more of the same,
they leave little to constitute the basis of dynamic interactions between them,
and such interactions otherwise constitute the speed, the registration of history
(Curran, 2007; Goldman, 2011; Hodson and Marvin, 2009; Kirkpatrick and
Smith, 2011; Monstadt, 2009; Shatkin, 2008).

The chipping away of residential and commercial districts built up over many
years to accommodate a great diversity of activities and people produces multi-
farious dispositions – different gradations of gentrification, renewal, decay,
resurgence, and dissipation. Here, different actors, agendas, aspirations, games,
and tricks produce a variety of interim solutions that go on to last a long time.
While injustice could hardly be more glaring and the poor more discounted,
maneuvers to foster more comprehensive integration into urban systems often
prove intensely exclusionary. On the other hand, spatial polarization often
proves the condition under which the marginalized, weakened or threatened
work out operational spaces – however temporary – to establish more effective
terms under which to participate in corporate modalities of governance (Auyero,
2007; Hansen and Verkaaik, 2009; Heller and Evans, 2010; McFarlane, 2008;
Roy, 2011).

Within such conditions, how do the majority of urban residents in the postcolonial urban world put together ways of inhabiting the city? The specifications
of land use, the conditions of tenure, the financial procedures for accessing housing, and the calibrations of labor markets are structural devices that generate a
specific framework of possibilities. But there are also deep inventories of various
social practices, ways of interpreting urban conditions, modes of social support
and stabilization that have long "guided" urban residents. Using Isabelle

Stengers' notion of an ecology of practices (Stengers, 2010), residents do not simply adhere to norms and rules either as prescriptions for action or as frameworks for deciding what is viable or not. In part, this is because what those norms and rules consist of is usually defined in majority terms or are distillations of specific interests of the powerful. They become instruments of silencing in face of the "weight" that norms carry as the crystallization of the best way of doing things, and where refusal of adherence is a judgment (bad) of the individual who refuses rather than a judgment of the norms themselves.

Practices, says Stengers, entail obligations – obligations to pursue a particular path as opposed to others, but as a means to induce thinking, to build up a perspective over time and which generates a sense of efficacy, a sense of belonging to something capable of absorbing individual action and effort. A practice is more than a particular way of doing something, more than simply technique, for it entails obligations to others who have also "practiced." Thus, practices introduces a temporality of hesitation, of thinking through what is entailed in the process that practice elaborates, and hesitating in face of the scenarios that practice opens onto, of knowing what works and what is useful or not (Latour, 2005).

What I want to do in this contribution is to explore some of the practices that residents have used to make viable forms of inhabitation in the postcolonial urban world. Most of these reflections are drawn from several years of research, activism and community organization in Jakarta – now part of one of the world's largest urban regions. While these reflections are specific to Jakarta, other work that I have done over the past thirty years in Africa's major urban areas, as well as in Bangkok and Phnom Penh, makes me think that many of these maneuvers undertaken by residents, nominally "belonging" to the working poor, working class, lower middle class, are also applicable more widely. Here, I focus on infrastructures of relationality. In other words, the ways in which relationships themselves constitute an infrastructure for inhabitation. These relationships are not just social events or descriptors of exchanges and transactions. They are not simply embodiments of sentiment or vehicles for organizing work, expenditure, attention and recognition.

Rather, they are materials themselves to be articulated in various forms in order to construct circulations of bodies, resources, affect and information. They are vehicles of movement and becoming, ways of mediating the constantly oscillating intersections of various times, spaces, economies, constraints and possibilities making up city life. Relations are also the tools through which political imaginations and claims are exerted and thus are the embodiment of force. Here, force, regardless of how it is mediated or institutionalized, exists in its potential as a means of urban change. More than notions of social capital, care, support, economy and livelihood are entailed in the efforts inhabitants make to work on and with relations. For what is also entailed are the circumvention of domination and the keeping open of many different trajectories of what life could be all at once (Amin and Thrift, 2002; Nancy, 2002; Virno, 2009).

## Mimetic zones

In variegated neoliberal urban conditions, probabilities, accountancy, and the stochastic modeling of risk are the things that really matter – not only because they are the instruments that work with large assemblages of data and uncertainty to specify the positions, the hedges, and the arbitrage that are critical for any urban economy, but also because they are the seemingly proficient instruments of dissimulation – they cover up for the fact that no one knows quite what is going on. This efficacy is derived from the way they make everything count, everything accountable; the ways in which large volumes of raw data can be scrutinized in order to establish the visibilities, the patterns that are worthy of being discerned, that will constitute the locus of intervention. Everything else that falls outside of such modeling does not matter (Callon et al., 2007; Cooper, 2010; Foucault, 2008). For large numbers of residents in cities of the majority world, then, the dilemma is how demonstrate that where they live and what they do matter, when the possibilities of translation, visibility and value become more problematic. On the other hand, it is important, and to a large extent has been important for a long time, to stay outside the count, not to get sucked into the game of who and what is eligible and who is not (Bayat, 2009; De Boeck and Plissard, 2006; Gooptu, 2001; Roitman, 2005; Whitson, 2007).

One course of action for not getting sucked into the game is to act as if one is very much involved in it, in a kind of mirroring process. The idea here is for particular communities, populations, or networks – otherwise considered to be divergent or incapable – to reflect back to hegemonic actors aspects of the practices that are acknowledged as playing a critical role in the reproduction of that hegemony. This constitutes an implicit acknowledgement by the weak of the capacities of the strong but also inevitably signals that, in the hands of the weak, these practices can never be implemented in ways sufficient to challenge the strong. The very same kinds of practices that in the hands of those with power are construed as calculating, daring, and innovative, in other hands are seen as impetuous and self-destructive. These are the very behaviors, then, which would seem to disqualify "ordinary residents" from being eligible to participate fully in a wide range of managerial, decision-making processes. Yet, in this process of mirroring, limited spaces of maneuverability are opened and for much of the very same reasons they are opened for those supposedly much more well-versed in using them (de Certeau, 1998; Goldstein, 2004; Taussig, 1999; Williams, 2002).

In this process, the "devices" associated with the incursions and re-compositions engineered by global capital – such as speculative finance, cut-and-paste modularization of spatial products, translocal configurations of production mechanisms, and the privileging of surface maneuvers emptied of historical reference – also are appropriated by collective actors as a means to substantiate practices of creating space and opportunities that ensue from different logics and aspirations. Under certain urban conditions, residents of lesser means and subject to the arbitrary constrictions on anticipating the future due to race, ethnicity or other attributes have often used the very bodies of household and kin to hedge against uncertainty. Spreading out across different locations, institutions, careers and exposures, households extend themselves across different sources of opportunity (Cross and Morales, 2007; Kothari, 2008; Meagher, 2010; Roitman, 2005).

While socio-psycho dynamics may account for differentiations within the household in terms of varied distributions and balances of power and responsibility, the ways in which members of a single family may be situated in higher education, factory work, the prison, the military, the hospital, or the corporation may reflect an unfolding infrastructure to connect different positions as a means of securing household livelihood. If one position doesn't pan out, others might. In situations where an individual's sheer identity – rather than skills or capacity – make them vulnerable to downturns, attritions, and scapegoating, this infrastructure of hedges proves necessary (Haber, 2006; Menjívar, 2000; Small, 2009; Stack, 1997; Telles and Hirata, 2007).

Games of anticipation are also mechanisms for taking on the profitability of risk. In everyday transactions, interactants anticipate the likely responses of each other as the basis on which to style particular overtures and interventions. Individuals are not likely to act when they feel unable to anticipate the likely range of responses their behavior is likely to elicit. They attempt to anticipate what the likely response will be to a forthcoming action. But rather than constituting a straightforward narrative of behavior shaped by a response that confirms the confidence of the actor to anticipate, there is always the presence of a certain dread. The recipient of the behavior can also use his or her response as an anticipation of the anticipation of the initial actor. This not only provides the scenario that the initial actor seems to want but, more importantly, provides confirmation of the initial actor's ability to correctly have read the situation – having made the right anticipation (Garfinkel, 1991; Goffman, 1986; Taussig, 1992).

Thus, this is a game full of potential duplicities, steering interactants into false confidence and subsequent vulnerabilities. In the accretion of these projected anticipations, actors can lose a sense of what it is that each other "really" anticipates. In such circumstances, actors may speculate about what might happen when they show behavior which is not what on the surface is anticipated. Instead, this behavior addresses an anticipation that is masked by the surface anticipation, so that the interaction becomes a moment of simultaneous discovery or surprise. Here, the other is momentarily disarmed by being addressed in a way that she discovers that she really wants and either must decide to quickly re-mask this desire or allow themselves to be addressed within it. This maneuver carries certain risks, especially when those in weaker positions of power attempt to deploy it.

But this is precisely the maneuver played out day after day in many markets of cities in the majority world, as well as in the overtures made by individuals seeking inclusion in some kind of business or economic opportunity to which they are otherwise ineligible. Appeals are made to the possibility that the ways in which the recipients conceive stable livelihoods and businesses, security for their enter-prises and schemes – while effective, normal or customary – are perhaps too limiting for the aspirations they might have. Here, there is the attempt to construct a sense that an extra body, an extra contact or activity might have a higher payoff. If one listens to the conversations at different conjunctions of work activities – carters who deliver boxes of goods to the market, mobile hawk-ers selling wares across various commercial landscapes, a journeyman looking for part-time work in some new workshop, factory workers talking to their supervi-sors about various aspects of work on the factory floor, minivan drivers ferrying workers back home from an office, low-level local officials collecting fees from market stalls – they are replete with such appeals (Fawaz, 2008; Guyer, 2004; Lindell, 2010; Peters, 2009; Prag, 2010; Wu et al., 2010). The attempt is to try and steer the transaction into an opportunity for inclusion in some other, some-times undefined, opportunity. The risks entailed is that the person initiating these appeals – these speculative anticipations of a possible more "real" anticipa-tion than the one being most apparently performed by the other – will lose the current position they have. This is what I mean by taking on risk.

The impetuous, speculative involvement of many urban residents across the majority world in gambling, loan sharking and ponzi schemes is well known. Traditional urban markets are increasingly becoming the locus for more system-atic, organized speculative ventures folding in the dimensions of the derivation process centered on the linkages among different kinds of assets. Here, the appar-ently naturalized link between economic efficacy and specific urbanized styles of calculation and individuation may also be broken. Economic success need not necessarily connote an overarching desire for individual material gain or the absence of it need not necessarily rule out the ability of individuals to assume what might be seen as a highly urbanized demeanor. Within a given street, there may be people who work constantly, stringing together a plurality of small jobs and their work may enable others to seemingly do nothing, even as this "noth-ing," this removal from work is the vantage point from which information is retrieved and coordinated enabling specific jobs to be created. Meager earnings are sometimes pooled together and seemingly "wasted" on games and improvised festivities which become the only means for a neighborhood to attract a wider "audience" to it, and then use that audience as a means of finding out what is taking place at larger scales. Individual accumulation, in face of being embedded in contexts of overwhelming economic vulnerability, may give way to excessive displays of expenditure intended to enfold diverse others into relationships that may have no other concrete basis for existing (De Boeck and Plissard, 2006; Guyer, 2004; Wilson, 2008).

Periodic displays of excess of all kinds can be a means to refuse modernist emphases on examining individual insufficiency and the need for continuous "upgrades" and improvements, as well as the associated compulsion for individu-als to progressively dissociate themselves from their surrounding human and material environments (Tassi, 2010). In ramshackle environments it is often queried why improvements are not made; why residents do not pool their resources to make various public spaces "nicer." Piles of discordant materials sometimes accumulate for years with apparently little use and that seemingly could be easily discarded, yet "hang on" as if exerting some excessive force (Latham and McCormack, 2004). Indeed, attempts at "community improvement" are often made, but even when they are not, it is not a matter always of a lack of resources or cooperation, but rather a sense of letting histories run their course, of retaining memories of all the ways a particular space and deteriorating object or infrastructure have been used, and in this history, maintain a sense of its accessibility, its availability to be used in many different ways by many different combinations of people. These are environments that not only show the excess of past use, but convey the possibility of an order in conditions where explicit attempts to impose structured orders are too vulnerable to inequities of power, porous interchanges with various externalities or the absence of authority able to instantiate itself over the long run (Bouzarovski, 2009; Jansson and Lagerkvist, 2010; Pile, 2005).

The process of derivation in finance is a multifaceted process organized around both minimizing and maximizing risk. On the one hand, the valuation of certain commodities is delinked from the conditions that otherwise would specify their supply, as contracts attempt to lock in a price of access at a future date. As such, these contractual relationships attempt to minimize risk. As these contracts themselves have become increasingly traded as options, abstracted from any underlying asset, risk as a character of mutating conditions becomes the driving motor of profitability. The dissociation of value from the relationship between supply and demand, as well as the range of uses of concrete things, opens up possibilities for the articulation of vast discrepancies. Things that do not belong together otherwise can be linked, brought into the same orbit. Various gradations and sources of debt can be pooled and then organized into specific tranches, reflecting different degrees of risk (Cheah, 2008; Lee and LiPuma, 2004; Pryke, 2006).

Aspects of this process have been incorporated into so-called traditional urban markets. While discrete items of a particular kind and quantity continue to be sold as the market's primary economic activity, there are increasing "excursions" into more "exotic" items. Here, different kinds of items and services are bundled together and sold as an overall package. Large volumes of non-perishable foodstuffs, repair services for future contingencies, and second-hand knock-offs of electronic goods that have yet to enter the market may be collected from different distributors and sold as a package to raise finance for the acquisition of future goods by these distributors, to guarantee work over the course of a future period of time, and/or clear out inventories. While access to existent or future goods and services becomes available for a price that is advantageous under present conditions, the risk largely centers on enforcing future delivery – which is mitigated in the way in which these transactions are focused on long-term relationships between specific consumers and communities with the given market.

In many African neighborhoods residents will collectively pool money to invest in a container of goods whose contents they may specify through orders in advance directed to a known trader. Some will also "buy options" to acquire the contents of any container – where the contents are unknown in advance – that manages to be unofficially offloaded by complicit contacts at the local port. Still yet, opportunities to acquire a contract for work or procurement from a public organization, to access a place in a given school, to have first access to bunkered oil or food assistance that has been diverted to private markets, to access electricity at a cut price for a given neighborhood, can be bundled into a single package and offered to a "consortium" of buyers who go in together for the sole purpose of investing in such bundles. Here, individuals who share common long-term residency in a given district, or who may be members of a specific religious organization or community association, use this commonality as a platform to accommodate certain measures of risk in order to reposition themselves in relationship to various prospective economic opportunities. In another example, enterprise becomes not simply a matter of profit and price but of collective experimentation that is not officially institutionalized for these purposes, but ensues as a by-product of situating, even suspending, the administration of markets and sectoral specializations between various logics of control.

For example, local markets in Jakarta for the most part are not the purview of municipal market administration – Pasar Jaya. Rather they fall under a municipal department established for the administration of small enterprise which treats traders not as a collective block but as small-scale individual street entrepreneurs that just so happened to be grouped as a "market." The use of facilities entails payment of nominal daily fees, but otherwise the administration of the space is the purview of a local "leader" who manages the security of the market and usually garbage collection. As salaries for these workers, on average numbering 40 for a market of 100 traders, are not insignificant, so too is the volume of trades. Local managers are established over the long run, and they secure their status by their willingness to fight over unwanted incursions and act as repositories of stories they willingly collect and share. They may organize the under-invoicing of trade volume reported to municipal authorities so that traders can retain a larger share of receipts. Thus, they maintain low prices that in turn capture consumption from both poor and middle class alike, often at rates 75 percent below those of major supermarket chains. As such, they constitute a space of temporary mixing of consumers from a large area.

At times, such markets are situated on land of uncertain and contested status, and operate in a cat and mouse game of expansion and retreat in face of ritualized surveillance by various authorities. But these authorities, too, at times come to view these unofficial expansions as opportunities for accumulation. They deploy their regulatory authority by maintaining doubled prerogatives. In some poorer sections of such mixed districts, certain households will parlay connections to larger-scale businesses, such as bakeries and restaurants, to prepare and package particular food items. With no access to commercial space other than the narrow lanes in front of their residences, these economic activities are visible to all, and often expansion will literally enroll neighbors in the pursuit of similar activities, either as extensions of the original business or as "competitors" who develop their own networks. As these forward linkages often vary greatly in terms of demand, the contiguous enterprises can then be mobilized as a coordinated unit, sharing labor, tools, and contacts. The differentiation between households and enterprise, while continuously marked, also bleeds into each other, where it is sometimes not evident where one household or enterprise begins or ends. At times, contiguous operations may be marked by common ethnicity; at other times, may involve very different residential histories and external networks.

## Practices of the incremental

Inhabitation in urban postcolonial worlds has depended on practices of incrementalism, where residents seem to add on to built environments, livelihoods, and social networks "a little bit" at a time. The incremental has long been a feature of sites and services programs – where basic demarcations of plots and skeletal services were provided that would be "filled in" over time through the initiatives and resources of the poor themselves. Similarly, pay-as-you-go, transitional, phased development, and core housing schemes also embody the notion of development in increments, whether it involved the physical construction, financing, or regulation of built environments (Greene and Rojas, 2008).

But the incremental usually encompasses a diverse range of practices. Instead of earnings, accumulation, and savings being directed toward a single developmental agenda or aspiration in an overarching maneuver of completion, the practice of the incremental is aimed at providing small supplements to whatever a household or individual has access to. These increments could be viewed as stages of some larger goal. But they could also be deployed as exploratory devices to see what opportunities or directions they might open up. Instead of committing resources and efforts to the realization of a "complete" project, these increments are instantiated to elicit particular kinds of attention and recognition. Residences may be added onto or altered, small financial investments may be made in selling items in front of the house or in a wide range of other commercial ventures, and investments of time and effort may be made in running various social welfare or political programs as a means of testing waters, indicating that someone is "on their way" somewhere or available for subsequent investments. The interest in eliciting attention and recognition is not so much to issue a signal that one has "arrived" at a particular status or destination, but rather to make "something" happen without a clear notion about what will happen as a result. The point is not so much to consolidate a position that then has to be defended, but to communicate that movement is underway as well as to launch a vehicle through which an individual or household can move.

At times multiple increments are initiated as a means of covering a spectrum of needs. Households may require physical expansion of their living space and their livelihoods. While the available resources, connections and opportunities may be sufficient only to adequately address one need at a given time, the household, nevertheless, spreads itself across multiple projects knowing that only partial outcomes are possible in order to concretize its commitments. Here, the household is concerned to set things in motion, to propel trajectories of development that leave it little choice but to continue its efforts across multiple projects. At other times these multiple increments become ways of hedging bets. If one project – a small enterprise, a change in employment, involvement in a specific association or political party, the accommodation of additional family members, the attempts to elevate social status – does not work, then investments have already been made in something else that could potentially cover the losses or simply constitute a concrete path to an alternate future.

In Jakarta, many districts founded with a certain commonality of population base, land certification and economic development 20–40 years ago usually experienced marked internal differentiation. They became replete with stories of accumulation and loss, of expansion and contraction. These stories are embodied in the shape of land disposition and the built environment. Households beginning with similar platforms of residency pursued different forms of calculating and concretizing opportunity. For example, investments may have been made in consolidating contiguous plots into facilities which combine residential and economic activities. In other instances, plots may have been subdivided to accommodate expanding family size or sold off with residential expansion developed along a vertical trajectory. Original pavilions may not have been altered since their construction, while neighboring plots have "witnessed" several projects, owners and occupiers come and go. Single streets are often the inventories of discordant values embedded in the very selection of materials used to sustain or remake built projects. The selection of roofing, tiling, or frontage – such as ceramics, wood, tin, steel, cinder block, aluminum – not only reflects differences in affordability and assessment of environmental conditions, but also social status and commitment.

Some residents aim for a "summation" of their residence – i.e., they wait until they have the financial resources, certification and permits to realize their project "all at one go." Others may "take their time," construct things in stages, aiming to instantiate "facts on the ground" – i.e. additions that aim to secure a *fait accompli* in terms of particular claims to land use or economic activity. They may not have yet secured permission to build or operate but select ways of "going ahead" that convey the sense that erasing what has been done will be too complicated for everyone involved. Yet if eviction does happen, the particular materials used and ways of trying to "implant" these facts will not incur a debilitating financial loss or loss of prestige. Still others may simply build slowly over time, adding some increments to a basic frame or multiplying the use of particular asset or space.

These differences in the surface of the built environment represent different stories, calculations, and ways of doing things. Yet, once concretized, they do not have to be used or apprehended in ways directly related to the histories these surfaces "tell." While this surface may have been produced from particular economic conditions and cultural practices, its existence as a surface is not dependent upon them; it operates as its own series of relays, channels, circuits that instantiate particular points of view, ways of doing things, and convictions among those who operate across this surface. It is a de-signed built environment, an act of fabrication in both senses of the word – i.e. something that is put together from available materials and something that need not tell the "truth" of a given situation, whether that situation refers to the process through which the built environment was constructed, what it was intended to be used for, or what use can be made of it.

Perhaps the easiest way to illustrate this point is to take the example of Ujung Padang, a central city district in Jakarta that is replete with differentiated surfaces. Ujung Padang was one of the first settled areas of this part of Jakarta and attracted large numbers of inhabitants of different backgrounds. There is a long-standing joke about the way in which the area was constructed – that the demarcations of plots and the design of living spaces were so jumbled up that residents kept waking up in the wrong bedrooms. The area is replete with different construction styles and most plots have undergone various successions of remaking, readjustment, add-ons, tearing down one house to completely remake another, and incessant divisions and consolidations. Again, all of these surfaces point to various stories about accumulation and loss, as well as multiple increments that have been elaborated, abandoned, or stalled. As to be expected in an area of such intensely multiple histories, there is no easy fit among discrete components of this built environment. It is often difficult to discern the integrity of discrete components themselves – i.e. where a particular construction or project begins or ends. Without room for horizontal expansions, space often has to be shared to contain varying uses and alternate times. Constructions that have an apparently lesser status because nothing has been done to them in decades suddenly become premium space for storing materials for workshops in cramped upper-level apartment buildings or whose frontage is able to accommodate local meetings.

The more recent consolidation of plots to built large single family houses enclosed by high walls interrupts certain continuities in the built fabric but also constitutes interstitial zones in the lanes and streets on which they are situated and on which certain economic ventures or local contestations are waged. Accommodating new and temporary residents is a major economic activity across Jakarta. Residents will often consolidate their living spaces in a small portion of their homes in order to rent out rooms or parts of kitchens. In some instances, residents who share a lane will pool their money and buy a building in the local area and then either add on to the existing edifice or tear it down and construct a multi-story dwelling, dividing it up into rooms for rent with each neighbour responsible for managing a particular proportion of the building. At times this is done to concentrate newcomers in an intensive relationship with each other in order for long-time residents to see what might occur in these deal-ings and how they might intersect with them. At other times, mosques may be inserted into a residential fabric as a means of concentrating local interactions. Residents continuously "play with" the textures of the surface; they connect wires and cables across different sites and kinds of ownership and use; they fill-in vacancies and recesses with provisional structures and activities; they "skip over" interruptions, blockages, and cul-de-sacs to expand various projects. While the fabric can look chaotic, ill-managed, and often on the verge of collapse and over-use – and indeed often is – there are also incessant recalibrations, adjustments, and repair. In order to make discrepant uses and environments work together, there needs to be various negotiations and deals from which it is difficult to exclude inhabitants simply based on their background or identity. These things, too, must be put into play. In other words, they become potential resources for the continuous process of working things out, of managing the tensions and over-loads. Spacing-out the built environment requires that the facets of it remain available for repositioning – i.e. for entering into relationships with other facets beyond those delineated by official spatial plans, zoning, and land use regula-tions, which, even if they apply, may not be functionally applicable either in addressing the reality or in getting residents to take them seriously.

The play of surfaces is also evident at the peripheries of large Southeast Asian cities constituting what some analysts have considered a particular kind of urban formation (Bunnell et al., 2006; Kelly, 1999; Laquian, 2005; McGee, 2009). As one crosses these peripheries – no longer economically or socially peripheral to the contemporary megacity region – there is a seemingly arbitrary arrangement of built environments, of ascendancy, renewal, ruin, erasure, and mixture in densely proximate relationships. Without systematic examination of cadastrals and demographic profiles, it is nearly impossible to piece together a functional prospective reading of what is likely to happen. Failed and new projects exist side by side, some even replacing the other – e.g. new developments replacing failed developments without any discernible difference in their appearance; high end mixed use commercial and residential mega-structures sit side by side, one with full occupancy, the other struggling to fill even half of the available space. Seemingly dynamic mixed use and social class neighborhoods reach quick "tipping points" and virtually disappear overnight, while contiguous districts, much more problematic in their economic and social histories, continue to hang on, even thrive.

Here, one might as well just give up trying to figure out what contiguities in place actually mean. What does it mean for particular kinds of built and social environments to be "next to each other," enjoined in a common designation of being part of the same city or urban region? Although political economy can provide a framework for understanding this intensified sense of disjunction, it is possible that the apparent disjunction itself obscures some form of distributed agency at work. The vast peripheries, with their new factories that come and go, with their agricultural plots that come and go, with their dense agglomerations of people that sometimes act like the city we know and sometimes not; the messy lines where the warehousing of the poor expelled from other parts of the city crosses the ambitions of suburban towns to become major urban centers which, in turn, cross the entrepreneurial juggernaut in search of cheap land for back-offices, warehouses and polluting industries which, in turn, crosses the lines of flight of the elite – all represent the tentativeness of urbanization, a new form of trying to keep the mess away from resplendent downtown skylines. What will these jumbles make out of each other; what kinds of specific municipal politics are at work to "space out" discordant functions and populations?

These surfaces of the periphery, on the one hand, can be maintained in a typical array of exploitation and marginalization. Wages are kept low, residents are kept scrambling for one provisional economic advantage after another, parochial social ascriptions are continuously reproduced to preclude mass mobilizations, and residents learn to rely upon their own wits rather than make sustained demands for a better life. These surfaces regulate relationships with various forms of control, most particularly with that of the state – the state that registers, surveys, accounts, disburses, and accords a range of various right and responsibilities. But there are other surfaces as well. There are those that face inside to a particular enfolding of populations and space – not necessarily communities or administrative districts – but zones of a felt commonality or shared past and present.

Across these surfaces different kinds of affective and material economies are performed. Whereas predominant forms of regulation may compel residents to provide "accounts" of themselves and to be accountable in terms of their management of households, expenditures, proclivities and associations, the ways in which residents and workers deal with each other is full of deals – i.e. constantly remade accommodations and collaborations seldom based on strict notions of eligibility or social status; reciprocities of all kinds without the necessary incurring of obligations. Constellations of actors that worked together yesterday may not do so tomorrow, or may indeed repeat their cooperation day after day; decisions, repairs, and innovations may be exercised by a changing cast of characters as no one particular function is the purview of a specific individual, status or territory.

Infrastructure then is not only the materialization of specific practices but a surface of interchanges and transactions that largely "discover" themselves, enacting their own potentialities in moments of unanticipated densities. At the same time, infrastructure is the materialization of anticipation – that sense of timing of knowing how to make a "next move," of the incremental accretion of capacity and possibility. While infrastructure sets lines of articulation and instantiates particular conceptions of space and time, it always engenders shadows, recesses, and occlusions that can be occupied as staging areas for unscripted incursions. All of these need not necessarily emerge from practice *per se*, but are rather implications of infrastructural acts.

## Temporal increments and acts of captivation

As Ackbar Abbas (1997) puts it, urban politics is a politics of dis-appointment – about the "not there" in what is there, or perhaps, more that of "dis-appointing" – being transported to a place you didn't think you were at. Looking at the situation of residents across the postcolonial urban world today, it is possible to construe them of a large sense of disappointment. All of the effort that urban majorities have made disentangling and individuating themselves in order to become eligible for different inclusions, access, participation, security, and accumulation often produces a sense of dissipation – a sense that "this is nowhere," and that it is too late to do anything about it. All of the investments in property, education, legibility have just gotten people deeper in debt, further from where the economic action is, more isolated, more insecure.

Yet, if the persistence of dynamic, if not always thriving, heterogeneous districts with long histories in places like São Paolo, Jakarta, Karachi, and Bangkok – to take a few examples – is any evidence, then the politics of disappointment have been kept at bay. If this is the case—that disappointment has not yet been incorporated as a debilitating recognition of inadequacy and bad calculations—then what kinds of practices have residents relied upon to continue to produce viable spaces of inhabitation? Many of these have already been taken up here. But particularly salient to this question is the way in which relationships to time and movement have been addressed. Here, the incremental refers to momentary consolidations of position that are opportunistically occupied with the knowledge that they are only momentary. Obligations to them, while necessary in the short term, will eventually "run out," for their use is to propel residents somewhere else, into some different disposition that requires different obligations, resources, and ways of paying attention (King, 2008; Kudva, 2009).

For residents who believed that their present and futures rested largely in their hands – whose reliance on formal full-time work decreased or was non-existent, and whose livelihoods had to take place across a broader expanse of space, work sectors and networks, it was important to keep moving. Even when a particular form of income generation seemed to work, it was always going to be insufficient in terms of contingencies that one could not quite get a handle on. From this perspective, then, everything becomes insufficient. It may be enough for now, but as the city grows more complicated, competitive, and opaque in terms of the powers that drive it, anticipations of change always had to be incorporated into decisions about what to do and whom to do it with. Consolidations of support and collaboration were temporary, but movement was impossible without them (Bayat, 2000; Benjamin, 2000; Chatterjee, 2004; Eckstein, 2000; Elyachar, 2011; Garmany, 2010; Gray, 2004; McFarlane, 2011).

In a series of household surveys being conducted across central Jakarta with long-term residents of mixed use, mixed income districts, it is evident that people recognized that they couldn't "go it alone," that relations of mutual obligation, investment, and support had to be put together from what was at hand. While residents had relationships with people of common ethnicity, in origin from specific villages and cities across Indonesia, those with whom they worked (and where frequently these were one and the same thing), such relations had their strengths and weaknesses. For example, in the convergence of occupational and ethnic identity, residents often worked with those coming from the same ethnic and geographical location. This commonality was a means of securing employment – both in terms of accessing and keeping jobs. It also entailed a series of unavoidable obligations whose duration was seemingly without end. Belonging was aimed at shoring up particular territories of operation or concretizing particular standards through which individual efficacy was to be evaluated. As such, these commonalities could be limiting in terms of the pragmatic actions necessary to keep pace with changing conditions.

In residential districts where compositional homogeneity was spatially limited if even existent, inhabitants invariably witnessed the quotidian actions of households whose backgrounds and ways of doing things were different from their own – often discovering that differences in background did not translate easily into differences in the ways they approached everyday livelihood and social life. Just because residents found themselves situated in heterogeneous places did not necessarily mean that people did or needed to interact with each other outside basic practices of conviviality. People could and invariably did keep their distance. But this distance itself could be instrumental in configuring a temporary coalescence of attention and effort among households marked by different statuses, backgrounds, occupations and social networks. When one asks households to identify the people with whom they spend time, get information, assess possibilities with, and take seriously as purveyors of evaluation, there are usually a significant number of co-residents who are neither immediate neighbors nor share any surface features of commonality.

While the persistence of these relationships over time waxes and wanes, in inquiries as to the composition of social networks in the past, there seems to be always a space set aside for such relationships. Often nothing is concretely done with them, but there are times when residents brought together in these relationships collaborate to identify economic opportunities, access contacts important to a specific task or aspiration, and even enroll each other as labor or investors in mutually elaborated projects.

This kind of logic has been built in to the functioning of some key medium-scale economic sectors. In the massive motorcycle parts and repair district of Taman Sari in central Jakarta, there are continuously oscillating relationships among individual retailers, often grouped through joint ownership or family relationships, but more importantly intersected through changing calculations of value and opportunity accorded to each potential transaction. For example, for those outfits situated at the poles of the district and along the major thoroughfare entrances, the priority may be to quickly capture particular kinds of needs – such as the rapid acquisition of small parts and accessories – or to gear transactions to the making of assessments of the largest volume of flow-through traffic as possible about what aggregates of demand look like – how many are looking for repairs, new or used parts; how many seem to know the nature of what needs to be fixed, and how many are less certain. Outlets also have to anticipate how potential customers think about the different reputations that have been made and lost among them, and where to situate themselves in relationship to each other.

While each outlet exists as a distinct entity, these are continuously being reassembled into various chains of cooperation – the conjoint buying from specific wholesalers, sharing certain skilled labor, and investing in particular kinds of engagements with customers in terms of what can be gleaned from their background, and then passing them on to other outlets that might be better prepared to capitalize on that background. In this way information and reputations about the district and particular groups of outlets within it might more easily amass and spread across a larger territory. Even if a given outlet is capable of fixing a particular problem, it may know that the outlet across the street has better mechanical capacity, and if they find out, for example, that the particular motorcycle and driver come from a pool in a specific company, they may attempt to capture some of that larger pool for sales of another kind – parts or accessories – by virtue of steering this particular customer to the best possible deal. Outlets don't only want to grab onto traffic passing through, looking for specific goods or services, but also want to use these moments as particular opportunities to reach out into and tap both the larger collective dynamics of hundreds of outlets – with different suppliers, skills, networks, and reputations – and the larger city itself.

Many of these relationships are entered into with a sense of their provisionality, a sense that in the long run little may actually come out of them but that they potentially open up residents to information, networks, places, and opportunities that they otherwise would have limited access to. They become perceived as vehicles of learning – expanding knowledge about the city and what is taking place across it. The opportunistic character of these relations mitigates the sense of mutual obligation; there are limited expectations of reciprocity and fairness, but one need not commit to developing them; the ease of entrance and exit continuously reframes their value.

These provisional consolidations act as breaks and detours – what Quentin Meillassoux (2007) calls in a philosophical context, time not "all at once" – a way of looking here and not there, of orientation to a sense of "here and then, afterwards, there." This is a sense of the incremental, of forging moments of accomplishment and assessment, and then moving on. But where does one go from here? Especially in cities where it becomes increasingly difficult to know the widening range of factors and places that affect what it is possible for one to do. It is important to have a sense of timing, not to settle in too much with a given way of doing things and with a specific set of cooperants. There is a need for trust and stability. But also there is need to be able to upend and move on, often with little notice.

The incremental then is partly enacted through these momentary *captivations*. These captivations have nothing to do with making accounts or making things legible, but are a way of paying attention to things as if they are not what they are – seeing one's neighbors, co-workers as something else and that require a momentary holding in place. As I have written in other publications, these captivations become a way of anticipating what might happen if a person decides to take an unfamiliar course of action (Simone, 2009). When we act, we do so only if we have some sense about what is going to happen to us if we do something in a particular way otherwise, we won't do it. This is why we are hesitant to take risks or do something new. So what I am talking about here is the way that people invent probable outcomes for experimental actions in situations that no longer have a strong relationship to reliable institutions to interpret what is going on. Thus what is involved here are ways of making connections among people and ways of doing things that don't seem to go together. This, then, opens up possibilities for individual residents to make new affiliations and collaboration, and take risks with them.

This does not mean that central Jakarta and other cities across the so-called Global South are not replete with tight strictures of control largely activated in displacing the criteria of survival upon the shoulders of individual households. Competition for jobs, money and contracts are intensifying. Local government systems sometimes closely scrutinize and monitor the activities of their constituents in ways that are claustrophobic and cut off the possibilities for innovation. Populist movements based on geographical and religious backgrounds can easily whip up the sentiments of overstretched households and induce quick fractures in long-term solidarities across various divides.

Still, in the districts within which I work in central Jakarta, residents shy away from social calibrations based on accounts of which group gets to do what, and under what circumstances. They don't want to be tied down to common rules or behavioral styles – after all, who would define them, and what would have to be left out in terms of developing something recognizable and accessible for residents to get a hold of? Making it in the city is more a process of experimentation than following the right procedures. Collaboration and reciprocity are largely experimental devices whose aim is not usually to cohere an emergent social body or concretize a collective-to-come. The range of practices described here do not produce a zero-sum game of clearly identifiable winner or losers, nor do they necessarily work toward enhanced levels of solidarity aimed at securing clear political objectives. The assessment of what is at work here clearly demands a sense of hesitation – both on the part of participants and observers. For the deployment of practice is essentially volatile – i.e. there are no guarantees as to the results, implications or trajectories set in motion. Practices may be implemented to attain specific results, but whether they are generous or manipulative, generative or destructive, good or bad, useful or useless cannot be determined in advance, and require a spirit of hesitation. But this volatility is critical to capacities of things and people to move with each other in both same and different ways; it is important to keep things from being foreclosed, which across the post-colonial world has been a critical and accessible agenda (Pease, 2010).

In situations where everyone has to find a way to get along, the sheer plurality of actions and backgrounds is seen as being a good bet, precisely because the excess means that if some residents are doing something that isn't readily measurable or understood, then what you are doing puts people in the same situation; and there is simply too much going on for it to be worth any one resident feeling like their own lives are being judged, constrained, or made insecure by the diversities going around. Heterogeneity is important not so much in terms of a locus in which to manage intensifying divergent demands or as a social ideal. Rather, it is a platform capable of absorbing different ways of doing things all at the same time without individuals concluding that they are less well equipped or less eligible to continue doing what they are doing or to try something else without necessarily committing to it over the long run. Everything attempted has the possibility of changing course without bringing the entire household or neighborhood down with it.

## Infrastructure and urban life

Infrastructure is a complex surrounds. Urban residents put together and are themselves put together through a continuous interchange of materials and the expressions these interchanges make possible. These are expressions of physical exertion, visible arrays, and symbolic arrangements – all of which constitute possibilities and constraints for what can be done. Infrastructure exerts a force – not simply in the materials and energies it avails, but also the way it attracts people, draws them in, coalesces and expends their capacities. Thus, the distinction between infrastructure and sociality is fluid and pragmatic rather than definitive. People work on things to work on each other, as these things work on them.

So, the incremental efforts discussed above are temporalities of remaking life through continuing adjustments, of adding on – the calibration of expectations concerning what can work, what is viable, and when. Decisions constantly have to be made in terms of the length of time necessary in order to determine whether investments in people, projects, and efforts will have a discernible pay-off; about when to shift things around; how to hedge against high risk experiments. Decisions have to be made about the division of labor, about who does what and under what circumstances; about how to forge reciprocal transactions; how to link up various livelihood "projects" in ways that generate synergistic effects and do not overburden them with too many obligations or factors. These decisions take material form as these forms in-form what kinds of decisions might be viewed as possible.

Residents have to support the necessary myths of given authorities – to sustain the impression of an overarching order – while, at the same time, acting as if everything is to be invented. They must render themselves to be counted and

accountable, and generate the appearance of administrative structures and procedures and; at the same time, buttress their survival with a wide range of
adjustments that are "off the radar." Thus, there are intricate arrangements and
mobilities across different sectors of organization, different logics of authority and
work. Values must be consistently remade and stabilized, and this requires a
plurality of engagement between residents and different urban institutions.

How these arrangements and practices intersect with the intensifying capital-
ization on ground rent values and the corralling of emergent middle-class
aspirations into highly individuated built forms and valorization through
consumption is a challenging story. In the past, while money circulated through
many hands, these hands at least knew that a proportion of what circulated was
theirs – it was their money to put into play, and even when pooled, participants
in various projects tended to take charge of those facets in which their money
was deployed. The long-term stability of the spaces in which the intricate
economies described in this chapter take place – the land, built environment and
local enterprises – will probably require various forms of corporatization. Here
residents will be reframed as investors, stakeholders, and members. The collective choreography of highly differentiated transactions will have to also take on
consolidations able to at least slow down the onslaught of big development and
speculation. This will mean investments for future gains – for example, in collective tenure, community-held assets, integrated development planning. These are
all technical devices that have been put to work to concretize the aspirations of
low- and middle-income residents across the cities of the majority world. None
of them functions without problems, and often they raise more problems than
they address.

The power of financialization completely elides situation-specific realities and
values. The collusions among developers, investment banks, management
companies, hedge funds, and property investors primarily use the built environment as a "shell" around which elaborate financial manipulations take place.
Even if the actual resultant built development is itself empty of significance, this
financial game eats up substantial urban space. If residents of mixed-use districts
are to preserve their hard-won efforts, this may require collective efforts where
resources put into projects are no longer always visible. Here, the traced circuits
of exchange disappear behind various corporate screens and contracts where the
labor of a district is hedged across various forms of income generation and ways
of exerting influence. Who then makes these decisions; who has sufficient clout
and trust to mobilize local effort and resources? These are increasingly critical
questions in Jakarta.

It is probably too simple to say that planning and governance must take
greater cognizance of these relational infrastructures in times where the long-
range futures of cities become more precarious. Regardless of the limitations in
any system of accountancy, there must be ways to enable the efforts that residents
make to sustain and redo their inhabitation count more in the ways in which
governmental decisions and policies are deliberated and structured. Relational

infrastructures must also intensify the possibilities of making visible capacities and aspirations that otherwise remain occluded, either for tactical reasons on the part of those who deem that the efficacy of what they do requires to remain under the radar or because they simply are not recognized by the optics of power. Much emphasis has been placed on inhabitants participating in a wide range of decentralized planning and governance processes. Work must also take place that thinks strategically about how to fold in the multifaceted, multiscaled institutions of planning, resource allocation and political decision-making into the infrastructures of relational practices, even if only to issue new complicities and dilemmas.

## Bibliography

Abbas, A. (1997) *Hong Kong: Culture and the Politics of Disappearance*. Minneapolis: University of Minnesota Press.

Amin, A. and Thrift, N. (2002) *Cities: Re-imagining the Urban*. London: Polity.

Auyero, J. (2007) *Routine Politics and Violence in Argentina: The Grey Zone of the State*. Cambridge: Cambridge University Press.

Bayat, A. (2000) "From 'Dangerous Classes' to 'Quiet Rebels': Politics of Urban Subaltern in the Global South," *International Sociology*, 15: 533–556.

Bayat, A. (2009) *Life as Politics: How Ordinary People Change the Middle East*. Stanford, CA: Stanford University Press.

Benjamin, S. (2000) "Governance, Economic Settings and Poverty in Bangalore," *Environment and Urbanization*, 12: 35–56.

Blundo, G. (2006) "Dealing with the Local State: The Informal Privatization of Street," *Development and Change*, 37: 799–819.

Bouzarovski, S. (2009) "Building Events in Inner-City Gdańsk, Poland: Exploring the Sociospatial Construction of Agency in Built Form," *Environment and Planning D: Society and Space*, 27(5): 840–858.

Bunnell, T., Muzaini, H., and Sidaway, J. (2006) "Global City Frontiers: Singapore's Hinterland and the Contested Socio-political Geographies of Bintan, Indonesia," *International Journal of Urban and Regional Research*, 30(1): 3–22.

Callon, M., Millo, Y., and Muniesa, F. (2007) *Market Devices*. Oxford: Blackwell.

Chatterjee, P. (2004) *The Politics of the Governed: Popular Politics in Most of the World*. New York: Columbia University Press.

Cheah, P. (2008) "Crises of Money," *Positions: East Asia Cultures Critique*, 16(1): 189–219.

Cooper, M. (2010) "Turbulent Worlds: Financial Markets and Environmental Crisis," *Theory, Culture & Society*, 27: 167–90.

Cross, J. and Morales, A. (2007) "Introduction: Locating Street Markets in the Modern/PostModern World," in *Street Entrepreneurs: People, Place and Politics in a Local and Global Perspective*. New York: Routledge.

Curran, W. (2007) "'From the Frying Pan to the Oven': Gentrification and the Experience of Industrial Displacement in Williamsburg, Brooklyn," *Urban Studies*, 44: 1427–1440.

de Boeck, F. and Plissard, M-F. (2006) *Kinshasa: Tales of the Invisible City*. Antwerp: Ludon.

de Certeau, M. (1998) *The Capture of Speech and Other Political Writings*. Minneapolis: University of Minnesota Press.

Eckstein, S. (2000) "Poor People Versus the State: Anatomy of a Successful

Mobilization for Housing in Mexico City," in S. Eckstein (ed.) *Power and Popular Protest: Latin American Social Movement.* Berkeley, CA: University of California Press, pp. 329–351.

Elyachar, J. (2011) "The Political Economy of Movement and Gesture in Cairo," *Journal of the Royal Anthropological Institute*, 17(1): 82–99.

Fawaz, M. (2008) "An Unusual Clique of City-Makers: Social Networks in the Production of a Neighborhood in Beirut," *International Journal of Urban and Regional Research*, 32: 565–585.

Foucault, M. (2008) *The Birth of Biopolitics: Lectures at the Collège de France, 1978–1979.* Basingstoke: Palgrave Macmillan.

Garfinkel, H. (1991) *Studies in Ethnomethodology.* New York: Polity.

Garmany, J. (2010) "Religion and Governmentality: Understanding Governance in Urban Brazil," *Geoforum* (August). doi:10.1016/j.geoforum.2010.06.005.

Goffman, E. (1986) *Frame Analysis: An Essay on the Organization of Experience.* Evanston, IL: Northeastern University Press.

Goldman, M. (2011) "Speculative Urbanism and the Making of the Next World City," *International Journal of Urban and Regional Research*, 35: 555–581.

Goldstein, D. (2004) *The Spectacular City: Violence and Performance in Urban Bolivia.* Durham, NC: Duke University Press.

Gooptu, N. (2001) *The Politics of the Urban Poor in Early Twentieth-Century India.* Cambridge: Cambridge University Press.

Gray, O. (2004) *Demeaned but Empowered: The Social Power of the Urban Poor in Jamaica.* Kingston: University of the West Indies Press.

Greene, M. and Rojas, E. (2008) "Incremental Construction: A Strategy to Access Housing," *Environment and Urbanization*, 20(1): 89–108.

Guyer, J. (2004) *Marginal Gains: Monetary Transactions in Atlantic Africa.* Chicago: University of Chicago Press.

Guyer, J., Denzer, L., and Agbaje, A. (eds.) (2002) *Money Struggles and City Life.* Portsmouth, NH: Heinemann.

Haber, P.L. (2006) *Power from Experience: Urban Popular Movements in Late Twentieth-Century Mexico.* Philadelphia, PA: Penn State Press.

Hansen, T. B. and Verkaaik, O. (2009) "Introduction – Urban Charisma: On Everyday Mythologies in the City," *Critique of Anthropology*, 29: 5–26.

Heller, P. and Evans, P. (2010) "Taking Tilly South: Durable Inequalities, Democratic Contestation, and Citizenship in the Southern Metropolis," *Theory and Society*, 39: 433–450.

Hodson, M. and Marvin, S. (2009) "Urban Ecological Security: A New Urban Paradigm?" *International Journal of Urban and Regional Research*, 33: 193–215.

Jansson, A. and Lagerkvist, J. (eds.) (2010) *Strange Spaces: Explorations in Mediated Obscurity.* Princeton, NJ: Princeton University Press.

Kelly, P. (1999) "Everyday Urbanization: The Social Dynamics of Development in Manila's Extended Metropolitan Region," *International Journal of Urban and Regional Research*, 23: 283–303.

King, R. (2008) "Bangkok Space, and Conditions of Possibility," *Environment and Planning D: Society and Space*, 26(2): 315–337.

Kirkpatrick, L. O. and Smith, M. P. (2011) "The Infrastructural Limits to Growth: Rethinking the Urban Growth Machine in Times of Fiscal Crisis," *International Journal of Urban and Regional Research*, 35: 477–503.

Kothari, U. (2008) "Global Peddlers and Local Networks: Migrant Cosmopolitanisms," *Environment and Planning D: Society and Space*, 26: 500–516.

Kudva, N. (2009) "The Everyday and the Episodic: The Spatial and Political Impacts of Urban Informality," *Environment and Planning A*, 41: 1614–1628.

Laquian, A. (2005) *Beyond Metropolis: The Planning and Governance of Asia's Mega-Urban Regions*. Washington, DC: Woodrow Wilson Center Press/Baltimore, MD: Johns Hopkins University Press.

Latham, A. and McCormack, D. (2004) "Moving Cities: Rethinking the Materialities of Urban Geographies," *Progress in Human Geography*, 28: 701–724.

Latour, B. (2005) *Reassembling the Social: An Introduction to Actor-Network Theory*. Oxford: Oxford University Press.

Lee, B. and LiPuma, E. (2004) *Financial Derivatives and the Globalization of Risk*. Durham, NC: Duke University Press.

Lindell, I. (2010) "Informality and Collective Organising: Identities, Alliances and Transnational Activism in Africa," *Third World Quarterly*, 31: 207–222.

McFarlane, C. (2008) "Postcolonial Bombay: Decline of a Cosmopolitanism City?" *Environment and Planning D: Society and Space*, 26: 480–499.

McFarlane, C. (2011) *Learning the City: Knowledge and Translocal Assemblage*. Oxford: Wiley-Blackwell.

McGee, T. (2009) "The Spatiality of Urbanization and the Policy Challenges of Mega-Urban and Desakota Regions of Southeast Asia," United Nations University-IAS Working Paper 161.

Meagher, K. (2010) *Identity Economics: Social Networks and the Informal Economy in Nigeria*. London: James Currey.

Meillassoux, Q. (2007) "Subtraction and contraction: Deleuze, Immanence, and Matter and Memory," *Collapse*, III: 63–107.

Menjívar, C. (2000) *Fragmented Ties: Salvadoran Immigrant Networks in America*. Berkeley, CA: University of California Press.

Monstadt, J. (2009) "Conceptualizing the Political Ecology of Urban Infrastructures: Insights from Technology and Urban Studies," *Environment and Planning A*, 41: 1924–1942.

Nancy, J-L. (2002) *L'Intrus*. East Lansing, MI: Michigan State University Press.

Pease, D. (2010) "The Crisis of Critique in Postcolonial Modernity," *Boundary 2*, 37: 179–205.

Peters, R. (2009) "The Assault on Occupancy in Surabaya: Legible and Illegible Landscapes in a City of Passage," *Development and Change*, 40(5): 903–925.

Pile, S. (2005) *Real Cities: Modernity, Space and the Phantasmagorias of City Life*. London: Sage.

Prag, E. (2010) "Entrepôt Politics: Political Struggles over the Dantokpa Marketplace in Cotonou, Benin," Danish Institute of International Studies, Working Paper 2010:03.

Pryke, M. (2006) "Speculating on Geographies of Finance," Centre for Research on Socio-Cultural Change, Open University, Working Paper #24.

Roitman, J. (2005) *Fiscal Disobedience: An Anthropology of Economic Regulation in Central Africa*. Princeton, NJ: Princeton University Press.

Roy, A. (2011) "Slumdog Cities: Rethinking Subaltern Urbanism," *International Journal of Urban and Regional Research*, 35: 223–238.

Shatkin, G. (2008) "The City and the Bottom Line: Urban Megaprojects and the Privatization of Planning in Southeast Asia," *Environment and Planning A*, 40: 383–401.

Simone, A. (2009) *City Life from Jakarta to Dakar: Movements at the Crossroads*. New York: Routledge.

Small, M. (2009) *Unanticipated Gains: Origins of Network Inequality in Everyday Life*. Oxford: Oxford University Press.

Stack, C. (1997) *All Our Kin: Strategies for Survival in a Black Community*. New York: Basic Books.

Stengers, I. (2010) *Cosmopolitics 1*. Minneapolis: University of Minnesota Press.

Tassi, N. (2010) "The 'Postulate of Abundance': *Cholo* Market and Religion in La Paz, Bolivia," *Social Anthropology*, 18: 191–209.

Taussig, M. (1992) *The Nervous System*. London: Routledge.

Taussig, M. (1999) *Defacement: Deception and the Power of the Negative*. Palo Alto, CA; Stanford University Press.

Telles, V. da Silva and Hirata, D.V. (2007) "The City and Urban Practices: In the Uncertain Frontiers between the Illegal, the Informal, and the Illicit," *Estudos Avançados* 21: 173–191.

Virno, P. (2009) "Angels and the General Intellect: Individuation in Duns Scotus and Gilbert Simondon," *Parrhesia*, 7: 58–67.

Whitson, R. (2007) "Hidden Struggles: Spaces of Power and Resistance in Informal Work in Urban Argentina," *Environment and Planning A*, 39(12): 2916–2934.

Williams, G. (2002) *The Other Side of the Popular: Neoliberalism and Subalternity in Latin America*. Durham, NC: Duke University Press.

Wilson, A. (2008) "The Sacred Geography of Bangkok's Markets," *International Journal of Urban and Regional Research*, 32: 631–642.

Wu, F., Shenjing He, and Webster, C. (2010) "Path Dependency and the Neighbourhood Effect: Urban Poverty in Impoverished Neighbourhoods in Chinese Cities," *Environment and Planning A*, 42: 134–152.

# Chapter 2

# Infra-city

## Speculations on flux and history in infrastructure-making

*Vyjayanthi Rao*

## Infra-city

To talk about infrastructure is to invoke both the promise of a future as well as imminent trauma. Underground or above ground, systems that make urban flows possible are always a threat, even when black-boxed and separated from the smooth flow of conscious urban life (Graham, 2010). The city might be turned into a weapon or the city is constantly broken and must be fixed. The city is overflowing and must be contained or the city is too contained and must grow and let off steam.

The story of infrastructure always begins with one or another of these historical moments—it is never a story of which infrastructure is itself the subject but a narrative about growth, decay or the end of the city, in which infrastructure happens to play a leading role. This chapter grows out of eavesdropping on many conversations about infrastructure not the least of which are the shrill cries of despair about the "infrastructure problems" of the mega-cities of the South. My intuition is that part of the context for these conversations is a fundamental disconnection between the "real" of infrastructure as the organizational medium of urban life and the various models and propositions from which urbanism is seen to derive, such as the metropolis, the global city, the mega-city and the world city to name just a few popular models that dominate urban theorizing. This disconnection gives rise to numerous ethical challenges on how to reconcile oneself to the ongoing and actually existing practices of urbanism in cities today when the normative horizons provided by models have given way to an incessant present of speculative practices, detached from ideas of the "near future" (Guyer, 2007) that dominated mid-twentieth-century planning imaginaries.

My point of departure is an understanding of the city as territory consolidated through a structural coupling of people and infrastructures and an assumption that this structural coupling is historically specific in different urban contexts. In the contemporary moment, we are drawn by this problem of coupling because of the visibility of the displacement of massive numbers of ordinary residents in places like Mumbai, Cape Town, Rio, and Beijing, to name only a few, to make way for new infrastructural formulations. My suggestion is that an ethnographic investigation of these moments of infrastructural (re)formulation together with a theory of history that attends to issues of causality, contingency and anticipation in everyday action will provide a platform to clarify the ethical challenges under which urban life-worlds are formed and inhabited by various actors who become "city-makers." These include planners and policy-makers, private sector barons and politicians as well as the ordinary residents of places like Mumbai whose displacement makes way for new infrastructural formulations on a massive scale.

Specifically, such an ethnographic investigation opens the door to considering the feedback effect of the propositions through which the structural coupling of people and infrastructure occurs, considering these propositions as acts of reconditioning the urban environments from which infrastructure systems are circumscribed to produce regularity, predictability and territorial consolidation towards specific, instrumental or utopian ends ranging from surplus generation to participatory democracy. Such propositional acts are increasingly visible in cities today as citizens participate in rethinking their neighborhoods through self-conscious proposition-making acts at different scales – from small-scale data-gathering exercises to versions of "design charettes," irrespective of whether or not these acts have any measure of success considered in the instrumental sense. The idea of the imminent end of the city, that is so present in contemporary urban discourse (especially regarding cities of the Global South) invokes a response that is now familiar in cities across the world: incessant talk of infrastructure building and financing, talk of movement and flow, constant disjuncture and permanent flux.[1] This idea also increasingly informs urban activism that focuses its attentions on infrastructure building. So what is given about infrastructure? Only this, it would seem – that infrastructure is never given *a priori* but it must be produced, it must be made, incessantly, through various discourses and experiences, most prominently those of destruction, decay and inadequacy. Might there be discourses other than those of destruction, decay and inadequacy that inform the production of infrastructure, material and conceptual?

I suggest here that a deeper examination of propositional, pragmatic actions provide sites at which the history of (infra)structure becomes visible as a reformulation that feeds back specific ideas about the future into an urban imaginary and is therefore a significant site for investigation. Even as a clear physical trace that confirms to a plan for creating infrastructure and a discourse that delineates "a series of norms and procedures ... that align provision and consumption with minimal mediation" (Simone, 2008), infrastructure is always an achievement, an outcome of a battle against nature or against specific social forces as in Haussmann's Paris and therefore, at some level, an act of design. Infrastructure making or coding the specific disposition of infrastructure (Easterling, 2011a) is thus an act of design that then constitutes a new relational agency in the urban environment.

For example, the switch from tank and well-based water supply in the early history of South Asian cities to tap water supply, delivered into the home, severed social and political relations that were coded around rights to water shares in a well. However, because of the scarcity of taps in relation to the burgeoning population, the tap as an actant effectively consolidated a different set of hierarchical and exclusionary relations in comparison with the tank. When considering such effects as "feedback" effects or loops into the infrastructure-making process, we are able to see how significant it is to consider the histories of infrastructure-making in relation to its coding.[2] The uses of infrastructure, active assertions in relation to infrastructure, are also what renovate its meanings and dispositions so that the "form" of infrastructure lies not in its object-ness but in the operations that inform and renovate infrastructure ceaselessly. These renovations too must be considered in the realm of design rather than viewing design as finally constituting fully formed and normed objects. In the cities of the Global South, various "small acts" of design are constantly renovating urban environment and also, further widening the disjunctures between surface and underground, to use the metropolitan metaphor. What they do is to introduce new imaginaries of infrastructure-making, which challenge the "mega-project" imaginary (see Benjamin, 2008) and introduce new forms of political claims, which draw on languages other than those of rights and entitlements.

In relation to infrastructure, acts of design generally draw on three distinct propositions about the structural coupling of people and infrastructure – the first emphasizes the determinism of technological systems in consolidating urban territories, the second concerns cities as zones of affect constituted by the everyday actions of people to achieve regularities[3] normally attributed to the mediation of infrastructural technologies; while the third proposition builds on recent theoretical positions that argue for recognizing the "I" as a compound of the traditional ontological categories of human and non-human (see Latour and Hermant, 2006; Bennett, 2009). In this chapter, I do not consider the feedback effects of these self-conscious acts of design but rather those moments at which socio-cultural and political specificities of the structural coupling of people and infrastructure might become visible. Such moments emerge in the course of pragmatic, everyday acts of making the city as life-world, on the one hand, and in course of the dramatic collapse of infrastructural systems, on the other. These are situations of a different order than acts of design and yet they also make visible a different understanding of history – not as an ordering of significant events but as the constitutive feedback of everyday acts of infrastructure-making into the urban environment that in turn affect the urban system, even if in minor and imperceptible ways.

To study these moments, I deploy the concept of urban density which seems particularly salient in Mumbai, a city that is said to have some of the highest human densities per square kilometer in the world. Here I interpret density not as a given attribute of urban space, a passive calculus that arises as a function of numbers and their normative environmental needs but as active spatio-temporal configurations that make visible styles of structural coupling, between human and non-human actors, and cultural-conceptual histories with the dispositions of non-human actants. Density, in other words, enables us to be "attentive to practical problems posed by the coexistence of such large numbers of people on such a small surface area" (Latour and Hernant, 2006) but its consideration in the cases I present here specifically highlights the ways in which loops are created between experience and concept that provide avenues for decisions to be based on different causal ideas relating to the future – including, most starkly, temporal anticipation or structural reproduction and, at a further remove, speculations about contingency and its effects on the system's ontological stability.

I turn now to an archive of ethnographic observations, or, contextual, situated observations of the ways in which people intersect with infrastructural formulations in everyday life. This archive is established, in the first instance, from the personal experience of participant observation, both as an anthropologist and as an ordinary resident of Mumbai. As the latter, I have rich memories of being in different kinds of crowds, always aware and awed by the sensory experience of being within. As a high-school and university student in Mumbai, I commuted 3 hours each day on the rickety and infrequent "Harbour Line" service of the Central Railways. The journey in the morning in the packed ladies' compartment listening to housewives describing their routines to each other on their way to offices was broken only a few stations later when my friend and namesake joined the compartment. Our favorite way to "pass time" (or timepass, which is a distinct word and concept in many Indian urban pidgins) was to sing to each other, showing off our most recent lessons in classical music, turning a rather dreary journey into a routine of pleasure. When others did the same and annoyed us, we came to understand in turn our own status as irritants to the compartment as a whole, even if this was a whole fragmented into distinct groups intent on seeking their own forms of pleasure.

Yet these daily journeys rarely broke down into discordant or cacophonous noise. At lunchtimes in downtown Mumbai, flowing along with the crowds on the sidewalks of the business district, I often caught bits of tunes hummed by someone in the crowd, always perfectly in tune. But these peaceful, sometimes even pleasant everyday experiences were jarred once in every while when the train service broke down or the city outside was occupied by a massive crowd of protesters. I look back at experiences, which were not connected to my later analytic life as an anthropologist when I developed a conceptual vocabulary to handle such experiences as part of an archive. However, to narrate these very personal experiences I turn here to the voices of others and their particular, lyrical abstractions of similar experiences, wagering that these voices render possible a view of the sociality of subjective, phenomenological experience and thus enable us to connect experience to an ethical order whose subjects are diffused in space yet connected in a phenomenological sense. I find my own voice in an act of ventriloquism, through the published fragments that reflect my own felt archive.

## Proximate distances: density and the "effective city"

In Kiran Nagarkar's novel, *Ravan & Eddie*, set in a prototypical Mumbai chawl, we find the following description of a Mumbai commuter train, seen through the eyes of one of the novel's two child protagonists:

> [Ravan] had reached the Byculla bridge. A local train swept past without stopping at the station. Like a sponge being squeezed, the people on the platform shrank back. There were commuters hanging from the bars of the carriage windows. Some stood precariously on god alone knows what between compartments. Every once in a while a trousered leg or an arm swung wildly but hurriedly got back to its owner when a signal pole of the support of a bridge rushed past. The sides of the train were bulging with the pressure of people packed into it (How many passengers does a Bombay "local" hold anyway? Twenty-five thousand? Thirty? Forty?) Any moment now that speeding solid iron shell was going to split open and thousands upon thousands of bodies were going to be flung all over Bombay, all the way to Borivali and Virar, some falling into the Thane creek, some into the Arabian Sea. Almost by rote, Ravan had stuck his head into one of the diamond-shaped openings in the gridiron of the bridge. This was, after all, one of the most exciting places in the universe.
>
> (1995: 20)

The sense of perverse excitement conveyed in this passage is a wonderful example of the ways in which a dominant, mythic image of Mumbai comes to be felt and experienced, even by a child growing up in the city. Ravan's Bombay[4] is a place in which these congealed images of awesome crowds and pressure are ubiquitous and overbearing, everywhere in the public discourse about the decline of the city and its bulging infrastructure. The train, seen through Ravan's eyes, is a solid iron shell that is also bulging and elastic, a melding of the human commuter with the solid iron shell. On the platform, the mass of commuters waiting become one as a sponge, shrinking back in unison from the speeding monster. This endless elasticity and melding with matter are finally mirrored by Ravan's act of squeezing his head between the railings of the bridge. The everyday experience of the city for the child, as one of the most exciting places in the universe, is one in which infrastructure is alive, not merely functional or even magical (as many interpretations of technology in the colonial and post-colonial world are apt to suggest).

The chawl itself – in which the drama of *Ravan & Eddie* is set – is, of course, one of the most potent images of crowding and density in Mumbai. It is a site, not only of new forms of sociality – intense and intimate relations forged by the very architectural form of the tenement structure – but also therefore a site at which the conceptual notion of the private is materially negotiated and the infrastructure through which the norm of private experience is coded. The tiny chawl rooms of Mumbai seem endlessly elastic to many observers, ever expanding to accommodate multi-generational families. Most literally, such expansions take the form of lofting and adding in private washing and bathing facilities and sometimes even private bathrooms (a more recent feature of chawl modifications).

These additions radically alter the metabolism of the building even as the expansion of families and the influx of new members into chawl space require the occupation of all common spaces such as the verandahs that run along the length of the buildings and even the stairwells at all times of day and night. Portions under the stairwells are often turned into shops and accommodations for tradesmen. These spaces double up for other uses by night. These spaces and the relations they engender have been interpreted as half-way points between the familiar social life of the village and the anonymity of the metropolis in the worlds of early migrants. The intimacy between strangers, marked by caste, language and region is one of the celebrated characteristics of chawl life in the films and literature which emphasize forms of sociality and affiliation that are not based on kinship ties alone.[5] However, as Nagarkar's novel emphasizes, the same qualities also turn the chawl into a site of conflict and mutual contempt, bred by familiarity, proximity and of course by the mutual recognition afforded to strangers of each other's ethnic or linguistic or caste provenance.[6] Indeed, one could interpret the private as an intensely conflicted zone between communion, community and conflict. The plot of *Ravan & Eddie* in fact turns around a deadly conflict set in the "Central Works Department" chawl number 17 whose floors are divided between Hindu and Roman Catholic families.

This melding of people with the built environment continues to define a visual-conceptual apprehension of the urban density of Mumbai today. During his first visit to Mumbai in 2004, Daniel Liebeskind, the well-known architect and a designer of the Ground Zero site in New York, remarked: "Mumbai is clearly a city that eludes architects who see the city as a material object. It's a city where human beings are far more important than brick and mortar, concrete, glass and steel." Mumbai disappears as sheer material fact to be substituted by sheer demographic density that constitutes its visual overlay, taking over even the traditional space of infrastructure as the city's substrate. In terms of numbers, it is well known that Mumbai's neighborhoods have some of the highest human densities per square kilometer in the world. In recent years, these densities have been conceived as infrastructural "problems" to be manipulated in order to produce an overarching argument for redesign and redevelopment. However, the train compartment and the chawl are manifestations of what historian Jim Masselos (2003) has called the "effective city," a city in which bodies are continuously in motion and, thus, the structural coupling of people and infrastructure acquires a functional dimension, making the city hang together, as an economic and social machine. According to a study quoted by Masselos, during the 1990s, Mumbai's local trains carried nearly five and a half million people each day, or roughly half the number of people carried by the entire national railway system.

This visual-conceptual effect of the dense massing of bodies overwhelms the architectural sense of "space as an implication of objects … [and] as the medium of our relationships" as the architect-philosopher Lebbeus Woods puts it. What sorts of relations, then, are possible when density defines the structural coupling of people and infrastructure, a density that visually overwhelms space itself as a medium of experience? In the passage from *Ravan & Eddie*, the train is a speeding, solid shell, a universal and neutral container of bodies that it would be flung into different parts of Mumbai. This description might conjure up the image of an amorphous mass, of bodies without identity, merely sharing a common destiny through a common journey. The imaginary of the mass, associated in social theory with exceptional demographic states such as those of the crowd and the mob, is an everyday experience in Mumbai though its "reality" effectively differentiates it from the concept of the mass. If the crowd and the mob are treated in social theory as exceptions specifically associated with violence, the local train appears as a container for a mass that is in fact peaceable on more or less a daily basis. This understanding is spelled out in Suketu Mehta's best-selling book on Mumbai, *Maximum City* (2004):

> If you are late for work in Mumbai and reach the station just as the train is leaving the platform, don't despair. You can run up to the packed compartments and find many hands unfolding like petals to pull you on board. And while you will probably have to hang on to the door-frame with your fingertips, you are still grateful for the empathy of your fellow passengers, already packed tighter than cattle, their shirts drenched with sweat in the badly ventilated compartment. They know that your boss might yell at you or cut your pay if you miss this train. And at the moment of contact, they do not know if the hand reaching out for theirs belongs to a Hindu or a Muslim or a Christian or a Brahmin or an Untouchable. Come on board, they say. We'll adjust.

In this passage, Mehta adds a more nuanced sociological dimension to the amorphous, pulsating mass described by the child protagonist, Ravan. Although Mehta's take on the crowd has been criticized by many as romantic, this passage is useful in that it makes visible a practice of "adjusting" as a principle means of claiming a place in the crowd. Adjusting implies a practice of persons with already formed and distinct identities rather than with those strangers who come to populate the canonical texts of urban theory, best described by Robert Musil's term, "the man without qualities," ambivalent and without a moral spine. The "badly ventilated" compartment becomes the site of another drama, that of physical proximity between citizens whose everyday ethos is, by implication, geared towards avoidance and social distance between castes, communities and classes. The train compartment, packed with this seemingly amorphous mass is, in reality, a complex intermingling of otherwise disparate universes. The idea of cohesive densities, with common goals and interests is supplemented by a practice and a philosophy of "adjusting" which turns out to be a key social practice in the creation of everyday density in Mumbai in the chawl as much as in the railway compartment.

In direct response to the above passage from Maximum City, Rohit Gupta, a blogger from Mumbai, wrote:

> Being a Bombay resident, I do not like the crude exoticisms offered by tourists like Mr. Mehta ... These hands that pull you upon the train is a particularly interesting case in point. Normally when this happens, it is because you are being pulled by a work-buddy, since you work in the same office/factory, get on at the same station or whatever, and you do this every day ... When the evening rush hour trains leave from Churchgate, what people standing near the doors (these are open trains) do is that they create a human door, an impenetrable blockade so that they can at least breathe for the next hour of the journey ... What he ascribes altruistic motives to are mainly phenomenon found everywhere in social chaos.

These criticisms do not detract from the observation about "adjusting" but rather add another layer to it. Instead of specific motives – such as altruism – guiding the process of adjustment, we see other, more micro-dimensions at work within the behavior of the crowd that highlight two aspects that are salient to this discussion. First, they point to the underlying violence of these practices of "adjusting." Second, they also add a material dimension to adjusting as an everyday practice of the structural coupling of people with infrastructure. The formation of the "human door" blockade, for example, is not an unconscious practice but rather one that is generative of both spatial and social relations at once.

Other ethnographic moments reveal and supplement this literary and journalistic sense that orderliness is a hard-won and carefully achieved quality of the Mumbai crowd. For example, when a poll conducted by the magazine *Reader's Digest* voted Mumbai the "rudest city" in the world, there was an outpouring of protest not only from residents of the city but also from admirers of Mumbai living in other cities. The tipping point or the threshold at which the crowd turns into a mob is the product of careful management and practice of adjustment of interests, both within the crowd and as it conjoins with the technologies of the "effective city." These practices serve as a counterpoint to the image of sheer numbers of people and the magnificent, terrifying dimension of being caught in the flow of persons in the city. The fragile reversibility of the crowd from the violent substrate of modern political society to its quotidian counterpart of "adjusted differences" is a key feature of the local train as a distinct site of density understood as shared urban destiny of people coupled with infrastructure. Density here becomes a complex phenomenon involving dynamic intersections between the amorphous mass created through the movement of persons across city space, the vehicles of such movement and the embedded potential for social conflict and disaster.

This ethos of everyday adjustment has also been usurped by agents of state bureaucracy from time to time and rearticulated as a practice of "calibration" or fine-tuning. A black comedic situation, described in the British sardonic magazine, *Private Eye*, attests to such moments and I quote it here to illustrate the social potential of such actions as the one that an official spokesman of the Indian railways is describing in the following passage:

> [F]rom now on, our first class compartments will be fitted with hundred watt lights, but the second class compartment will only have sixty-watt lights. Considering that an average second-class fare is one-third that of a first class fare, they ought by rights to be getting only thirty-three watts. So in reality, our administration is being kind and generous in giving them almost double that power, with no matching increase in fares ... We have a number of ideas, which will be taken up in stages for implementation. Take the case of fans. The second class already have fewer fans, naturally, but a commuter standing under a fan in second class currently receives as much air as a first class passenger similarly placed. So, to reflect the difference in fares, we are planning to reduce the speed of fan rotation in second class compartments, and our engineering department is currently modifying their design.

The fine-tuning of the mass and its adjustment to various criteria of social difference inscribe the possibility of generative social potential into seemingly simple acts of design such as reducing the speed of fan rotation or changing the light bulbs to a lower wattage to signify class status. Such adjustments, both those practiced within compartments as well as those practiced by bureaucratic designers of human and material hierarchies suggest that the mass is a site at which the structural coupling of people and infrastructure embed potentials for both producing peace on an everyday basis as well as turning a situation violent. Rather than an anonymous crowd, the literature of and on Bombay/Mumbai reveals a highly socialized crowd, attuned in relation to infrastructural codes, existing as a function of where one lives (Borivali, Vihar, and so on), or of social differences "adjusted" to the materials of the "effective city" or of differences that are fine-tuned by the top-down actions of the state and the bureaucratic apparatus. These practices of adjustment and fine-tuning underlie the phenomenology of the effective city as it appears and disappears, clad in or melding with the iron armor of technologies of mobility. These effective densities or points and propositions of structural coupling between people and infrastructure generate, as their predicate, the order of the effective city. But this order is fragile and indeed characterized by a temporality that is very different from the temporality of "progress," which is imagined to be marching inexorably forward yet detached from eschatological imaginings of end times (Koselleck, 1990). In the contemporary city, these fragile orders are frequently reversible, rendering the city constantly open to the risk of the accidental and the unanticipated. In the following section, I consider an instance of infrastructural collapse, a moment when the effective city is reversed, with blockage replacing movement.

## Inside-Out: Streets and the Extension of Private Life

While the Mumbai local train serves as a container for the crowd and a site for the placid expression of density as an attribute of the "effective city," a city that hangs together, at least for the moment, the urban street provides a different lens from which to examine the structural coupling of people and infrastructure. Apart from gatherings and processions, that take place with regularity on the streets of Mumbai, in the last decade, the streets have also turned into expressions of a different kind of density, defined by disconnection and immobility. On two recent occasions of "network failure" – first, the devastating flood on 26 July 2005 and second, the serial bomb attacks on 11 July 2006 – we see this new form of density that stops the flow of the effective city and the street into a frozen representation of the effective city. For even in these moments of collapse there is a dynamic at work, one that reveals something of the environment and ecology of the effective city. On both occasions, the centralized infrastructure of mobility – the street and the train system – turned into a weapon in the hands of inimical forces. These events reveal the form of the functional city as a sociotechnical system achieved through action and movement. In their own way, these events underlined the idea that the effective city exists as a function of movement rather than existing *a priori* as a normative abstraction. The blockage of the passages of circulation extended a private world onto the street, creating, for a brief period, an awesome manifestation of the actually existing city.

The downpour of nearly one meter of rain, on the afternoon of 26 July 2005, led to the sudden flooding of streets across northern Mumbai. Blocked stormwater drains made it impossible for most of the water to drain into the sea, leading to a situation where both naturally low-lying areas and areas newly rendered low-lying due to the construction of new roads and buildings turned into lakes, trapping people, animals and vehicles. Around 500 people drowned while millions of commuters, who used the railway and bus system, were trapped with no alternative but to walk home from their workplaces, traversing distances of between 10–40 kilometers on foot. The flooding in many parts along their path led to massive slowdowns in their movement with those living farthest away taking days to reach home. Their paths were marked by the kindness and comforts afforded them by strangers who opened their homes and passed out food and drink to the walkers. All these actions were lauded by the press, citizens and politicians as exemplars of the "spirit of Mumbai," its essential kindness and cosmopolitanism. According to this rhetoric, this "spirit" was manifested in the breaking down of many social barriers, with slum-dwellers who lived along the highways helping stranded motorists even as their own homes were sinking and with middle-class housewives opening their homes to strangers, disregarding the usual fears surrounding the stranger in the home. But these acts of charity and kindness on the street must be considered against the everyday streetscape of Mumbai, a teeming, crowded, competitive space marked by displays of inequality as well as defiance of the norms of civic space.

Mumbai's streets are constituted by a visual cacophony of activities – both domestic and commercial – that would normally belong in interior, enclosed spaces. From travelers and scholars both, the accounts of Mumbai's visual field are characterized by a consistent reversal of inside and outside, private and public. Domestic lives might be conducted entirely on the streets, sometimes in the open or inside tiny, temporary shacks. Moreover the pavements can serve as unfurling scenic backdrops as the active, mobile subject takes in a variety of activities unfolding in the background, such as cooking, washing, bathing and sleeping or work-related activities like shoe-shining, welding or general repairing or widespread vending activities. These forms of extending "inside" space and activities, of reversing inside and outside, make the street vulnerable to a kind of living that exposes and calls into question the meanings of the interior or the private, in relation to the public or the outside. The conceptual cross-mapping of these categories has been wonderfully explored by Sudipta Kaviraj in his (1997) essay "Filth and the Public Sphere," in which he generates a concept history of the public in the context of colonial and post-colonial India. He writes that during the early colonial period, the street in relation to the home was not understood so much as a material-geographic distinction but as a conceptual one. The street was physically outside the home but it was also conceptually understood through the category of the "outside," distinct from the concept of the public, as a space lacking any personal association and identification through common civic norms and therefore lacking association with any kind of obligation, constraining its use to only certain activities. In the Indian context, Kaviraj shows that, for the bourgeois middle classes, the street/outside is understood as a "conceptually insignificant *negative* of the inside" (emphasis added), which explains the phlegmatic response to the people treating the street as a space to dump their household filth as well as why the middle classes did not really react until recently to the domestication of the street by an influx of people with nowhere else to go.

In his (2005) autobiographic novel, *Shantaram*, the Australian writer Gregory David Roberts describes Mumbai street life, extensively drawing on his experiences as a fugitive convict fleeing Australia and finding refuge in the slums and streets of Mumbai, losing himself in the crush of humanity so thick that even a very large and conspicuous white man could escape notice from the city's police. Here, Roberts describes the night:

> The nights, at least, were quiet … the beggars, junkies, and hookers who weren't already home or hiding were chased from the footpaths. Steel shutters came down over the shop windows. White calico cloths were thrown over the tables in all the markets and bazaars. Quiet and emptiness descended. In the whirl and crush of people and purposes in Bombay's daylight scramble, it was impossible to imagine those deserted silences. But each and every night was the same: soundless, beautiful and threatening. Bombay became a haunted house.
>
> (Roberts, 2005: 179)

It is telling that Roberts uses the metaphor of haunting to describe the reversal of night and day, of purposeful crowding and silence. Night is not only, in other words, radically unlike day, rather it is like an afterimage of a street by day, teeming with activities of all kinds, a mixed-use zone in the social rather than the technocratic sense. The extensions of the inside to the street, to make space for the slowly moving and sometimes immobile crowds during the two events of network failure I mention here, can also, similarly, be read through the idea of haunting. What I am suggesting is that this incessant, everyday extension of private lives onto the street as part of the city's efficacy, creates its own textures of density of and on the street against which the crowds created by incidents of network failure might be understood. The place and position of the middle class, the relatively more privileged commuter, are made visible and evident only when juxtaposed against the existing fabric and meanings of the street upon which they are superimposed.

A contrast here, with the North-East US and Canadian Blackout of 2003 as experienced in the city of New York might be useful. Numerous observers have commented that during this event, the crowds that filled the city – residents walking home – were orderly and obedient, especially in contrast with the events marking an earlier Blackout in the 1970s. The contrast is a measure of how the city itself has changed during the interim, especially in terms of its demography and the material qualities of its space. The increased privatization and fragmentation of space as a consequence of increasing gentrification of mixed and low-income neighborhoods have produced an overall interiorization of the street. Thus, one might suggest that the orderly files of residents walking towards home during the Blackout were in a space already transformed and rendered inscrutable to the manipulation of the masses as a political force. In Mumbai, by contrast, the experience of the flood of July 2005 was haunted both by the everyday uses of the street as well as by the contemporary experience of urban spatial transformation and its history – of deindustrialization, ruin and the spectacle of conspicuous wealth – writ large. As historian Gyan Prakash (2006: 78) writes, "It was as if the water had forced the city to bring its innards out in the open, exposing its decaying, putrid secrets." Yet this brief, and for some, all too brief, exposure of those innards and secrets was immediately covered up by a discourse celebrating the "spirit of the city," and, more specifically, the unifying effects of the flood on a deeply divided citizenry.

A popular news channel, broadcasting flood stories live served up headlines like "Dreams of Shanghai are broken." Such headlines suggested that the flood had exposed the fundamental inability of the city to "improve" or to catch up with Shanghai, its most recent role model and ideal. Shanghai dreams were particularly significant from the standpoint of politicians and elites engaged since 2003 in a massive urban renovation project to turn Mumbai into a "world-class" city. The stories of the city's "spirit" were especially important to sell the idea that these dreams could not be broken even if "practical difficulties" like the flood were a setback. The generally poignant imagery of the orderly crowds trudging homeward through water and mud, amid floating animal carcasses, garbage and the debris of household goods, and the stories of help received by these unfortunate thousands (many of whom spent more than 24 hours return-ing home) are subsumed in this discourse of the "spirit of Mumbai." This spirit, of course, became all the more evident when contrasted with the experiences of residents of New Orleans after Hurricane Katrina wreaked similar havoc upon their city. Buried within this discourse about the "spirit of Mumbai" is an image of an orderly density, able to function even in the absence of the "effective city."

The "effective city," in the reading of historian Jim Masselos, is "one defined and patterned by the daily commuter journey through which, every morning, Mumbai redefines itself in an immense collective awakening … the daily commuter journey constitutes a defining moment in urban life; an affirmation of city unity" (2003: 31). This daily commuter movement thus gives a pattern, purpose and destination to the crowd constituting the "effective city." In a star-tling inversion, the "effective city," formed by movement through the streets ended up occupying the street as an immobile mass, thereby turning the street into a concrete, visual expression of density instead of a conduit for its circula-tion and dissemination. Network failure thus rendered the effective city into a city on the street and the effective city became a delivery system of victims as infrastructure turned into a weapon against the city.

The effective city was temporarily suspended in the moment of the flood. Tales of the flood also evoke a different sense of orderliness and effectiveness, one that is patterned by the floating debris of household goods and shack frames, animal carcasses and human waste, whose presence in the water brought to the fore the city's intimate spatial formation through reclamations of various sorts – of land from the sea, of land from marshes and of land from landfills of garbage and construction debris. All of these reclamations were exposed effectively as the foundations of the city over which the "unifying" commuter communities that Masselos speaks of were formed.

The experience of density in the moment of the flood is therefore qualita-tively different from that in the daily journey which I examined in the earlier section both from the outside (through the eyes of the child-protagonist, Ravan) and from the inside (as in the descriptions of Suketu Mehta). The inside and the outside of the crowd – that ur-construct of density, massing and space-lessness which constitutes the effective subject and social manifestation of urban density – formed by the flood can similarly be analyzed through the lens of the "effective city." From the outside, this mass formation, the manifestation of urban density turned inside out, appears orderly and appears to be following well-defined paths, mapped through the experience of countless daily journeys to and from work, in the service of the productive city. Viewed from the inside, however, this formation's sociality can be described through its encounter both with the material debris and with the everyday life-world of the street, both described above.

In sharp contrast to the reports in the media, my friends who were among those walking home and taking days to return, as well as others I interviewed in the aftermath of the flood,[7] have described the fear they experienced during their nightmarish journeys home. This fear was not just of being electrocuted by a stray live wire or of falling into an open drain (as did happen) or of being trapped in one's own car and drowning, but what was also described as a fear, specifically of strangers. The very strangers with whom accommodations or adjustments might be made in a train compartment despite harbored suspicions, are the ones who were feared out on the streets. Youth gangs roaming the streets, ostensibly extending a helping hand, were doubly suspect. Their mischievous, violent and dangerous abandon, an extension of their "normal" behavior – interpreted sometimes through the concept of *masti* (a dangerous abandon) – was also in evidence as their everyday life-world in the street was temporarily extended by the flood to include people normally considered too respectable to share in their own, dystopic and violent experiences of the city.

Journalist Dilip D'Souza wrote in his column on the Rediff website a few days after the flood,

> I found myself accosted on the flyover by a gang of drunk toughs, laughing but faintly threatening as they demanded I take a photograph of them. "You didn't take it," said one belligerently when I was done, "you just looked at us through your lens!" "Yeah, yeah, go on," said another, with a hint of menace, "you're going to show the world how dirty Bombay is!"
>
> (D'Souza, 2005: 28)

This idea of being looked at through another's lens is clearly intriguing for a whole social group of disenfranchised youth who know that their own experiences are made available to the public only as emblems of the city's problems while the suppression of their voices and images is necessary for anticipating the city's future as a proper bourgeois metropolis (Chatterjee, 2004).

Predictably, such encounters within the crowd, between, for example, youth gangs and walkers, normally removed and protected from such encounters with the faces of violence, brute, masculine physical strength and hooliganism, were quickly suppressed in favor of more "celebratory" stories of the indefatigable spirit of Mumbai. This spirit itself is considered the means by which the poor and disenfranchised citizens of Mumbai are expected to pull themselves into the emerging "world-class" Mumbai shaped by dreams of Shanghai. Viewed from the inside, the flood orchestrated multiple encounters, juxtapositions and proximities among groups normally carefully separated and socially distanced despite their physical proximities. We might thus say that the experience of density is, therefore, not just about physical proximity but the social and infrastructural engineering of proximate distancing.

Two days after the flood, rumors of a tsunami directed only towards the poor in the slums, caused a stampede in Nehru Nagar, a slum colony that was already very badly affected by the flood. But such events only served quickly to re-establish the social distance as they reinforced the views and stereotypes held by the rich about the poor, by the middle class about migrants and squatters, and by the poor about the elite, and by pushing all against the awesome wrath of nature. The close brush between classes and groups that had occurred as people sheltered wherever they could only served to highlight actual distance even though many, if not most, slums intimately share physical space with more "permanent" structures, through the practice of packing housing into every available open space, through sanction or aggression. Nehru Nagar, for instance, is packed up against the more prosperous western suburbs like Santa Cruz and Juhu. Many middle-class families in these areas, for instance, were dismayed to find the families of their household help sheltering in the public spaces of their buildings as their shacks were drowned or washed away even though these people had intimate connections to their everyday lives and entered and exited their buildings freely as household labor.

Thus, the undifferentiated mass of those making up the "effective city" in Jim Masselos's terms, can be further distinguished by the nature of these encounters that reinforce what we might call the experience of proximate distance as a social diacritic of urban density. Similarly, one can analyze the encounters of the crowd with the debris described above, each of which might be read as fragments of a social history of existing in the city. The mattresses, pots and pans, the television sets, radios and armoires, the corpses of animals kept at the abattoir or at home, the tarpaulin, sticks and tin frames from which the temporary architecture of the city is fashioned and the abandoned bicycles, cars and scooters, marooned buses and trains stopped dead in their tracks – are all turned, in the moment of the flood, into ephemera, material ruins through which the life-world of the city could be grasped by its weary masses. Here, the phenomenological experiences of the crowd and practices of adjustment encounter those of aspiration and achievement, through the life and death of objects that may have been discarded anyway through the cycles of personal histories of consumption or may have been picked up as debris by others too poor to consume except the trash and debris discarded by the better off.

## *Jugaad* or actually existing urbanisms

These ethnographic descriptions of moments in which the structural couplings of people and infrastructure become visible or, are made visible by following certainly rapidly circulating traces[8] point to the ways in which infrastructure, as a medium of social relations, is produced or made incessantly in pragmatic acts of inhabiting the city. The systemic consolidation of urban territory as a terrain of work, production, desire, pleasure and consumption occurs through the information gathered, processed and transmitted through the medium of infrastructure. In this concluding section, I would like to explore the examples presented above in terms of what information is being transmitted and the manner in which such information is systemically processed. In both cases – whether infrastructure is the medium of connectivity or of collapse – the social is traced in its formation, bringing up an old anthropological conundrum about the relationship between structure and event or between structure and memory. For the problem of structure is one of continuity, predictability or, at any rate regularities, which would produce the co-existence of large numbers of people on a daily basis and even enable them to survive catastrophic events as a group. In his classic book of essays on island societies, Marshall Sahlins (1987) offers two propositions about the relation between structure and event – the first is that the "transformation of a mode of culture is a mode of its reproduction," and the second is that "cultural categories acquire new functional values in acts of reference" (ibid.: 138). These propositions, offered in relation to culture as a system of categories which structure acts of subjective reference, however, position structure as a synthetic, analytic concept. By contrast, infrastructure is a fundamentally realist concept, peculiarly detached from the conditions that produce meaning for the subject or the observer – at the very most, referentiality is obtained but in a broken fashion, directed by forces other than the human and by media other than language.

The sense of the real that emerges through systematic theorizations of infrastructure is one of a field of forces, constantly transformed not only by conscious acts of fabrication and design but also less visible phenomenological practices drawing on the potential expressed in material dispositions inherent in infrastructural formulations. Thus the remarkable series of "innovative fixes" that define the public spaces of most South Asian as well as other cities – ranging from the transformations of sidewalks into active marketplaces to the use of large diameter sewage pipes as building materials for propping up homes to using the railway compartment as a site for practicing forms of "adjustment" as precursive forms of conviviality – should be noted but outside of the usual discourses of despair or redemption achieved by being able to celebrate the ingenuity of the poor, the marginalized and the excluded in their practices of inhabitation.

These practices, born of necessity, do have a quality of artfulness about them, which is undeniable. Many practicing contemporary artists based in India turn to such situations routinely for "inspirations," ranging from recreations of situations and experiences (Hema Upadhaya, Meera Devidayal, Bose Krishnamachari, to mention only a few) to the production of situations in which networked forms of community might emerge as a work of art (Raqs Media Collective). Such practices bring visibility to the diversity and creativity of life-worlds emerging in the shadows of poverty and deprivation. The problem, however, is to move from images and representations to propositions, which requires considering a range of ethical questions. The celebration of *jugaad* or innovative, improvisational urban practices and the objects they produce as temporary "fixes" or solutions to systemic problems is problematic in that such celebration either assimilates innovation to the sphere of capitalist entrepreneurship (which includes the vast majority of professional design practices as well) and, even more perniciously, turns the conditions for contemplating necessary ethical problems into permanently speculative and provisional ones.

In his historical anthropology of media technologies in urban Nigeria, Brian Larkin (2008) argues for "treating media technologies as parts of a much wider logic and form of infrastructure," which, in turn enables him to "open up new ways of thinking about the production of Nigerian urban space over time." The logic and form of infrastructure are connected, in turn, to the "institutional discursive contexts that accompany objects and which establish them as facts in the world." These contexts, he suggests are similar to Foucault's concept of "archive," "not as a collection of documents or things but as the form of political exteriority that makes objects appear to have certain meanings and not other ones" (ibid.: 247). I began my own discussion of infrastructure under the sign of "crisis," in need of renovation and then proceeded to examine situations of urban density that made visible different dimensions of the structural coupling between people and infrastructure as contexts within which different forms of sociality emerge. When a continuous discourse of crisis about the loss of instrumental efficiency in the city's underground norms the practices and imaginaries of infrastructure-making, it becomes the form of "political exteriority that makes objects appear to have certain meanings and not other ones."

It is important to remember that particular forms of sociality emerge, however, in conjunction with and indeed, inseparable from the qualities of infrastructure as material forms or the dispositions of materials as constituting their form (Easterling, 2011a). In turn, if we think of infrastructure through the logic of media or as "media objects," as Larkin suggests, we might also use these emergent forms of sociality and their effects as interpreted above as evidence for the ways in which infrastructure serves as a medium of spatio-political reconditioning (Easterling, 2011b). Infrastructure as organizational medium might constitute the "real" underlying the ideal of the modern metropolis, the mega-city, the global city, and so on.

Yet, as media objects, infrastructures are not mere carriers of information but also conditioners of systems through their capacity to process information and to feed it back into the urban system, thereby influencing its goals and orientations. The acts of urbanism analyzed in this essay are spatio-political reconditionings of a particular sort – they depart from normative understandings of the effects of the structural coupling between people and infrastructure and build affective arguments for inhabiting the city. The emergent forms of sociality must always be considered against the backdrop of an archive as the "form of political exteriority." This raises, once again, the specter or the trace of the public as an archival substrate for ethical discussions of the city and its future rather than the metropolis as technical achievement in which the public on the surface is coded and constituted by the instrumental efficacy of the technological underground.

In a place like Mumbai, the disjuncture between surface and underground is vivid – it is most palpable in the visual experience of the city as a messy and ad hoc agglomeration of forms bearing no formal, relation to one another, reflecting a particular aesthetic based on geometric regularities of objects implicated in space. Such messy forms signal a ludic element at work – the play of changing urban development regulations, investment flows and business cycle caprices and the desires of powerful urban residents for upgraded neighborhoods coming together to modify the city's development plan, bit by bit. But they also signal a politics of gridlock at work – a snarl brought about by the continual renovation and modification of the underground itself by alternative imaginaries of infrastructure-making, coexisting with and pushing up against the imaginaries of the "mega" (Benjamin, 2008). Critiques of such gridlock are forced to draw on the metropolis and its ghosts, to confront the immanent and imminent death of the city either as in the fully realized utopia of the metropolis or in the shattering of the ideal of the metropolis. The reflective ethical framework of the public, essential to this understanding of time is being replaced by a speculative ethical framework that operates through the embrace of predictable uncertainty as a force shaping everyday life and reflected in situations of infrastructural flux. I do not have the space here to develop this point further but only to say that in order to understand this emergent speculative ethos better, it is necessary to recognize those moments at which imaginaries of infrastructure making meet the relational agency of material infrastructures in the urban environment as constitutive of the ethical conditions for inhabiting the city today.

## Notes

1   Architects and urban designers, however, continue to be ever hopeful of detecting patterns amidst the seeming chaos and articulating propositions in relation to these emergent patterns. For one interesting and critical perspective on emergent urban form, see McGrath and Shane (2012).

2   Eyal Weizman (2004) shows how Haussmann's infrastructure-making coded the disposition of serving as a battlefield into every modern city, everywhere. This coding comes to fruition now in the way that cities are turned regularly into battlefields.

3   As Simone (2008) puts it, these are "regularities that ensue from a process of incessant convertibility – turning commodities, found objects, resources, and bodies into uses previously unimaginable or constrained."

4   Bombay was officially renamed Mumbai shortly after the publication of Nagarkar's novel, an acclaimed biographic sketch of a particular universe of working-class neighborhoods that were about to be radically transformed in the coming decade. On the politics of naming and renaming, see Hansen (2001).

5   These new forms of community – at once social and political – are discussed in detail by Kaviraj (1997), in his essay on the development of the public sphere in colonial and post-colonial Calcutta. Kaviraj is specifically concerned with the "modernity" of colonial and post-colonial cities and with the transformations of concepts of public and private as they are translated into the vernacular of Bengali society and into the pragmatics of everyday urban living. While Kaviraj does an admirable job of considering the history of these concepts in relation to material, spatial practices, he does not specifically consider the field of technological infrastructure as a medium for the consolidation of territory. Nevertheless, his essay is crucial and instructive in reminding us of the detournements or inversions that make possible the emergence of new understandings of concepts that urban theory often considers to be settled.

6   Rajnarayan Chandavarkar's writings on working-class Mumbai and the material contexts of its neighborhoods also warn against the romanticization of chawl life and against the homogenization of community in those contexts. His work is a powerful

reminder of the conflicts that inform the construction of working-class identity everywhere.

7    I myself spent the days after the flood trapped rather comfortably, albeit without running water or electricity, for several days in my apartment on a high floor of one of the recently constructed high rises. When the flood rushing down my street slowed a little, I was out among the crowds rushing to help neighbors further "downstream" in our neighborhood's overflowing stormwater drainage system but without much cost to myself since I could always trudge back up to my apartment.

8    As Latour and Hermant put it:

> There is not exactly an outside to the social, if by this word, already more precise, we mean a certain form of rapid circulation of traces. The outside, the general framework, is not what dominates me; it is what I dominate with my gaze. But what I dominate I don't see unless I refrain from looking outside, otherwise I am immediately limited to my own point of view. Hence there is never much sense in distinguishing the individual and the context, the limited point of view and the unlimited panorama, the perspective and that which is seen to have no perspective. It is better to distinguish the person looking from a window and not seeing anything, who has no idea who they are or what they should do, from the person who, in a continuous flow of traces, picks out an image that will teach them both who they are, in particular and the global frame in which they should be situated. Either I really see and I see nothing, I am nothing; or I see nothing directly, I look at a trace and I begin to really see, I gradually become someone.
>
> (2006: 11: emphasis added)

## Bibliography

Benjamin, Solomon (2008) "Occupancy Urbanism: Radicalizing Politics and Economy Beyond Policy and Programs," *International Journal of Urban and Regional Research*, 32(3): 719–729.

Bennett, Jane (2009) *Vibrant Matter: A Political Ecology of Things*. Durham, NC: Duke University Press.

Chandavarkar, Rajnarayan (2005) "Introduction," in Neera Adarkar and Meena Menon (eds) *One Hundred Years, One Hundred Voices: The Millworkers of Girangaon, an Oral History*. New Delhi: Seagull.

Chatterjee, Partha (2004) *The Politics of the Governed: Reflections on Popular Politics in Most of the World*. New York: Columbia University Press.

D'Souza, Dilip (2005) "Give Me Bombay Every Time." Rediff, July 28. Available at: www.rediff.com/news/2005/jul/28dilip.htm.

Easterling, Keller (2011a) *Extrastatecraft: The Power of Infrastructure Space*. New York: Verso.

Easterling, Keller (2011b) "The Action Is the Form," in Mark Shepard (ed.) *Sentient City: Ubiquitous Computing, Architecture, and the Future of Urban Space*. Cambridge, MA: The MIT Press.

Graham, Steve (ed.) (2010) *Disrupted Cities: When Infrastructure Fails*. New York: Routledge.

Guyer, Jane I. (2007) "Prophecy and the Near Future: Thoughts on Macroeconomic, Evangelical, and Punctuated Time," *American Ethnologist*, 34(3): 409–421.

Hansen, Thomas Blom (2001) *Wages of Violence: Naming and Identity in Postcolonial Bombay*. Princeton, NJ: Princeton University Press.

Kaviraj, Sudipta (1997) "Filth and the Public Sphere: Concepts and Practices about Space in Calcutta," *Public Culture*, 10(1): 83–113.

Koselleck, Reinhart (1990) *Le futur passé: contribution à la sémantique des temps historiques.* Paris: Éditions de l'École des Hautes Études en Sciences Sociales.

Larkin, Brian (2008) *Signal and Noise: Media, Infrastructure, and Urban Culture in Nigeria.* Durham, NC: Duke University Press.

Latour, Bruno, and Hermant, Emilie (2006) "Paris: Invisible City." Available at: www.bruno-latour.fr/node/95 (accessed March 1: 2007).

Masselos, Jim (2003) "Defining Moment/Defining Events: Commonalities of Urban Life," in Sujata Patel and Jim Masselos (eds) *Bombay and Mumbai: The City in Transition.* New Delhi: Oxford University Press.

McGrath, Brian and Shane, Grahame (2012) "Metropolis, Megalopolis, and Metacity," in C. Greig Crysler, Stephen Cairns, and Hilde Heynen (eds) *The Sage Handbook of Architectural Theory.* London: Sage.

McGrath, Brian and Shane, Grahame (forthcoming) "Introduction," in *Handbook of Architectural Theory.*

Mehta, Suketu (2006) *Maximum City: Bombay Lost and Found.* Mumbai: Penguin Books India.

Nagarkar, Kiran (1995) *Ravan & Eddie.* New York: Viking.

Prakash, Gyan (2006) "After the Deluge," *Sarai Reader* 06: 77–83.

Roberts, Gregory David (2005) *Shantaram: A Novel.* Basingstoke: Macmillan.

Sahlins, M. (1987) *Islands of History.* Chicago: University of Chicago Press.

Simone, Abdou Maliq (2008) "The Last Shall Be First: African Urbanities and the Large Urban World." in A. Huyssen (ed.) *Other Cities, Other Worlds: Urban Imaginaries in a Globalizing Age.* Durham, NC: Duke University Press, pp. 99–120.

Weizman, Eyal (2004) "Military Operations as Urban Planning," in E. Cadava and A. Levy (eds) *Cities Without Citizens.* Philadelphia, PA: Slought Books.

# Part II

# Infrastructural violence and dispossession

Chapter 3

# Water wars in Mumbai

*Stephen Graham, Renu Desai and Colin McFarlane*

## Beyond the pale

The *Mumbai Mirror*, Friday, 8 January 2010.[1] A photograph (Figure 3.1) shows a line-up of proud Mumbai police officers standing behind row upon row of what appear at first sight to be rusted machine guns. But this is not one of the arms caches regularly unearthed to demonstrate the Force's acuity against the myriad of terrorist networks that regularly target urban sites in contemporary India. The objects, rather, are water booster pumps, pulled from the ground in Mumbai slums in a new campaign of dawn raids against 'illegal' water theft within the city's burgeoning informal settlements in the city's Shivaji Nagar and Govandi districts (see Figure 3.2 on p. 65).

*Figure 3.1* Mumbai police stand proudly by piles of water booster pumps removed from informal settlements in the Shivaji Nagar and Govandi districts of the City the previous night

'Stealing water to earn a few bucks?' the article's headline reads. 'Pay a hefty price!' It details how the raids are being backed up by new legal moves to criminalize people 'stealing' water. Hundreds of people, arrested for installing and using the pumps, are to be prosecuted under draconian and non-bailable laws such as the Damages to Public Property Act. All this is portrayed unproblematically as a heroic response to the threat that water theft in slums poses to the wider, formal, legitimate and law-abiding city. 'Pilferages, if not controlled,' writes the author, Abhijit Sathe, 'could exhaust the potable water reserves before the next monsoon.'[2]

Such statements tap into a mainstream discourse where recent monsoons have led to a major 'water crisis' in Mumbai which necessitates radical, emergency measures to address widespread 'water theft' or 'water pilferage' – especially by the urban poor. What such discourses occlude, however, are the ways in which current systems of urban water provision work to systematically dehydrate and profit from urban slum communities while water wastage by the affluent and their preferred urban facilities goes unchecked.

On a rapidly urbanizing and increasingly thirsty planet, contemporary Mumbai is one possible harbinger of a stark global future. The majority of humans, already, are urbanites; some estimate that 75 per cent will be by 2050. The inevitable result is that water, like everything else, is being urbanized: larger and larger swathes of the Earth's 'natural' hydrological systems are being orchestrated to sustain burgeoning metropolitan areas.[3] This transformation challenges the easy separation of nature and the city that is a legacy of modernist thinking, because the Earth's water is increasingly metabolized through the pipes, channels and sewers of urban areas (and, of course, the bodies of the people that live in them).

With urban residents largely unable to provide for their own water needs, access to technological systems providing water of adequate quality and quantity is now arguably the most basic element of the right to a decent urban life. This is especially so for the world's billion or more slum dwellers, who are usually denied access to formal water supplies because their claims to space are deemed illegitimate or illegal. For such communities, the challenge of even very basic hydration, sanitation, or washing often involves the negotiation of complex circuits of predation, corruption, and patronage, arrangements which seek to fully exploit both the nature of urban water as the ultimate, inelastic, life-giving commodity, and the distance of such communities from adequate formal water infrastructures.

Crucially, slums and slum dwellers are demonized and criminalized in many megacities of the Global South. Indeed, often, they are portrayed as not actually of 'the city' at all. Another *Mumbai Mirror* article, for example, published three days later,[4] recounts the systematic destruction of another network of 'illegal' pipes improvised by slum dwellers in the Dahisar district, 12 miles to the North West of Shivaji Nagar and Govandi. Here a punitive act of state violence against one of the poorest and most vulnerable communities in Mumbai, undertaken after protracted lobbying by nearby affluent communities, is sanitized as a heroic act of water conservation, 'saving water' for 'the city.'

In this case, 'the city' signifies, crucially, not the whole of Mumbai but the formal city of apartment blocks, malls, corporate towers, technology centres, and leisure parks organized to meet the needs of elites, middle classes, foreign investors, and tourists. All else – the majority of the population living in self-built slums on a mere twentieth of the city's land – is here discursively cast out from the modern rights, entitlements and promises of city life. The urban poor are rendered instead as a parasitic threat requiring increasingly violent response and draconian control. Given the most essential nature of urban water, Giorgio Agamben's notion of 'bare life'[5] – human existence reduced to a biological process that can be extinguished through sovereign power with impunity – has rarely been so apposite.

In the essay that follows, we draw on an in-depth ethnographic field study into the water and sanitation practices within informal settlements in Mumbai to excavate further the complex politics of water in contemporary Mumbai.[6] We demonstrate in particular how the contemporary situation in Mumbai reveals the costs of marginalizing the majority urban poor in global megacities: in public health, death rates and communicable and water-borne diseases; in the burden of waiting for and carrying water (especially for women and children); in the burden of incurring high expenditure on water; in water extortion against the poor by predatory water rackets; and in the problems of systematic dehydration. Beyond this, we also show how these costs are often obfuscated in dominant discourses of the urban water crisis emanating from governing elites, security and police forces, and the mainstream media. In Mumbai, as we shall see, these discourses often tend to demonize informal settlements and their residents as the ultimate *cause* of the wider water crisis afflicting the city. They portray informal settlements and their inhabitants as spaces that must be reclaimed and reconstructed in the production of Mumbai as a new 'global city' to rival Shanghai.

For example, the influential and controversial (2003) report by McKinsey and Company and the organization Bombay First, entitled *Vision Mumbai: Transforming Mumbai into a World-Class City*, and subsequently taken up by the Maharashtra State Government, argues that Mumbai needs to transform its infrastructure and governance in order to become a 'world class city'.[7] It draws on examples from Shanghai, Singapore, New York, and London, and emphasizes high-impact projects with public–private partnerships, largely ignoring informal settlements and sanitation. When slums do feature in the report, they are as sites of proliferation that mark Mumbai's 'slippage' down the rankings of 'top' Asian cities, and as spaces that must be removed because they do not fit with the image of the world-class city. The report argues 'the percentage of the population living in slums must fall to 10–20 percent' (2003, p. 20), and says very little about the causes of slum formation beyond housing prices being too high. It does suggest building more low-income housing, creating 'Special Housing Zones' for 300,000 people, reforming existing schemes such as the controversial market-led Slum Rehabilitation Authority (SRA) scheme by increasing contributions from slum residents to the cost of construction, ensuring that housing prices should be no more than 3–4 times the annual household income, and insisting that no post-1995 slums should be allowed (i.e. they should be demolished). Not only are these minor interventions that are nowhere near significant enough, they also insist on slums as spaces outside the project of 'worlding' Asian cities to meet global aspirations of market competitiveness and aesthetics.[8] The political agendas around the promotion of a new Shanghai continue to reverberate in the city, not just from elements of politico-corporate Mumbai but by public NGOs like Citispace and mainstream journalists. For example, one *Times of India* journalist celebrated Shanghai over Mumbai for its expensive hotels and shopping malls that beat 'even Singapore', for its 'new overpasses, metro rail links, a dream subway system', and for the fact that the 'unruliness visible on Indian streets is almost absent'.[9]

Finally, dominant discourses surrounding Mumbai's contemporary water crisis tend to simplistically equate the city's poor citizens with the interests of a powerful and shadowy 'water mafia' in Mumbai. This term, which is very vaguely and loosely deployed by elites and mainstream media outlets, refers to a set of loose alliances to exploit water scarcity among Mumbai's population. It involves corrupt municipal officials, police officials, and middlemen (some of whom are better-off residents of informal settlements). This complex set of arrangements, practices, and rackets works to profit from Mumbai's water shortages by organizing, for high levels of kickbacks and payment, both legal and illegal water connections, including the deliveries of private water tankers.

By failing to reveal how such corrupt water practices impact negatively on Mumbai's poor, the 'water mafia' discourse further compounds the vulnerabilities of informal city dwellers, especially in the context of increasingly extreme water scarcity. In the process, the exploitative power relations linking the police, the Brihanmumbai Municipal Corporation (the city's municipal government), politicians, private water tanker companies, influential middlemen, and residents of informal settlements are rendered all but invisible. Our analytic strategy here is thus to deliberately juxtapose elite, discursive, invocations of 'water crises' in Mumbai with ethnographic research exposing some of the lived materialities surrounding accessing to water among Mumbai's most marginalized inhabitants. We adopt such an approach in order to illustrate some of the jarring collisions that characterize both the research process and the nature of hydropolitics in Mumbai.

## Parched city

In 2008, some 19.5 million people were squeezed into the 438 square kilometres of Mumbai's tiny island-peninsular and its immediate hinterland (Figure 3.2). The city was thus the fifth biggest in the world by population, its population

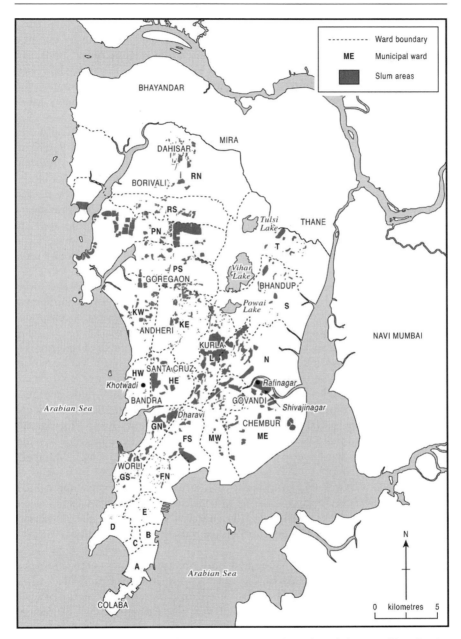

*Figure 3.2* The city of Mumbai, 2011, showing municipal wards and the main *Zopadpatti* or 'slum' areas mentioned in the text

having quadrupled in a mere four decades. Dominating this growth overwhelmingly has been Mumbai's burgeoning population of people living in informal settlements. Indeed, one estimate suggests that, while in 1861 only 12 per cent of Mumbai's population could be classified as 'poor', by 1991, this figure had risen to 51 per cent.[10] (Such definitions are contested, however, and are complicated by the fact that Mumbai's extremely high real estate prices force many lower middle-class people to live in informal settlements.)

Mumbai has a fragmented and polarized metropolitan landscape.[11] The World Bank estimates that 54 per cent of Mumbai's population – around 9 million people – are now concentrated into the city's archipelago of dense informal settlements or *Zopadpatti*, forced to occupy just 5 per cent of the city's land.[12] Such places have among the highest population densities on Earth: the biggest and most famous – Dharavi – squeezes over a million people into just one square mile. Mumbai's slum-dwellers are the city's most vulnerable population: they are the prime victims of environmental pollution, a whole spectrum of water-borne and other diseases, and suffer inadequate housing conditions, infrastructure services, and waste disposal routes.

Within 30 years, moreover, most projections suggest that Mumbai's extraordinary rate of continued growth will lead it to become the world's second largest city (after Tokyo), with over 26 million people. The majority of this new population is expected to squeeze into informal cities.

Mumbai's polarized social landscape is reflected in the politics of water provision in a city which, despite having copious monsoon rains, has never been able to provide decent, piped water for all. Instead, Mumbai's water politics are labyrinthine. A complex colonial and planning legacy of half-built improvements laces a shaky and partial piped system. Based on a crumbling, century-old network of fragile pipes, Mumbai's water system is already at crisis point. Ongoing efforts to build new reservoirs north of the city have faced delays and funding shortages and have so far failed to increase supply to match Mumbai's burgeoning population. Such a situation has been compounded by a series of failed monsoons as well by continuously high levels of water leakage and regular pipe ruptures. All this means that while Mumbai, with a *notional* per capita water availability of 180 litres, is theoretically endowed with more water per person than London, which has 150 litres, it fails even to offer its most affluent citizens 24-hour piped water services.[13]

Mumbai currently receives about 2,500 million litres of water per day from the jungles, lakes, and mountains in the north of the Maharashtra State within which Mumbai falls. This has been estimated to represent only around 65 per cent of demand.[14] In 2009, this deficit led the Brihanmumbai Municipal Corporation (BMC), the city's municipal government, to limit the hours of water supply to all users in the city.

Mumbai's water crisis means that even many wealthy residencies are now supplied with piped water for only two or three hours a day. Around 20 per cent of all the city's piped water escapes into the ground through leaks. Another 20 per cent or so is tapped illegally by water tanker providers, the construction industry, or informal and formal settlements. Periodic ruptures in the mains supply add to the sense of a pivotal urban resources being wasted before reaching its rightful users. Complete bans and rationed quotas are regularly introduced during relatively dry monsoon seasons.

The presence of the burgeoning *Zopadpatti* – informal settlements – dominates Mumbai's water politics. Many such places have, for generations, been denied adequate linkages to formal, piped water supplies, and are thus the most vulnerable to the current water crisis. The BMC offers inhabitants of informal settlements water connections with a daily notional amount of 45 litres per person per day, 30 per cent of what is allocated to a resident living in formal residential areas (135 litres per person per day). But even this amount is often unavailable. Informal settlements rely on unmetered municipal standposts, metered municipal group connections, wells, boreholes, tanks, tankers, filtration systems and improvised pipes, as well as many other efforts to seek water of adequate quality and quantity. Meanwhile, a complex world of organized crime, which overlaps with the world of municipal officials, works to build high profits from illegal piped supplies and water tanker deliveries, focusing especially on the poorest slums. Their practices also delay efforts to extend adequate formal piped water supplies to slum communities.

Recent proposals to plan and improve Mumbai have not even attempted to universalize decent water for the city. Instead they tend to disguise or camouflage the problem. Strategies like *Vision Mumbai*, commissioned by the elite citizens group Bombay First from the McKinsey management consultants, seek, instead, to superficially 'clean up' or 're-brand' Mumbai, improving the quality of life and services for affluent and middle-class citizens yet doing little or nothing for the impoverished communities who have such dire basic needs. Planners and the local government officials hope that such changes will help Mumbai reproduce the success of 'global' cities such as Shanghai or Singapore. The result is an increasingly authoritarian stance against Mumbai's slum dwellers, including mass demolitions (particularly intensive in the winter of 2004–2005), declarations that newer slums will not receive any water service, and efforts to remove the poor from public spaces.

The growth of revanchist urban politics in Mumbai relates closely to the broader construction of a xenophobic, nativist, Marathi-centred, regional political party – the Shiv Sena – which has dominated both municipal and state government in recent years.[15] As Matthew Gandy points out,[16] the embourgeoisement of public policy has also been fed by an increasingly moralistic discourse among Mumbai's media and public institutions. This tends to demonize the poor migrants from elsewhere in India as imposters within Mumbai and to legitimize authoritarian and punitive policies against them. It therefore tends to weaken already feeble concepts of civil society, citizenship and human rights within the city. The Shiv Sena has long argued that immigrants in informal settlements are the main reason for Maharashtrians being unemployed, and has consistently invoked the figures of the migrant and the Muslim as a source of crime and social disorder. The Sena's grip over the municipal corporation since the mid-1990s has entrenched this politics, and closely linked them to the election of councillors across the city. As a political movement, the municipal success of the Sena has been part of a wider marginalization of and disproportionate targeting of Muslim groups in the city, evidenced not just in the pogroms of the early 1990s (which helped the Sena's rise to power in the city and state) but the ongoing demolition or infrastructure denial and removal of Muslim informal settlements, for example, in Rafinagar (a neighbourhood we discuss in detail later) and surrounding areas in north-east Mumbai.[17]

In the context of water, this politics of denial, violence and disconnection has also been made possible because of perceptions that the municipal water shortages faced by many of Mumbai's middle-class residents are caused by slum dwellers. Moreover, the water-borne diseases that increasingly afflict slum dwellers – Surat plague, malaria – tend not to directly endanger middle-class residents who can access a range of clean water alternatives far more easily. As a result, rather than the emergence of a broad-based campaign for citizenship and human rights for all urban residents in the context of water, there has been a further fragmentation of civil society in Mumbai. Not only are there competing claims on the city's water resources, but the embourgeoisement of public policy has supported the view that affluent groups have more legitimate claims on the city's water than the urban poor (see Baviskar, 2002, on bourgeois environmentalism[18]). As with the example of the New Link Road Residents' Forum detailed below, organizations of middle-class residents in Mumbai increasingly mobilize to protect and further their interests at the expense of the urban poor, while organizations working for the rights of the poor find it ever more challenging to make themselves heard and realize systemic change in the city's water policies.

Mumbai's water crisis means that water protests increasingly convulse the city; water scarcity increasingly dominates political mobilization and debate; new legal sanctions are mobilized against transgressions to cope with the new sense of emergency. In addition, water engineers are regularly attacked and regularly complain that they get no protection from the police. Political parties often mobilize their loyal mobs on water demonstration against water engineering departments and officials; local groups have beaten up neighbours accused of locking collective taps, parading them around streets with their hair shorn in humiliation. 'The city's water crisis,' warned the *Mumbai Mirror* in December 2009 at the height of a particularly acute shortage, 'seems to be turning Mumbaikars into monsters'.[19]

This politics of water scarcity and the systematic denial of water to the poor is quickly translating into a militarized struggle to control and protect Mumbai's water supplies. Thus the status quo of effective hydrological apartheid, forged through lesser water entitlements for residents of informal settlements as well as predation on them by the water mafia, is sustained rather than undermined or overturned.

This is being done through a campaign to blame and criminalize *Zopadpatti* dwellers, and their attempts to gain even minimal access to water, for the city's water crisis as a justification to 'take back' or 'reclaim' the city's water for elite and middle-class 'tax payers' and real estate interests. Such a campaign works to obscure the origins of the current water crisis and deny the stratification of supply which starves the majority of the urban poor of water.

In making this argument, we are not suggesting that this eviscerated hydropolitics is itself new. Mumbai's water and sanitation infrastructures have always been deeply fragmented and politicized. While colonial investments made clear their biopolitical choice in which neighbourhoods were metabolized through water and sanitation and which were not, nationalist discourses emphasized an egalitarian focus that envisaged a modern urbanite in need of civic transformation.[20] The Nehruvian view of the city as an important site for the expression and negotiation of modernity was in practice always heavily prescribed both by the inequities of India's capitalist urbanization that consistently drove surpluses away from infrastructure investment for the poor, and the piecemeal will of India's political elites. The city has never, for example, come close to providing full and adequate sanitation coverage. The colonial legacies of disinvestment in the extension of sewer coverage to poorer areas structure the possibilities of contemporary sanitation intervention, where public toilets are provided to informal settlements off the sewer grid and at nowhere near sufficient number for most neighbourhoods.

A 2001 survey, for example, found that 63 per cent of those living in informal settlements depended on often defunct toilet blocks, and a variation in people to toilet seats of 273:1 in A ward to 56:1 in F/S and S wards, often resulting in queues lasting two hours or more and an untold range of small and serious health complaints.[21] There is a complex story to be told around the changing logics and imaginaries which have shaped this deeply unequal metabolic geography, which exceed the scope of this chapter, but it is important to be clear that the present moment is a particular intensification of unequal water politics for certain neighbourhoods (often 'unauthorized', often predominantly Muslim) over others.

What is new, however, is the intensification of a bourgeois urbanism that is both revanchist in its aims – seeking to seize urban space from the poor, often to realize property prices – and splintering in its form, as elites increasingly shift to infrastructure-rich gated tower blocks and as political imaginations all but abandon more progressive urban projects in favour of investments for the wealthy.

Indian cities increasingly reflect the logic of what Amita Baviskar calls 'bourgeois environmentalism' – disparate efforts to remove informal settlements, street hawkers, and (often Muslim) immigrants from spaces across the Indian city, which depend partly on notions of urban contamination and beautification, and the often violent removal of the poor.[22] As Baviskar argues in relation to Delhi, a lack of public toilets means that any open space with sufficient shelter becomes a potential place to defecate. She uses the example of the public park. To the expanding middle classes, however, the park embodies a sense of 'gracious urban living', a place devoted to leisure and recreation; to the poor, it may be the only environment where defecation with relative safety and dignity is possible. Baviskar uses this conflict to point to the increasingly powerful presence of bourgeois environmentalism as an ideology shaping urban landscapes in India, a notion that combines political, economic, social and ecological dimensions. Bourgeois environmentalism discriminates between 'good' and 'bad' natures, such as between the park and the 'unsanitary slum', and privileges commodified socionatures, and if it is a discourse with a long history, it is nonetheless intensifying. It is clear that there is now a growing impetus to 'cleanse' the streets of India's major cities, whether through violence or through regulation, and to focus infrastructure resources on high-end residential and industrial secessionary network enclaves that disproportionately benefit the wealthy, including roads, fly-overs, air-conditioned malls, and telecommunications and media infrastructures.[23]

## Water wars

As with the *Mumbai Mirror* articles detailed above, the official discourse surrounding Mumbai's water crisis offers a simple tale of a malign and burgeoning informal population threatening the order, security and public health of the formal city of legitimate, tax-paying citizens through their criminal theft of water. One report by the Mumbai High Court, published in July 2009, stipulates that the number of encroachments on the mains pipelines in Mumbai has grown from 6,687 in 1995 to 15,780 in 2009.[24] It sees these 'encroachments' as a 'health and security hazard' which can 'puncture the entire system' – what they term 'the real lifeline of the city'.[25]

A powerful revanchist logic is at play here: if only 'we' – i.e. the middle-class and elite consumers and corporate investors – could reclaim the city's hydrological – and urban – commons from the mass of illegitimate slum dwellers, Mumbai might attain civil order, a high quality of life for elites and the middle classes, and its aspiration, solidified in 2003 with the 'Bombay First' and 'Vision Mumbai' strategies for the city, to emerge as a truly 'world class' or 'global city' to compete with the likes of Singapore and Shanghai. Bombay First, a powerful corporate coalition which commissioned the influential *Vision Mumbai* report[26] from McKinsey and Company in 2003, have since lobbied hard for the wholesale privatization of Mumbai's water industry, part of what Matthew Gandy[27] has called its 'Neo-Haussmannite' agenda of forcibly reengineering Mumbai through slum clearances into its vision of a 'global' city.

These policies powerfully reinforce the message that slum dwellers are not actually of Bombay; that their presence acts as a pathology and an obstacle to the legitimate aspirations of Mumbai's elites. Thus, no political effort is made to address the root causes. Crucially, for example, no adequate alternative, public or formal water supplies are made available for the communities whose water supplies are destroyed in the raids. Thus, acute water shortages and extreme reliance of already vulnerable communities on water rackets, are further accentuated.

Powerful residents groups representing affluent areas have been especially vocal about the need to destroy the 'illegal' taps and end the complicity of local municipal and water officials in the so-called 'water mafia' operations that construct them at huge profit. The New Link Road Residents' Forum, for example, which represents affluent communities in an area of Mumbai's North Western suburbs (see Figure 3.2), mentions these efforts to provide basic hydration in the same breath as what they term 'terror threats to Mumbai's water network'.[28] Criticizing a huge slum by the name of Ganpat Patil Nagar which has been built recently on the New Link Road, the group has filed many legal complaints about thefts of the mains water that previously flowed unencumbered to their communities. The group has been 'consistently filing complaints of alleged water theft by the slumlords and unsocial elements who indulge in puncturing the MCGM [Municipal Corporation of Greater Mumbai] lines laid under the link road'. The result of the 'water theft', they argue, 'is being faced by the honest tax paying citizens of Borivali and Dahisar who often face water cuts and shortages and inconsistent supplies'.

Fuelled by such allegations of ineffectiveness, corruption or complicity, the BMC have recently joined forces with the police to launch draconian raids against slum settlements during which improvised water pumps, tapping into the city's formal water system, have been destroyed (the results have been the startling press conferences discussed at the start of this chapter) and supposedly illegal pipes have been disconnected (Figure 3.3).[29] Certain slum settlements, portrayed as especially important centres of 'water theft', have been the particular focus of these activities. Raids in January, 2010, against the Dahisar slums identified by the New Link Road Residents, for example, were portrayed heroically in the *Mumbai Mirror* as being part of a 'save water' drive which successfully saved the city 400,000 litres of water.[30] Harish Pandey, Secretary of the New Link Road Residents' Forum, was 'thankful that the BMC has finally taken some action against this water theft'. He argued, however, that 'the civic body should look at a permanent solution as slums end up getting water in full pressure, while taps at the taxpayers' homes run dry'.

The most notorious slum for municipal raids, however, has been the predominantly Muslim settlement of Shivaji Nagar in Govandi in Mumbai's M-East ward, the poorest of Mumbai's 24 municipal wards (and a ward which has gradually become a concentration of poverty as people have been resettled here over 30 years of continuous slum clearance in central Mumbai). Here the BMC deems the destruction to be so 'successful' as to consider it a model to be followed around Mumbai's other informal settlements. After one raid in Shivaji Nagar in early December 2009, Senior Police Inspector Dundapa Jodgujari reported that his forces raided and destroyed 156 illegal water pipes which had been connected to the mains illegally. The police also seized 96 booster pumps. In the process they 'detained around 40 people. Of these, 21 were arrested, as they did not have valid documents to use the pumps. Many of those arrested sold water to the slum dwellers.'[31] Jodgujari, moreover, argued that local residents were relieved that the

*Figure 3.3* Water pipes cut in Rafinagar during the water raids in December 2009
Source: Photograph by Renu Desai.

'menace' of the water mafia was no longer hanging over their community. However, this argument masked the fact that because of the denial of adequate formal water connections in the area by the BMC and the high costs of acquiring even a legal water connection from the BMC, many residents were in fact forced to rely on the corrupt practices of water rackets to obtain water for their daily needs. Thus, while many local residents of Shivaji Nagar got better water pressure in their taps after the municipal raids, many others spiralled into a deepening water crisis since the BMC cracked down on their only source of water while not providing them with alternate adequate water supplies. And yet, the Shivaji Nagar experience was deemed to be so successful by Rahul Shewale, standing committee chairman in BMC, that they began to consider implementing similar programmers of continuous raids across the whole of Mumbai.[32]

Our research in Rafinagar, a predominantly Muslim informal settlement located at the edge of Shivaji Nagar (see Figure 3.2), suggests that water raids by the BMC have been a regular occurrence in some informal settlements. Almost every year, the BMC has cut some 'illegal' water pipes supplying water to Rafinagar's residents. However, this time around, these raids were not only carried out on a larger scale, with more intensity, but also for the first time involved the police. The water wars in Mumbai have thus evolved from routinized practices of a BMC crackdown on 'illegal' connections to militarized crackdowns. Initially, basic criminal law surrounding damage to public property or inhibiting public services was used to prosecute those deemed to be guilty of setting up illegal water connections. The discourse of 'water emergency', however, soon allowed political leaders to invoke the more draconian Maharashtra Control of Organised Crime Act (MCOCA)[33] against offenders. Not only were arrests made under these laws, but the militarized crackdown also translated into police harassment on the streets of ordinary residents trying to now obtain water from surrounding areas by foot or cycle. There is a sense among NGOs working in Shivaji Nagar, whose population is 70 per cent Muslim and increasingly comprises north Indian migrants (both Hindu and Muslim), that the water raids in the area reflect the religious and ethnic biases of Mumbai's municipal officials and the police.[34] The vehement anti-Muslim and anti-north Indian politics of the Shiv Sena, which has penetrated the work cultures of the municipal government and the police, thus also shapes how the broader revanchist politics against Mumbai's poor unfolds on the ground.

Beyond the use of draconian laws, further efforts to securitize Mumbai's water system are emerging. The Brihanmumbai Municipal Corporation has drawn up plans to physically demolish and erase informal settlements located alongside the city's water mains.[35] Even if residents are relocated under the city's controversial slum demolition and resettlement programme – which was launched by the Hindu nativist Shiv Sena Party when it was in power in the State of Maharashtra in the mid-1990s and which continues to be implemented under the Congress Party which is currently in power – it is likely that many will be excluded since only residents able to prove pre-1995 residency in the city are eligible for resettlement under the programme.

Ambitious, though still unimplemented, plans were also announced in late 2009 to place protective walls around every major exposed water main in the city, supported by a complex network of closed circuit television cameras and security guards. One BMC official revealed:

> We will float a tender for construction of a protective wall. At some places where this is difficult, we will put up a barbed wire. We have even planned to deploy security guards to keep a vigil and protect the pipelines, as we have received terrorist threats stating that the pipelines could be blown up. Besides, there is the peril of someone poisoning the city's water supply through the pipelines. We will take all possible measures in due time to prevent a disaster.[36]

The CCTV system, costing Rs. 2.3 million (around US$50,000), was put out to tender in April 2010.[37]

## Hydrological apartheid

Crucially, at no point does Mumbai's water revanchism allow for the provision of adequate alternative sources of formal, public or 'legal' water supplies to the majority of the city's population living in slums. What such discourses and actions mask is the inevitability of mass water theft among *Zopadpatti* dwellers in Mumbai in a context where political elites have long worked to use the systematic dehydration of such places as a deliberate strategy to discourage the formation, or force abandonment, of slums. Since 1996, the Maharashtra State Government – first under the Hindu nativist Shiv Sena Party and then under the Congress Party – has deliberately linked the right to water to the geography of tenancy in Mumbai. Slums deemed to have been formed after 1 January 1995 are considered unrecognized and have, consequently, been totally denied rights to access formal water mains.

Official, recognized slum-dwellers are entitled to water connections on provision of a photo-pass, name on the voters' list or ration card with the requisite pre-1995 date. However, these comprise of metered group connections, shared between 5–15 households, which are supposed to provide 45 litres per person per day (as opposed to 135 litres per person per day in residences in the formal city). Moreover, these connections do not always materialize and when they do, they do not always provide adequate water. The 1.2 million or more people living in post-1995 settlements,[38] meanwhile, remain unrecognized and consequently live under the permanent threat of the bulldozer and bereft of legal entitlements to water and other basic services.

Of course, this ruling has done nothing to inhibit the continued growth and formation of slums, as India's population burgeons and ever-more migrants move to Mumbai from impoverished areas and violent rural states in search of a better life. Indeed, in the absence of affordable housing in the formal city, many slums are brought into being through corrupt public officials working in liaison with elements of organized crime, the 'slumlords', and the 'vote-bank' politics whereby politicians seek to gain the votes of the city's majority slum dwellers in exchange for electoral promises.

In such a context, the demands among slum dwellers for even minimal hydra-tion have provided the motivation for the growth of the water racketeering sustained by the so-called water mafia. Both pipeline connections and tanker supplies are accelerated and made possible through large payments organized through the middlemen, in liaison with municipal officials, police officers and politicians. In Rafinagar, our research found that obtaining a legal water connec-tion from the BMC usually involves having to resort to a middleman and residents have to therefore pay between Rs. 20,000–60,000 (and increasingly more) to organize a legal water connection from the public mains. Not all resi-dents, therefore, can afford to get a legal connection and are forced to be dependent on those who can incur such costs. The middleman, who is sometimes a plumber, organizes the installation of the water pipe, giving a cut to municipal officials, and even the police and local politicians. Even after this, there is no guarantee of how long water will come in the pipe. Nonetheless, having incurred these high expenses, these 'tap-owner' residents then sell water at high prices to others in their neighbourhood, in order to recover their investment, pay the BMC's water bill, as well as make some cash for themselves. Our research in Rafinagar revealed that many residents paid between Rs.5–20 for a 35-litre jerry-can of water. This is between 30 and 200 times more than the official municipal water tariff for slums. Others paid for water based on the number of minutes they filled water from the tap-owner's connection.

Along with such formal connections are also 'illegal' connections organized by middlemen for some residents, who similarly sell water at prices that rise and fall with the seasons and the extremities of the water crises. Geographies of legal and illegal water provision thus become extremely blurred and materially entangled. During the raids in Rafinagar, for example, many legal connections were also cut by the BMC. Meanwhile, the raids created a deeper water crisis for those who had been forced to depend on these legal/illegal connections for water, and they increasingly had to pay more money to obtain water from inside Rafinagar. An increasing number of residents also had to go to neighbouring areas on foot or cycle to obtain cheaper water.

Mumbai's predatory water rackets have also grown through the involvement of municipal officials. An undercover investigation by the *Mumbai Mirror* in April 2010, for example, showed how 6,500 rupees delivered to hydraulic depart-ment and municipal ward officials, ostensibly to film a 'rain scene' in a Bollywood movie, was able to bring instant water tanker deliveries, filled illegally from the public water system by one of the 10,000 or so private water tankers in Mumbai. (Through official BMC means, such tankers take at least a week to arrive, cost only Rs. 600, and come through the BMC's over-stretched fleet of only 24 water tankers.[39]) The newspaper's investigations revealed a classic racket which forced slum dwellers – and, indeed, more affluent communities who often resort to private tankers as well – to pay extremely high prices to the illicit tanker companies for water – prices which rise and fall with the levels of supply and the depth of the city's water crisis. These arrangements are organized by geographic neighbourhood, with kickbacks distributed to key political, municipal and hydraulic department officials to keep everyone happy.

In such a context it is no surprise that city officials attempting to crack down on the water rackets surrounding pipeline or tanker provision have struggled to cope with the complex vested interests involved. And by destroying pipes built illegally in slum settlements, BMC official were, of course, further adding to levels of demand for highly profitable tanker supplies.

At the broader scale, and to compound the geographies of hydrological apartheid across Mumbai, the BMC has presided over the construction of a whole archipelago of massive water-hungry architectural edifices. These are geared towards Mumbai's powerful middle class and social and political elites and endlessly invoked as evidence that Mumbai is 'going global'. Most obvious here has been the complicity of the BMC in licensing the proliferation of private swimming pools within Mumbai's burgeoning array of upscale gated communities and apartment complexes.[40] But large-scale water theme parks are also being built across the city's suburbs. As ordinary Mumbaikers reeled under the 10 per cent supply cuts during the 2003 water crisis, Charubala Annuncio observed that, at the same time, the periphery of Mumbai was being ringed by complexes of water parks, theme parks, leisure parks, elite high-rise complexes, clubs, and bungalows with swimming pools rented out for Bollywood film shootings. 'Just the two dozen existing water parks in Mumbai and adjoining areas like Thane and Raigad use over 50 billion litres of water every day. Of this, Esselworld's Water Kingdom, which is spread over 24 acres, gets over 7 billion litres.'[41] Indeed, the water used by these water parks is twice the water supply to the whole of Mumbai.

India's burgeoning bottled water industry only adds to the city's deepening hydrological apartheid. As elsewhere, in Mumbai those who can afford it increasingly buy bottled water to try and insulate themselves from the perceived health risks of piped municipal water, which has often been found to be contaminated. Such strategies reflect a broader tendency among more affluent Mumbaikers to attempt to secede from the public city through complexes involving gated communities, new raised highways, private malls and the 'capsular' mobilities afforded by private cars.

The Indian market for bottled water, valued at Rs. 10 billion in 2010, is growing at an astonishing 40 per cent per annum.[42] The industry, which tripled in size between 1999 and 2004, is one of India's fastest growing. Over two hundred brands jostle for the market share, their utopian advertising looming large above the city's streets (see Figure 3.4). For those who can buy in, the latest 'premium' bottled brands offer the fantasy of a pure, 'natural', escapism amidst the dense urbanization of Mumbai. 'I was born in the Shivalik range of the Himalayas,' proclaims the label on the Tata Corporation's 'Himalayan' bottled water:

*Figure 3.4* A Bisleri bottled water advert looms large over Mumbai, north of the Fort
District
Source: Photograph by Colin McFarlane.

In a place most of you visit only in an Atlas. In a time that wasn't measured
by cuckoos that sprang out of clocks. In a silence that was sometimes
punctuated by howling winds and gushing streams. In a world that had
nothing to do with yours.

This mythologized 'journey' of Mumbai's premium, elite, bottled water, a Tata
press release argues, 'seeks to make the consumer one with its source – the
Himalayas – with its inherent and pristine goodness that sets it apart from ordinary water'.[43] The strap-line seems especially startling given the wider context of
Mumbai's water wars: 'Hydration with wellness.'
    The larger, corporate bottling plants, which are owned by companies such as
Parle Bisleri, Nestlé, Coca-Cola, PepsiCo, Manikchand, and Britannia, and are
given water at favourably low charges, are based on the urban fringes. Simpreet
Singh of the National Alliance of People's Movement points out that even
during water cut-offs and no water days for the rest of Mumbai, the BMC continued to supply over 800,000 litres a day of potable water to bottling plants – for
mineral water and soft drinks – geared towards the city's middle classes and

elites.[44] Indeed, despite the city's deepening water crisis, and the extreme scarcities suffered by its informal cities, the BMC supplied almost 300 million litres of water to 17 bottling plants in 13 months between January 2009 and 10 February 2010.[45] The largest of these, Duke and Sons, owned by Pepsi, used almost 80 million litres in the same period.

The middle classes and elites tackle the water crisis by a combination of groundwater from their borewells, calling in private water tankers, and, more recently, by installing rainwater harvesting and grey-water recycling systems, thus seceding from the public city when required.

## 'Can Shanghai be made on the graves of the poor?'

Mumbai's water raids have further accentuated the public health, economic and social impacts of systematic dehydration among already vulnerable communities. Paradoxically, the reliance of such communities on extremely expensive water provision organized through water rackets and, ironically, further 'illegal' piped supplies delivered through BMC corruption, has also been deepened still further.

The limited evidence available already paints a bleak picture of the health and social impacts of systematic water shortages among Mumbai's slum dwellers. Before the raids, for example, a study of 1,070 households in four slums in the year 2000, led by Hideki Harada of Nagaoka University of Technology, published in India's prestigious *Economic and Political Weekly*,[46] showed that where one water tap was provided between 13–30 households, it was woefully inadequate both quantitatively and in terms of quality. The median per capita daily water consumption per person in the four slums was found to be as low as 26, 27, 33 and 25 litres per day. Not surprisingly, slum-dwellers ranked access to water and toilet facilities as being the most important issues they faced. Among slum-dwellers living with such extreme water scarcity, the annual diarrhoea, typhoid and malaria cases were estimated to be 614, 68 and 126 per thousand people respectively. The study found that 'all types of water-borne disease are occurring with great severity' in all the four poor communities that were studied. Consequently, the authors calculated that at least 30 per cent of all deaths in Mumbai could be accounted for by water-related infections.[47]

Dr Ravindra Rathod,[48] of the Niramaya Health Foundation in Rafinagar, recounted to us some of the chronic health impacts from systematic dehydration that he has to treat daily among his patients. Diarrhoea, dysentery, scabies and typhoid are all extremely common. As desperation takes hold, many people dig their own wells, accessing limited supplies of extremely contaminated groundwater in the process. Tests by the World Health Organization have found cholera, hepatitis and, most disturbing of all, polio, viruses in water samples from such wells.[49] Nazia Sayed and Geeta Desai point out that, to date, the Indian state has spent Rs. 26 billion trying to eradicate polio, only to again expose residents to its virus because of the BMC's aggressive water raids policy. Sangeeta Yadav, a Mankhurd resident, discussed a newly dug well in her house with the journalists. 'How do they expect us to survive without water?' she asked. 'We have no option but to drink this dirty water. We will die if we don't drink water, and we will die if we drink this water. Whatever has to happen, will happen.'[50] Iqbal Shaikh, a social worker in the area lobbying for more municipal pipelines, stressed that 'The residents all know the water is contaminated but are helpless. For days we don't get water in the area and if we complain, the BMC people demand a huge amount of money for a pipeline. That's the reason why people opt for such illegal measures.'

Following the destruction of pipes serving Rafinagar in November 2009, our research demonstrated how the community was pushed more deeply into a water crisis. Two weeks after the raids, the BMC did install two temporary water storage tanks just outside Rafinagar. However, beyond the burden of long hours queuing, even this completely inadequate supply was next to useless for most residents as the arrival of the BMC water tankers to fill the tanks was extremely sporadic. In addition, many physical struggles occurred as residents fought over the inadequate water supplies, especially when the tankers finally arrived (Figure 3.5). 'Either beat up each other for water or die [without water] yourself,' a

*Figure 3.5* Rafinagar residents waiting at one of the temporary water storage tanks for the BMC water tanker to come and fill it

Source: Photograph by Renu Desai.

Rafinagar woman remarked to us caustically.[51] 'Those whose mouths have strength [to speak up and shout],' recounted another, 'those whose bodies are strong, those who can curse, they are the ones who can fill [water from the tanks].'[52] Even after a group of residents improvised a system for regulating the queues at the water tanks, various exclusions continued.

The extreme water scarcity in Rafinagar meant that, for the first time, private water tankers, organized through corruption and offering extremely expensive water to those who could afford it, began to be regularly called in. Many of the private water tankers also obtained water from borewells, pointing to profits being made through excessive and often unregulated groundwater extraction.

Water prices within Rafinagar increased after the raids. While water delivered through a legal connection is charged at Rs. 2.25 for 1000 litres, Rafinagar residents, the poorest of Mumbai's poor, were increasingly paying up to 100–200 times that amount just to fill one jerry-can of 35–40 litres. Some of our interviewees thus ended up spending over Rs. 600 per month on minimal water supplies, out of a total monthly income of Rs. 3000–4000. Most of our interviewees were unable to bathe on a daily basis, even in the unbearably hot summer months, leading to skin infections. Water was available for lower rates only if it was 'brown' or 'yellow' in colour.

After the raids, our interviews showed that more of Rafinagar's residents than before were forced to rely on sources of water outside the settlement, accessing these by time-consuming and exhausting 1–5 km journeys by foot or cycle. Many women and young girls, in particular, went by foot with water pots to search for water from outside while many men and boys went by cycle with jerry-cans. Children often had to forego schooling or paid work because of the imperative of accessing water, or took on multiple burdens.

These itinerant water-carriers, in turn, then became subjected to state violence and harassment. The BMC and police started to confiscate cycles and jerry-cans and even punctured jerry-cans. An additional problem was that the threats of arrest against those caught 'illegally' selling water meant that water-carriers found it harder and harder to gain supplies even beyond the community's boundaries. For instance, one male resident from Rafinagar (who used to often fill water from outside the settlement even before the water raids) told us: 'People in Shivaji Nagar aren't giving water. They say that if we give you water, then the police will catch us.'[53]

The systematic state harassment, and the active denial of an essential source of urban life, led to deep feelings of outrage and alienation among Rafinagar and Govandi inhabitants. 'I sold my jewellery to acquire this connection and now police have seized the motor. How can we live without water?' pleaded one Govandi woman who has a family of six to the *Mumbai Mirror*'s Nazia Sayed.[54] Many complained that they were not even aware that their connections, organized after all with BMC complicity, were technically illegal. Others were incensed that raids destroyed pipes that were legally supplied and for which they had been paying bills. A further group of residents actually backed the raids because the resulting increases in pressure further down the pipes meant that their supplies were improved.

Govind, a 17-year-old boy, visibly upset as he recounted his experience, discussed with us how, as a Rafinagar resident, he was violently assaulted by residents in neighbouring Gautamnagar: 'Once when I was coming back from there, some 5–6 men from there stopped me on my cycle and forcefully took the cans and upset all the water. They told me that if you people from Rafinagar come here to fill water, then Gautamnagar's connections will also be cut so don't come here again.'

Mumbai's slum-dwellers are painfully aware of the way in which their demonization has served the purposes of the city's political and economic elites. They are also not slow to see links between the wider political aspirations of reengineering Mumbai into a 'global city' or a 'new Shanghai', and the increasingly orchestrated state violence against them and their needs.

Salma, one of our Rafinagar interviewees,[55] discussing the ongoing threats of demolition against the settlement as well as the water raids, puts it bluntly: 'The government is not listening to us,' she says, 'because it wants to make [Mumbai into] Shanghai ... We don't oppose Shanghai. But [the government] comes and crushes us and goes away, like [one might crush] ants ... We would also like that Shanghai is made. We might not see it but at least our children will. Our children's dreams will be fulfilled.' But, Salma argues, if Mumbai's government and ruling elites 'try to make Shanghai at the cost of the dreams and aspirations of the poor, then this Shanghai will not be successful ... Can Shanghai be made on the graves of the poor? If there is a funeral opposite me and I play music, can I really enjoy it?'

Water protests by the urban poor in Mumbai have often targeted political parties whose vote-bank politics traditionally surrounds the politics of water provision for Mumbai's poor. Through these, election-cycles tend to coincide with promises to address questions of water provision to slums. After the municipal water raids in and around Rafinagar too, residents mobilized to approach their political leaders, reminding them of their election promises to bring adequate piped water to Rafinagar. However, instead inadequate temporary arrangements were made and the realization of these promises was continually delayed. This reveals an increasingly predatory vote-bank politics in which politicians on the one hand come to power based on their electoral promises to the urban poor and, on the other, are often involved in perpetuating the dependency of the urban poor on exploitative or predatory water rackets for their own financial benefit.

## The right to urban water

In Mumbai, water 'infrastructure' encompasses much more than pipes, aquifers, rivers, borewells and taps. It also involves, crucially, complex social and political arrangements and the very people of the city.[56] The fragmented nature of civil society has paved the way for water revanchism: an attempt by the middle classes to 'claim back' the city's hydrological commons from the poor through a discourse that casts themselves as tax-paying citizens who are denied their legitimate right to municipal water because this is diverted through vote-bank politics and corruption to 'encroaching' slum dwellers who have no legitimate right to the city's resources. This discourse erases the experiences of the urban poor of the hydrological apartheid as it does their right to urban water. This discourse further dovetails with attempts by powerful elites to 'claim back' the city from the poor majority under the spurious justification of competing with mythological cities elsewhere (Shanghai, Singapore …). As a result, civil society organizations that cast the city's water crisis through the experiences of the urban poor and argue for policies that would recognize their right to water face profound challenges.[57]

Mumbai's water wars reveal in stark detail what emerges when slum dwellers are cast out from the rights of a modern urban existence in the world's burgeoning mega-cities. Much less familiar than the now frequent attempts by terrorist groups and state militaries to interrupt the socio-technologies of flow and metabolism in contemporary cities, as a means to distribute shock and violence,[58] Mumbai's water raids reveal that revanchist politics extend to the systematic destruction of the means of hydration. Excavating them shows in startling detail how the complete denial of the status of water as a public good to be organized and distributed collectively to benefit all urban residents opens the door to the hydrological apartheid which surrounds the hyper-commodification of the ultimate inelastic good. Finally, our story demonstrates that apparently benign aspirations to 'Clean up' Global South megacities, to allow them to be reengineered into 'global' metropolises imitating some shining and mythical exemplar (so often Shanghai but, increasingly, Dubai) can camouflage extreme campaigns of violence, erasure, intimidation and plunder by political and economic elites against the vulnerable and poor.

The results of the water wars – dehydration, death, disease and desperation – demonstrate the urgent need to challenge the politics of water at its foundation. For, only by building a politics of water rights, addressing the legitimate needs of Mumbai's poor for clean, adequate water, will the city and state authorities ever hope to eradicate the symptoms of poverty and social fragmentation that their regressive and violent mobilizations are ostensibly designed to address. We are encouraged by the range of activist groups and organizations that attempt to draw attention to Mumbai's deeply unequal urban metabolism, but we have yet to see a broader movement in the city coalesce around water and sanitation that continually calls into question and offers robust alternatives to the nature of the city's development strategies.

## Notes

1   Abhijit Sathe, 'Stealing water to earn a few bucks? Pay a hefty price', *Mumbai Mirror*, 8 January 2010, p. 4.
2   Ibid.

3   See Erik Swyndegouw, *Social Power and the Urbanization of Water: Flows of Power* (Oxford: Oxford University Press, 2004); Maria Kaika, *City of Flows: Modernity, Nature and the City* (London: Routledge, 2005).

4   Virat A. Singh, 'How the BMC saved the city 4 lakh litres of water', *Mumbai Mirror*, 11 January 2010, p. 8.

5   Giorgio Agamben, *Homo Sacer: Sovereign Power and Bare Life* (Stanford, CA: Stanford University Press, 1998).

6   We gratefully acknowledge the support of the ESRC for the grant 'Everyday Sanitation, number RES/0360/7277', which made this research possible.

7   Maharashtra State Government (2003) *Vision Mumbai: Transforming Mumbai into a World-Class City.* Available at: www.maharashtra.gov.in/english/reports/taskforce.pdf (accessed 2 September 2014).

8   A. Roy and A. Ong (eds) *Worlding Cities: Asian Experiments and the Art of Being Global* (Oxford: Wiley-Blackwell, 2011).

9   J. Joseph (2005) 'What will make Mumbai into a Shanghai?', *Times of India*, 6 April. Available at: http://timesofindia.indiatimes.com/business/india-business/What-will-make-Mumbai-into-a-Shanghai/articleshow/1069800.cms?flstry=1 (accessed March 2012).

10  Sunil Kumar, Shigeo Shikura and Hideki Harada, 'Living environment and health of urban poor: a study of Mumbai', *Economic and Political Weekly*, 23 August 2003, pp. 3575–3586.

11  See Matthew Gandy, 'Landscapes of disaster: water, modernity, and urban fragmentation in Mumbai', *Environment and Planning A*, 40 (2008):108–130; Arjun Appadurai, 'Spectral housing and urban cleansing: notes on millennial Mumbai,' *Public Culture*, 12(3) (2000): 627–651.

12  World Bank, 'Bombay fights the markets, and more than half of Mumbai's residents live in slums', WorldBank.Org, 2009. Available at: http://web.worldbank.org/WBSITE/EXTERNAL/HOMEPORTUGUESE/EXTMAININPOR/EXTDATAANDRESINPOR/EXTRESINPOR/EXTWDRINPOR/EXTWDR2009INPOR/0,,contentMDK:21954976~pagePK:64168445~piPK:64168309~theSitePK:5593535,00.html (accessed 2 September 2014).

13  Lisa Bjorkman, 'Water and resettlement on the urban periphery: the case of Mumbai's M-East Ward', unpublished paper, p. 1.

14  Narendra Jadhav, 'Economic renewal of Mumbai City: opportunities and constraints' paper presented at the International Conference on Urban Renewal: Learning for Mumbai, Mumbai, 24–26 May 2005. Available at: www.drnarendrajadhav.info/drnjadhav_web_files/Published%20papers/Economic%20REnewal%20of%20Mumbai%20City.pdf.

15  See Appadurai, 'Spectral housing and urban cleansing'.

16  See Gandy, 'Landscapes of disaster', p. 122.

17  On the pogroms, see T. B. Hansen, *Wages of Violence: Naming and Identity in Postcolonial Bombay* (Princeton, NJ: Princeton University Press, 2001); Appadurai, 'Spectral housing and urban cleansing'; and R. Varma, 'Provincialising the global city: from Bombay to Mumbai', *Social Text*, 22(4) (2004): 65–89.

18  See Amita Baviskar, 'The politics of the city', *Seminar* 156, 2002. Available at: www.india-seminar.com/2002/516/516%20amita%20baviskar.htm (accessed 2 September 2014).

19  See Yogesh Sadhwani, 'Water war!', *Mumbai Mirror*, 17 November 2010, p. 2.

20  See C. McFarlane, 'Governing the contaminated city: Infrastructure and sanitation in colonial and postcolonial Bombay', *International Journal of Urban and Regional Research*, 32(2) (2008): 415–435; M. Dossal, *Imperial Designs and Indian Realities: The Planning of Bombay City, 1845–1875* (New Delhi: Oxford University Press, 1991); Gandy, 'Landscapes of disaster'.

21   See MW-YUVA, 2001 Slum Sanitation Project: Final Report (Municipal Corporation of Brihanmumbai, Mumbai); C. McFarlane, 'Sanitation in Mumbai's informal settlements: state, "slum", and infrastructure', *Environment and Planning A*, 40 (2008): 88–107.

22   Baviskar, 'The politics of the city'; and see P. Chatterjee, *The Politics of the Governed: Reflections on Popular Politics in Most of the World* (Delhi: Permanent Black, 2004).

23   For an excellent discussion of how these processes connect to the city's disparate but crucial film culture, see R. Mazumdar, *Bombay Cinema: An Archive of the City* (Minneapolis: University of Minnesota Press, 2007).

24   Hetal Vyas, 'HC pulls up BMC over state of water pipelines', *Mumbai Mirror*, 30 July 2009.

25   Ibid.

26   McKinsey and Bombay First, *Vision Mumbai: Transforming Mumbai into a World-class City* (Mumbai: McKinsey and Bombay First, 2003).

27   Gandy, 'Landscapes of disaster', p. 125.

28   Geeta Desai, 'Where does Mumbai's water go?' New Link Road Residents' Forum, 26 March 2010. Available at: http://newlinkroad.blogspot.com/2010/03/where-does-mumbais-water-go.html (accessed 2 September 2014).

29   This process links to the ways in which particular civic groups have become part of a broader architecture of exclusion in Mumbai. See, for example, Jonathan Shapiro Anjaria's study of exclusive Advanced Locality Management (ALM) and Local Area Citizens' Groups (LACG), 'Guardians of the bourgeois city: citizenship, public space, and middle-class activism in Mumbai', *City and Community*, 8(4) (2005): 391–406.

30   Singh, 'How the BMC saved the city.'

31   Vinay Dalvi, 'BMC, police begin crackdown on illegal water vendors', *Mumbai Mirror*, 1 December 2009, p. 2.

32   Geeta Desai, 'BMC wants ACB, cops to curb water thefts', *Mumbai Mirror*, 7 June 2010, p. 4.

33   Sudhir Suryawanshi, 'Water thieves to be tried under MCOCA', *Mumbai Mirror*, 10 April 2010, p. 2.

34   Personal interviews with Leena Joshi, Apnalaya (a community-development NGO).

35   Sudhir Suryawanshi, 'BMC to reclaim city's pipelines', *Mumbai Mirror*, 11 September 2009, p. 2.

36   Ibid.

37   Sharad Vyas, 'BMC kickstarts process to install CCTVs at pipelines', *Times of India*, Mumbai edition, 6 April 2010, p. 5.

38   Sukhada Tatke, 'Slum dwellers rely on ration shops for water', *Times of India*, 19 December 2010, p. 9.

39   Anil Raina, 'Water, yes, but at 10 times the cost', *Mumbai Mirror*, 12 November 2009.

40   Varun Singh, 'Pools to be built despite water crunch', *Mid.Day.Com*, 2 April 2010. Available at: www.mid-day.com/news/2010/apr/020410-swimming-pools-water-crunch-mumbai.htm (accessed 2 September 2014).

41   Charubala Annuncio, 'Watery divisions', *Outlook India.Com*, 26 May 2003. Available at: www.outlookindia.com/article.aspx?220265 (accessed 2 September 2014).

42   Gits4u.com, 'Bottled water industry in India'. 2010. Available at: www.gits4u.com/water/water16.htm (accessed 2 September 2014).

43   Tata Group, 'Mount Everest Mineral Water unveils the new Himalayan natural mineral water', 7 May 2008. Available at: www.tata.com/media/releases/inside.aspx?artid=Mw/mP8IlwTE= (accessed 2 September 2014).

44   Tatke, 'Slum dwellers rely on ration shops'.

45   Alka Shukla, 'Bottled up', *Mumbai Mirror*, 14 April 2010, p. 8.

46   Kumar *et al.*, 'Living environment and health of urban poor'.

47  Ibid.
48  Personal interview on 6 Feb. 2010.
49  Nazia Sayed and Geeta Desai, 'Thirst for water leading to polio', *Mumbai Mirror*, 29 December 2009, p. 1.
50  Ibid.
51  Resident, Rafinagar Part 2, personal interview, 8 Jan. 2010.
52  Resident, Rafinagar Part 1, personal interview, 12 Jan 2010.
53  Resident, Rafinagar Part 1, personal interview, 7 March 2010.
54  Nazia Sayed, 'Artificial water shortage in Govandi', *Mumbai Mirror*, 5 December 2009, p. 6.
55  Resident, Rafinagar Part 2, personal interview, 8 Jan. 2010.
56  See Abdou Maliq Simone, 'People as infrastructure: intersecting fragments in Johannesburg', *Public Culture*, 13(3) (2004): 407–408.
57  For a broader discussion of such mobilizations, see Arjun Appadurai, 'Deep democracy: urban governmentality and the horizon of politics', *Environment and Urbanization*, 13(2) (2001): 23–43.
58  See Vyjayanthi Rao, 'How to read a bomb: scenes from Bombay's Black Friday', *Public Culture*, 19(3) (2007): 567–592.

Chapter 4

# Waiting in the ruins
## The aesthetics and politics of favela urbanization in "PACification" Rio de Janeiro

*Mariana Cavalcanti*

## Introductory fieldnotes

On January 8, 2012, a massive six-building compound that had once housed a milk factory was blown up to give way to a low-income housing project, as part of the Federal Government of Brazil's Growth Acceleration Program, or PAC-Favelas (Programa de Aceleração do Crescimento). Located in the old industrial zone of Rio de Janeiro's north suburb, on the outskirts of the agglomeration of favelas known as Manguinhos, the old factory ruin had been occupied by hundreds of families since 2000. The implosion marked the end of a long process of relocating some residents and compensating others, a process wrought with delays, deferrals and moments of sheer despair for all involved. In the place of the old factory, a 600-unit housing project is to be built, to which many of the former occupation residents are to return. For now they get a monthly stipend of R$400 (US$200) to help them pay their rent while they wait for their keys. Since the beginning of the PAC works in Manguinhos in 2008, this has been the second occupied industrial site to be demolished in order to give way to a housing project for its former tenants. More are to follow.[1]

The implosion attracted considerable media coverage. Dozens of journalists crowded around the restricted area set up on top of an overpass that offered a privileged view of the implosion site. The state vice-governor (who is also Secretary of Public Works), and the Director of the State Public Works Department shared the spotlight with a number of community leaders, many of them representatives of other favelas in the region undergoing infrastructural upgrading and urbanization works under the aegis of the PAC-Favelas. The euphoria that followed the long-delayed but successful implosion of the massive factory ruins created the opportunity for an improvised stroll with the authorities through the PAC works in order to inspect their progress and to prospect future urbanistic interventions in the Manguinhos region.

I was at the scene shooting a documentary on the process of relocating the residents of the occupation, and happened to be directing the crew that had documented the steps of the community leader of the old factory throughout the morning of the implosion. So we joined the group as they set off towards the site where elevated train tracks were under construction. There were maybe two dozen people in the group, between local community leaders, politicians and assistants, plus our crew. As the entourage walked along the train tracks, the community leader we were filming disappeared into an alley.

*We immediately switched off the microphone we had on her, for there was no question that she had slipped out of sight in order to notify whoever was running the drug trade surveillance of the politicians' presence in the interstices of Manguinhos. It only took her a moment; she joined us readily and discreetly enough.*

*The group walked along the deteriorated train tracks that should have posed a stark contrast to the massive concrete structure running parallel to it, upon which new tracks were being laid (but not today; it was Sunday). Instead, the juxtaposition of ongoing construction work with the deteriorated landscape surrounding it seemed to confirm the aptness of the term the media uses to refer to the region – they call it the "Gaza Strip" because of the constant shootouts and armed confrontations in the region. This entire stretch of Leopoldo Bulhões Avenue fits the description of a war zone in the aftermath of a major battle. We stepped over layers of debris of different processes of ruination. The not-yet inaugurated structure of the new tracks already showed layers of graffiti. Occasional crack users nestled beneath the pillars of the new tracks as they slept in dirty bundles, or just smoked out of dirty plastic mineral water cups, oblivious to the presence of the authorities. Many of them had probably just been displaced from the old factory ruin; in its last days the shell of the old factory had turned into a scene of a zombie movie. Here on the tracks, however, the debris from the cracudos' (as the "crackheads" are locally referred to) improvised individual or collective campsites was moderate when compared to the other parts of Manguinhos where hundreds of them routinely congregate, including the recently paved roads and sidewalks surrounding a soccer field recently built by the same PAC-favelas that had just demolished the milk factory.*

*But the euphoric group strolled along the apocalyptic scenario with talks of the next factory they planned to convert into yet another housing project of colorful façades. And, in fact, if one turned one's back to the train tracks, and zoomed in on one particular corner of the avenue opposite it, two shining new buildings – one of housing units and the other, a high school – stood out among the ruins, lending some coherence to the reigning optimism of the public authorities and community leaders.*

*I wondered how long it would take those buildings to become incorporated into the general derelict atmosphere, like the housing projects and facilities built in the late 1990s in the neighboring favela of Jacarezinho, just a couple of hundred meters away.*

This episode renders evident the multiple scales of power relations and mundane negotiations that large-scale favela urbanization programs must come to terms with on a daily basis. From federal budget negotiations in Congress, to planners' blueprints, to their implementation "on the ground", such grandiose initiatives have to deal with concrete challenges posed by everyday life. And in Rio de Janeiro's favelas, daily life has sedimented, over the course of the past three decades or so, a logic of urban informality that defies any theoretical boundaries between the legal and illegal, the legitimate and illegitimate precisely because it constitutes an organizing logic that, as Ananya Roy has pointed out, governs the process of urban transformation itself, by connecting "different spaces and economies to each other" (Roy 2005, p. 148).

Urban informality as a "way of life" (Alsayyed, 2004) that itself shifts in time and space, has shaped what I refer to as the favelas' consolidation, that is, their incorporation into and increasing centrality in city politics and policies. Favela urbanization has become institutionalized and been legitimized in the public sphere as a response to their territorial dominance by highly militarized drug gangs, organized, on a city-wide level, in three major drug factions constantly at war. In other words, the rationale is that it is because they are violent that the favelas' material infrastructure should be improved. So somewhat paradoxically, violence and the stigma attached to the favelas end up creating the conditions for the favelas' material improvements but also for their residents' political recognition and leverage – while reproducing all sorts of stereotypes and power relations that reinforce the idea of their cultural alterity vis-à-vis the so-called formal city (see Cavalcanti 2007, 2008).

Thus, on an everyday level favela consolidation is experienced as the ever-precarious accommodation of often contradictory organizing forces, territorial logics, and modes of exercising sovereignty over particular stretches of urban space. Daily life unfolds in the interstices of the distinct territorializing efforts shaped simultaneously by drug trade disputes and by the irruptive presence of a violent, corrupt police force, but also by increasing state investments and service provisions, in spaces that nonetheless get taken over by the sights, smells and sounds of so-called "cracklands" – regions where crack cocaine is used continuously that take on a series of spatial and social dynamics of their own, sometimes at odds with the interests of the more institutionalized aspects of the drug trade. Between these different systems of relations that get played out and accommodate each other in the space of the favela, thousands of residents maintain their routines and go about their daily business.

This chapter is a broad ethnographic account of the PAC-Favelas urbanization program in the Manguinhos "complex," a grouping of 14 favelas and/or housing projects located in the heart of the old industrial zone of the north suburbs of Rio de Janeiro. I am particularly concerned with how the PAC works affected daily life and local politics in Manguinhos. What sorts of daily practices do these infrastructural works alter, affect, shift and produce? In a context of territorially based social relations largely mediated by violence, what sorts of power structures do the new landscapes challenge? How do they enable, or produce new modes of sovereignty? How does the appropriation of space and the production of new spatial practices, tactics or routines unfold? What are the stakes for the local politics, and how does the production of new spaces – as well as the destruction of old ones – affect long-standing power relations and structures of authority that govern politics of space here? What sorts of political mediations between different spaces and logics emerge in this context?

Asking these questions entails deconstructing the rhetoric that legitimizes public policies targeting the city's favelas in the public sphere, a rhetoric that builds upon the self-evident rationale of the virtues of the "arrival of the state" in regions where it was allegedly "absent" up until now. The problem is that both the history of Manguinhos and the sociology of Rio's favelas seriously challenge such convenient narratives of a redemptive state occupying an alleged power vacuum.

In Manguinhos – as in other favelas of the city – the state and its margins have constantly redefined their boundaries and relations for most of the twentieth century. The endurance of the favelas in time and space has itself produced a series of spaces for politics and social actors whose very existence is tied to the constitution of regimes of informality that have historically shaped the development of the city's favelas – *as favelas*, as opposed to the so-called "formal" city. Thus, local political brokers, the Catholic Church, labor union politics, clientist arrangements, community agents, the "violent sociability" enforced by the drug trade – and the possible and even necessary transits that different individuals operate between these subject positions[2] – have all had a stake in the favelas' social incorporation into the city, even if as its margin. The historical development of the 14 communities that today comprise the so-called Manguinhos "complex" is intricately connected to state-sponsored housing policies for most of the twentieth century: many originated from "provisional" housing projects to which residents of other favelas from the city were relocated between the 1940s and the 1970s; others constituted early experiments in infrastructural upgrading in the 1990s; now, the PAC works have officially incorporated illegally occupied former industrial spaces as communities to the "Manguinhos" complex, thus placing them in considerably more formalized relations to the state, relations that are articulated in accordance with the language of rights. From this perspective, Manguinhos emerges not as a region from which the state is absent, but as a place that has functioned as a laboratory for low-income housing policies for most of the twentieth century.

But if the state was already there, what is new about the PAC works? In this chapter I make the argument that the increase in the scale of the interventions targeting the favelas – of the PAC works in general but of the Manguinhos project in particular – constitute and are constitutive of a qualitative shift in the aims and outputs of current state policies vis-à-vis the city's favelas. Thus, in order to understand the effects of the PAC works in Manguinhos and elsewhere, it is necessary to move beyond the urbanistic interventions themselves and turn to the current conditions under which urbanization programs are conceived, performed, and connected to larger processes of social and urban transformation.

The PAC-Favelas was conceived in consonance with the exigencies of strategic planning and city branding efforts that the city administration has aggressively espoused in the last half decade or so. No matter how effective the conversion of the favela into a global trademark, the political, discursive and imaginary construction of the image of a city suited to host global events would inevitably have to deal with the so-called "public security crisis" of the past three decades. And the so-called public security crisis for the past three decades has coincided with the "favela issue" (see World Bank, 2012; Burgos, 2013). I am therefore arguing that the PAC works constitute one aspect of a larger syntax of favela "pacification" that is central to the city branding strategies currently reshaping Rio de Janeiro due to the city's winning bids to host global mega events like the 2014 Soccer World Cup and the 2016 Olympic Games.

"Pacification" here refers to the public security program launched by the state government of Rio de Janeiro in late 2008. It consists in the permanent occupation of certain strategically located favelas where Unidades de Policia Pacificadora – Pacifying Police Units, or UPPs, as they are known and as I shall refer to them throughout this chapter – have been established. In general, the favelas were initially occupied by the elite forces of the Military Police or by "pacifying forces" made up of army soldiers from different states. Once territorial control has been secured, special forces give way to recently graduated military police officers who become the representatives of law and order – thus anchoring "the state" – in the favelas. "Pacified" favelas, i.e. those with UPPs, become the preferred sites for public and privately funded social programs and as well as new, improved, legalized services. The spatial distribution of UPPs in the city leaves no doubt as to their privileging the touristic sites, the elite south zone in particular, and the areas where the Olympic Games are to be held.[3] It seals a new pact with the business sector in the running of the city, with the establishment of public–private partnerships that ensure what seem to be unlimited funds for the UPP program. Since 2008, 28 UPP units have been established to guarantee the pacification of about one hundred favelas.[4]

Obviously, addressing the shortcomings or long-term effects of the UPP program is beyond the scope of this chapter. What matters is that the coupling of the large scale of the PAC interventions with the UPP program speaks to a grammar of social control of the city's favelas that constitutes the larger political remakings of urban form prescribed by the project of Rio as an Olympic city: the grammar of "PACification," as it were. The effects of this simultaneous bundling together of urbanization and militarization and the upscaling of both these types of interventions opens up a series of venues of disputes, opportunities and challenges for exerting local powers. From the perspective of daily life in the favelas, it also sets in motion new key political brokerage relations that go with the governance of large-scale displacement of people and the distribution of keys to apartments in new housing projects, and also with the brokerage of employment opportunities in the construction works themselves.

In other words, if none of the interventions works of the PAC favelas are new in and of themselves, their very piling up and juxtaposition with the UPP program in the city at large amount to an experience of ongoing – and future – transformations on an unprecedented scale. In a word, they produce a sense of impending change. The UPP program matters here because it places change on the horizon of an everyday that is and has been for decades now constituted by routine uncertainty – residents have for years on end lived in expectation of the next shootout, the next police incursion, the next glimpse of violence down an alley (see Cavalcanti, 2008). Now the sources and meanings of daily uncertainty have shifted. And while daily life endures as riddled with uncertainty as ever – and very little changes despite the proliferation of debris from construction work that has been going on for more than three years – the juxtaposition of the spatial transformations of the PAC and the remote effects of UPPs produce a sense of anticipation; residents are, mostly despite themselves, waiting for something to happen. In Manguinhos, in times of PAC and UPP, everything is changing though nothing really changes, is what the residents feel.

Therefore, this study captures a moment in which long-established regimes of urban informality felt the impact of a series of disturbing phenomena.[5] And while this chapter makes an effort to deconstruct the commonsensical notion of favela urbanization as the "entrance" or "arrival" of the state in the favelas, one of its main claims is that the transformation that the PAC brought to everyday structures of authority in the favela has frayed long-established power relations. In particular, I am concerned with the role of new political subjects or mediators that operate precisely on the interstices between the multiple structures of urban informality that conform to daily life in Rio's favelas, usually in the guise of presidents of residents' associations, and how the uses and appropriations of space in the favela accommodate the new logic of production of urban space in pre-Olympic Rio de Janeiro.

In the pages that follow I shall pursue these questions first by providing an outline of how the PAC-Favelas and the Pacification program articulate a distinct regime of (in)visibility of the favelas in the urban landscape that deliberately resignifies the social contrasts and historically constituted, sharp social boundaries as a spectacle of their incorporation into the state. I then move on to provide a historical background of the recent history of Manguinhos, with particular attention to the recent transformations brought about by the arrival of the crack economy, by the PAC works themselves, and by the recent occupation of the favelas comprising the Complexo do Alemão in June 2010. I then turn back to my fieldnotes in order to highlight how these – the real and imagined; past, present and projected – have affected local politics and residents' future expectations. Finally, I sketch a few remarks about the subjective experience of waiting that seeps through the interviews, observations and experience of being in Manguinhos: the sense that major change lies just ahead, and the anticipation and uncertainty this context produces.

## The PAC aesthetics: inscribing the favela in the urban landscape

In January 2007, the Federal Government of Brazil launched the *Programa de Aceleração do Crescimento*, the Growth Acceleration Program, or PAC, as I refer to it throughout this chapter. Following the political wisdom of our times, it consists of a series of state investments in major infrastructure works throughout the country, with the aim of creating the social and material conditions for fostering private investments in strategic sectors, thus enabling economic growth. The PAC Program defines three strategic sectors for investments in infrastructure: the energy sector, transportation and logistics, and Social/Urban development.

The latter refers to favela and informal settlement urbanization works and infrastructural upgrading. Of the 3.9 billion Reais destined to the state of Rio de Janeiro in the first phase of the program, 860 million were allotted to urbanization works in four favela areas in the city of Rio: Cantagalo and Pavão-Pavãozinho, in the south zone; Rocinha, at the border of the south and west zones; the 13 communities comprising the Complexo do Alemão, in the north suburb not far from the 14 communities the Program considered to comprise the so-called Manguinhos Complex (see Trindade, 2007, 2012).

Large-scale investment in Rio's favelas as a means of fostering economic growth is by no means an unprecedented political strategy in the city. The history of public policies targeting the city's favelas dates back to the 1940s (see Silva 2005; Valladares 2005). In the 1960s, large-scale removal programs razed many favelas of the elite south zone of the city, and included the construction of massive USAID-funded housing projects in remote areas of the city, in an earlier national project for economic development.

In the late 1970s and all through the 1980s, favela removal programs virtually disappeared, giving way to urbanization efforts like the Projeto Rio of the 1970s (yet another federally funded initiative) and the Mutirão and Mutirão Remunerado programs. The latter were largely the result of improvised methodologies of favela urbanization – with the state financing the well-established practice of collective labor efforts by residents in improving both houses and the public spaces of the community (the *mutirão*). These small-scale experiments were, however, crucial in establishing the institutional conditions, routines and staff that would make up Municipal Secretary of Housing, set up in 1993 to promote favela urbanization. Its function and structure, however, consolidated the separation between the routines of urban planning for favelas and informal settlements, and the daily practices of the Secretariat of Urbanism, whose mission remains circumscribed to urbanistic interventions in the so-called formal city.

The Municipal Secretariat of Housing implemented the Favela Bairro Program between 1993 and the mid-2000s. This program played a key role in the consolidation of Rio's favelas. Its blueprints centered on urbanization works, improvements in favela infrastructure, the construction of public spaces and the provision of public services like day care centers and health centers. The program sealed the rupture with favela removal programs by resorting to displacements only in the case of families living in risk areas (those subject to floods and landslides in particular). It thus replaced former "removal" programs with the premise of urbanization with a "social" component, in that intervention projects include the provision of social services, in particular day care centers, schools, health centers and capacity building and income generation initiatives. In its first two phases, each funded by a 300 million IDB loan – the program targeted more than 150 medium favelas and some 25 informal settlements throughout the city. Its third phase was incorporated into the PAC works. Finally – and this is perhaps the Favela Bairro's most enduring and significant legacy – it created the conditions for increasing formalization of property and services in the city's favelas.

What this brief history spells out is a story of escalating state investments in the favelas, and increasing housing security for the poor. It is also the story of the construction of a consensus about how to deal with the "favela issue": if the increase in violence rates, and if the territorial control of the drug trade over considerable vast stretches of urban space in the city core are a result of an alleged "absence" of the state, then the "solution" to the "favela issue" is by definition, the "arrival" of the state in these territories. The Favela Bairro Program also coexisted with a smaller community policing program known as the GPAE in the late 1990s and early 2000s. So while neither favela urbanization programs nor their coupling with police occupations are nothing new on the political or urban landscape of Rio de Janeiro, the scale, scope and ambitious social outputs of the PAC and UPP are without precedent.

But there is one other feature that singles out the PAC interventions in relation to former favela urbanization initiatives: the monumental inscription of the favela into the city landscape. The juxtaposition of urbanization works with the discourses and performances of "Pacification" convey a powerful message. The PAC projects have had massive effects upon the urban landscape, by combining the following features: they emphasize the favela as scenery; they are visible from afar; they underline the connections or passages between the favela and the so-called formal city. Therefore, they produce an ambiguous regime of favela (in)visibility insofar as it is not the favela as such that is accentuated in the landscape, but the very spectacle of its "integration" into the city.[6]

This feature is particularly visible in the Oscar Niemeyer-designed pedestrian overpass that looms large at the western exit of the Zuzu Angel tunnel, that connects the consolidated elite south zone of the city to the western frontier continuously expanded by a proliferation of high rise towers in gated condominiums. The overpass connects the Rocinha – for decades now branded as the "largest favela in Latin America" – to a massive sports center built to cater to the community (see Figure 4.1). On the occasion of its inauguration, the lower part of the hill was painted in colorful tones.[7] The ensemble produces a powerful resignification of the sharp social contrasts that have long constituted the social imaginaries of social strife and urban violence associated with Rio de Janeiro in general and its favelas in particular. The overpass and outskirts of the favela at once mark the presence of the state and perform the spectacle of favela integration into the city.

On the hill that separates Rio's most famous beaches – Copacabana and Ipanema – a massive elevator built by the PAC now connects the favelas that spill down the slopes to the subway station on General Osorio Square (see Figure 4.2). Its futuristic design is visible from the beach, and from the Lagoa Rodrigo de Freitas, i.e., the lagoon waterfront in the heart of the postcard south zone of the city, again obliterating the favela from the urban landscape thus produced. The gaze is drawn to the connection, to an alleged model and discourse of favela integration into the city.

*Figure 4.1* Rocinha and the pedestrian overpass
Source: Photograph by Daniela Fichino.

*Figure 4.2* The Alemão cable car
Source: Photograph by Rosi Milliotti.

The PAC works, in short, inaugurate a distinct regime of (in)visibility of the favelas in the urban landscape insofar as they deliberately resignify the social contrasts and historically constituted sharp social boundaries as a spectacle of their incorporation into the city through grandiose infrastructural works and "pacification." This is particularly easy to grasp in the case of the landscape produced by the PAC works in the Complexo do Alemão. Its signature – the gondola cable car service – is visible from afar from the Linha Vermelha, the expressway that connects the international airport to the southern zone where the hotels and tourists concentrate (Figure 4.3). The Linha Vermelha also cuts across the favelas that comprise the Complexo da Maré, home to more than 100,000 residents allegedly benefitted with an "acoustic treatment" of the Expressway that also blocks the view of the favelas from those who drive through it. Many a social movement challenged the dubious measure, denouncing the ultimate aim of hiding the favelas from the eyes of tourists attempting to make their way to the paradisiacal south zone. The soundproof barrier proved even more incongruous once it was decorated with naïf paintings populated with Brazilian popular culture motifs, among which figure the city's favelas.

Thus, on the Linha Vermelha the new logic of (in)visibility of the favelas in the urban landscape is pushed even further: it replaces the "real" favela, hidden behind the "acoustic barrier" with a romanticized depiction. The tourist gaze is drawn to the naïf paintings that bar the short-sighted view of the surroundings.

*Figure 4.3* The Linha Vermelha
Source: Photograph by Rosi Milliotti.

But if one's gaze moves beyond the acoustic barrier, the favela catches one's eye yet again, now at a distance, sprawling at the foot of the cable car system that spreads across five different hilltops. The stations and general design of the cable car system were designed by architect Jorge Mario Jauregui, an award-winning native of Argentina whose name was built on favela urbanization practice and whose designs illustrate many "best practices" publications of policy think tanks, the InterAmerican Development Bank, the World Bank, and so forth. The model was initially attempted in Medellin, and imported to Rio by the PAC works. The stations are brightly lit by night eclipsing not only the favelas of the old industrial suburb beneath them, but also obliterating the old city landmarks such as the Igreja da Penha, one of the region's oldest tourist sites, that used to loom majestically alone above the hilltops.

In "pacified" favelas – Rocinha, Alemão, Cantagalo/Pavão-Pavãozinho – the UPPs come into play also as landmarks that are accentuated in the landscape, lit by night and brandished by day in large panels that loom over the hill slopes, next to shining colorful new housing projects and futuristic alternative transportation experiments. The UPP buildings are also highly visible from afar, from below in the so-called formal city, thus also "pacifying" the anxieties of the middle classes who for more than two decades also bore witness to the constant shoot-outs in the favelas and constructed themselves as virtual victims of drug trade-dominated favelas. The UPP sign reminds the favelas' neighbors of the marvels of "PACification" (Figure 4.4).

*Figure 4.4* The UPP providencia

In Manguinhos, the performance of the state evokes the idioms of the Spanish colonial plaza of which Angel Rama (1996) spoke: in the midst of vast expanses of favelas of the old derelict industrial suburbs, a large square with Cartesian grass lawns now houses a series of shining new social equipment. This large plot that formerly housed an Army Supply Depot – whose name remains the same, D-Sup, as residents still refer to the area – now houses a large model high school that functions in an old army building completely retrofitted and restored to its former monumental splendor (Figure 4.5). It stands across the square from a large public library that is well equipped and includes a concert hall and movie theater under construction. The Library shares the Jauregui-designed building with a Youth Center, a legal reference center and offices for several of the government programs being implemented in the Manguinhos area, including the PAC works. A small building in the middle of the square shelters the Casa da Mulher, a reference center for women. At the far end of the D-Sup plot, a large public health center makes its unmistakable presence in the landscape; to be sure, it is placed under a huge sign that is also lit up at night.

The message here is eloquent: the state has arrived. And its majestic "arrival" is to be confirmed by yet another former industrial site to be re-functionalized. Just a few hundred meters down the road, right in the center of the so-called "Gaza Strip," Manguinhos residents have witnessed, for more than a year now, the construction of the City of Police, a large complex that is to concentrate specialized police forces. The government refers to it as one of three large headquarters for police operations currently under construction of what is to become a Security Complex.[8] So despite the lack of any formal announcements for a UPP

*Figure 4.5* The D-Sup building in Manguinhos
Source: Photograph by Mariana Cavalcanti.

in Manguinhos at the time my research was conducted, a steady stream of rumors involving the City of Police or a UPP pervaded daily conversations. The incessant construction sounds that emanated from the formerly abandoned industrial site produced a sense of imminent change, that seemed to be confirmed by the proliferation of ruins and spatial change brought about by the PAC works.

In other words, I am suggesting that there is an aesthetic feature of the PAC works that was lacking in past initiatives: the ways in which it symbolizes favela "integration" into the city as urbanistic spectacle. This is quite different from the aesthetics of the Favela Bairro program, for instance. The former's urbanistic interventions aptly illustrated before/after images in many UNESCO and International Development Bank publications. The chief aesthetic effect here was one of producing comparative improvements on a small scale. Few of the Favela Bairro works are visible from outside the favelas.[9] To overstate my point, the Favela Bairro was Jane Jacobs; the PAC works are Robert Moses. Thus, if the Favela Bairro program's greatest legacy was the definitive plotting of the favelas on official city maps, the PAC works definitively inscribe the favelas into the urban landscape.

In what remains of this chapter, I seek to sketch an initial response to the question: what happens in the shadow of this monumental inscription of the favelas into the cityscape? I will suggest that the juxtaposition of the spatial transformations brought about by the PAC works coupled with the remote effects of the UPP program have affected sedimented power arrangements that have structured daily life for decades in Manguinhos – as I discuss shortly – the "arrival of the state," however, seems to reinforce the structures of authority of the drug trade in many ways. Thus local politics and future expectations are today shaped by forces that seem even greater or more far-reaching than the drug commands or local political actors. As the stakes of local politics are scaled up, the very certainties that grounded daily life in a context of pervasive uncertainty regarding the explosion of violence at any given moment are now frayed. It is to each of these issues – local politics and future expectations – that I now turn.

## Manguinhos, and its "complexity"

The so-called Manguinhos favela "complex" is located in the north suburb of Rio, and it holds the fifth worst position in the Human Development Index in the city. It refers to a cluster of 14 favelas, occupations and housing projects that, together, account for a population of 31,432 residents, according to the household census conducted by the PAC works in 2008/2009. As opposed to the archetypical hill favelas of the south zone of the city that produce a landscape of sharp social constrasts, in Manguinhos, the flat favela landscape extends as far as the eye can see. It incorporates housing projects and derelict, abandoned industrial plants, and spreads on to river banks into which raw sewage and waste constantly spill. It is surrounded by other large favelas, like Jacarezinho, or other favela "complexes" like Alemão and Maré, all of which share a common history of development tied to the implantation, in the 1940s, of a modern industrial zone in the north suburbs of the city. The factories of the region thrived well into the 1970s, feeding a constant flow of migrants to the communities surrounding the industries. In the 1980s and particularly in the 1990s, however, decline related to production restructuring occurred many times over with the intensification of the territorial-minded routines of violence and territorial structures associated with the drug trade.

Manguinhos constitutes the core of a vast region historically dominated by the Comando Vermelho (CV), the oldest of the three well-established drug "factions" in the city. This strategic location secured the area as a stronghold that buffered the core Manguinhos from both the police and rival factions. Thus the brazen appropriation of the public spaces of the favela here reached new heights when compared to the limited scope of drug-dealing activity in the south and north zones. All activities related to the drug trade are more visible, from sales to surveillance to consumption. Whereas in other favelas, the "*bocas*," or drug sale spots, are transient, here they have become permanent fixtures. Drugs are set out visibly on large market stands and the dealers have their own couches that make the sale of drugs an undisturbed leisurely activity. Sales and usage of marijuana, crack and cocaine take place openly in several areas across the favelas of the "complex", and concentrate on the sidewalks of the bars and brothels where crackheads of all ages prostitute themselves, spilling out onto the pavement and the surroundings of the community. The daily routines through which the drug trade reproduces and perform its power – such as exhibitions of weapons, of violent force, and the reiterative performance of their dominance over public space in the favela – ranging from occasional public executions in public areas to the material blockage of streets and alleys – are more obvious here than in most favelas in the city, even before the UPP program. This invisibility of what happens in Manguinhos also means that police incursions are, as a rule, more virulent and violent than elsewhere in the city. The police seldom enter Manguinhos or Jacarezinho without the aid of the Caveirão (or "big skull", as the Military Police's armored vehicles are known). The militarized atmosphere justifies the proliferation of war zone metaphors to name micro-regions of the favela (like Korea, or Gaza). All this four subway stops or a 20-minute bus ride from downtown Rio.

The overall sense of decline of the region only deepened in the wake of the 2005 lifting of the ban on the sales of crack cocaine in Rio de Janeiro by the CV and other drug factions (see Rosales and Barnes, 2011). Nearly overnight, "cracolandias" (or "cracklands") – as the media and neighbors of these spaces refer to them – sprang up wherever the drug trade let them become permanent fixtures. Manguinhos and Jacarezinho had, at the time of my research, the largest cracolandias in the city. Along the railroad tracks that cut across Jacarezinho and in the soccer fields built by the PAC in the region known as "Korea," in the core of the Manguinhos complex, hundreds of crackheads make their presence felt by the scores of garbage they produce and seem to thrive upon. The so-called cracolandias can be traced from afar by the scores of used water bottles that get turned into makeshift pipes, and where traces of crack users' livelihoods – like selling copper wires they steal from the railways on a nightly basis – pile up in the consumption and recycling and reselling of junk collected from abandoned factory sites. Informal markets of junk, stolen items and sex function operate on the imprecise outskirts of the cracolandias on a full-time basis. The sights and smells of the cracudos produce a series of disturbances, that range from conflicts with residents who live near the cracolandias to their occasional execution by the drug trade. The crack economy is itself somewhat marginal vis-à-vis the cocaine trade, with a parallel structure of sales that is also lower ranked in the trade hierarchies. The encroachment of the cracolandias upon the favelas of Manguinhos and Jacarezinho became problematic even from the perspective of the social control mechanisms deployed by the drug trade to secure their territorial hold upon their communities. In June 2012, after I had left the field, the local drug trade placed a ban on the sale of crack as a last desperate measure to take back control over the space of the favela, cleaning it of the cracolandias that attracted more constant police incursions.

All this seems to attest to the commonsensical narrative of the "absent state" as the cause of the disappearance of anything resembling public order in Manguinhos. But, as I have been insisting throughout this chapter, urban informality regimes are never that simple. The very idea of a "Manguinhos complex" is itself a reality effect of the social construction of this particular grouping of favelas – whose residents do not necessarily recognize themselves as part of a favela "complex" – as an administrative unit for purposes of governance by the state in the mid-1990s, i.e., as part of the larger process of favela consolidation in the city. Contrary to common knowledge – and residents' widely shared representations – of Manguinhos as a "forgotten" place, or a "depository of people" – Manguinhos' social and spatial history actually imposes a more complex analysis of the process of favela formation in the city. Actually, most of the communities comprising the so-called Manguinhos "complex" were set up, in some measure, by the state. They tell a non-canonical story of public policies vis-à-vis the city's favelas in the twentieth century. From this perspective, Manguinhos emerges not as a region from which the state is absent, but as a place that has functioned as a laboratory for low-income housing policies for most of the twentieth century, as I have already pointed out.

Now the latest chapter in the non-canonical tale of Rio's public housing policies remains as invisible as many of the other initiatives that initially populated Manguinhos, and it consists in the refunctioning of old abandoned industrial sites into housing projects. This is not an invention of the PAC works; throughout the old industrial suburbs, the names of the former factories continue to designate certain areas that are now sites of housing. These occupations of both private and publicly owned land, mostly sites recently divested of their original industrial functions, began in 1995 with the occupation of an abandoned site that belonged to the Postal Service in the Manguinhos region. In the 2000s a series of other occupations gave rise to new "communities" that were swiftly incorporated, for administrative and political purposes, into the Manguinhos complex.

Now the politics of these occupations are quite complex assemblages of different if not conflicting organizing logics that lay bare the structures of informality particular to Rio de Janeiro that are, in turn, to a great extent consequences of the long-standing territorial control of the drug trade. In cities like São Paulo or in downtown Rio for instance, occupations of abandoned buildings are conducted by social movements that engage in legal battles framed in the language of rights entailed by the Constitution of 1988 and the 2001 Statute of the City. But in the former industrial suburbs of Rio, "occupations" are, significantly, referred to by their agents, that is, the "occupiers" themselves, – as "invasions." These "invasions," one learns in informal conversations in the field, are often led or organized with the aid of the drug trade. There are reports corroborated by several residents of Manguinhos that, on the occasion of one particular occupation of a former abandoned factory site, members of the drug trade mimicked actions of the state in order to ensure that the neediest and most "hardworking and deserving" of those in line for a plot in the occupation got one. They produced written records of families, and secured that the occupation occurred in an orderly fashion. In other cases, such as the occupation of the old milk factory, the drug trade mediated an agreement between the leaders of the occupation and the former deliverers of the plant, who had secured their own tenure over a few warehouses with the owners of the factory themselves. The vice-president of the former milk factory community emerged out of the episode as a peacemaker, and that kept her "in command," as she put it, for the nine years between the alleged peacemaking breakfast and the January 2012 implosion of the old buildings (see Cavalcanti and Fontes, 2011).

And this is itself significant of how pervasive the drug trade's structures of authority have become. There are no financial or managerial gains directly involved in the constitution of such occupations. Yet these processes reinforce the overall structures of authority of the drug trade, and mainly their territorial control over the space of the favelas. What is so puzzling here is the uncanny coupling of the language of rights deployed by the drug trade and the ever contradictory ways in which a situation of violent territorial control ends up opening unexpected and unprecedented paths to the recognition of favela residents' citizenship rights. The PAC works incorporated two such communities into the Manguinhos complex. The invasion of the former headquarters of the extinct state telephone company EMBRATEL was removed in 2010, and the built structures plant was demolished after it was emptied of its residents. Like the residents of the old dairy factory I opened this chapter with, the tenants of EMBRATEL were temporarily assigned to the social rent program, and then reconducted to a brand new housing project of colorful façades in 2010. The housing project was swiftly incorporated into the territorial logics of the drug trade. As I write these lines, the residents of the imploded milk factory have been relocated, and await the conclusion of the buildings project currently under construction. These "invasions" as a mode of producing housing tenure in Manguinhos have been, from the perspective of residents, quite successful. Since the beginning of the PAC works hundreds of families have had their housing rights recognized by the state. In the process, thousands of former "squatters" have become home-owners.[10]

The advent of the *cracolandias* in 2006–2007, coupled with the beginning of the PAC works in 2008 had a considerable impact upon the public spaces of Manguinhos. Hundreds of houses were demolished, dozens of new public buildings erected. Established *cracolandias* got pushed from the outskirts of the communities to their core. At the time of my research the border region between the communities of Korea and Vila Turismo had become one large *cracolandia* that colonized three soccer fields, one of them built by the PAC but was already as run down and as covered with garbage as the ones that preceded it. Thus the advent of *cracolandias* and of the PAC presented considerable disruptions to daily life in Manguinhos. But these changes were "more of the same," as residents put it: façade urbanism, "cosmetic make-up" of the outskirts of the favelas that change nothing, were some of the most recurrent expressions we heard to describe the impact of the PAC works.

But nothing contributed more to the building sense of uncertainty and of waiting for something to change as the occupation of the Complexo do Alemão in late November 2010, as part of the Pacification Program. Until late 2010, the CV's strategic operations such as the stockpiling of weapons and the regional distribution of drugs to the favelas of the south zone were centered in the Complexo do Alemão. With the latter's occupation by the army, Manguinhos unwittingly and unexpectedly entered the UPP era, as it inherited many of Alemão's strategic functions in the Comando Vermelho operations.

The occupation of Alemão had two main effects upon the daily lives of Manguinhos residents: first, Manguinhos ended up harboring many members of the drug trade who had been hiding out in Alemão. The subject was brought up in several informal conversations, always as a source of anxiety. According to a 26-year-old mother of four, "Things are getting worse" because "we keep hearing of some John Doe or another who came from places where UPPs have been set up." The second concrete effect of the UPP program was that Manguinhos absorbed many of the drug customers of Alemão. This effect is mainly discernible in the overnight increase of crack users that expanded and multiplied the so-called *cracolandias* of Manguinhos.[11] Thus, the period that has been experienced in other favelas as "pacification" – or at least the virtual disappearance of heavy weapons in the hands of the drug trade – in Manguinhos translated into an increase in the scale and visibility of the drug economy, as well as in the flows of strangers in the alleys and corners of the community. Thus, in Manguinhos, residents express a great deal of anxiety about what appears to be a world where power balances that were precarious to begin with are now overtly unstable.

The effects of the occupation of Alemão extend beyond the economy of the drug trade itself. The occupation of Alemão made the idea of the UPP more tangible for Manguinhos residents. The spatial proximity between Manguinhos and Alemão brought the possibility of "Pacification" home, in many ways. One evangelical pastor who was clear in his support for the program sums up well the sources and rationale for this anticipation: "As far as I know, it is already coming here. The next one to be pacified is Mangueira, right? Which is very close to here. They are creating the City of Police, over there, in Jacarezinho, in Manguinhos. The state government is working … on dominating this entire community here, this whole place, all of Rio, right?"

This suggests the idea of the closing in of the UPPs, which amounts to a perception of the UPPs as a process that unfolds in time and space and is approaching Manguinhos. An old resident of Manguinhos used the future tense in his description when asked whether he thought the UPP was coming to Manguinhos: "There will be no weapons. The drug trade will be more discreet." The same resident acknowledged the difficulty in envisioning a different image of the police: "We will need to gather the children, show the young what the police are about … that they do not just come in to cause shoot-outs and arrest people. They need to see the policeman as someone who can help, not as a predator."

That residents can even fathom a world in which the drug trade is not the most powerful agent in the favela, and in which the police can be conceived as a rightful representative of law and order is itself a massive transformation in the life-worlds of Manguinhos. Yet old power structures tend to be stubborn and capable of constant readaptations.

## More fieldnotes: a chance encounter in the D-Sup

*Between June and August 2011 I was in Manguinhos at least once a week, doing research for two different projects. For the documentary on the former factory site, I did not need any "native" assistants, given of the nature of the space of the milk factory compound: because it was walled on all sides, drug trade activities here were extremely low. It was a safe haven in Manguinhos insofar as shoot-outs or police incursions were concerned. But mostly, I did not need a local assistant because I was constantly under the surveillance of the vice-president of the residents' association, and the attention the equipment drew was enough to keep us safe within the walls of the old factory.*

*In the other communities of the Manguinhos "complex", however, it was a different story. Not even the community agents of the PAC walked about without the company of an "authorized" resident with no formal ties to the City Hall. In order to conduct my field research I hired an old resident of the area, who worked as a research assistant at a nearby biological research and vaccine production center and had a long history of political and social engagement in several communities of Manguinhos. Her husband, moreover, was a well-respected leader of one of the old labor unions in the region, but since most of the factories had shut down and the drug trade dominated community politics had since become an electrician with a workshop in the vicinity of the favela of Jacarezinho. She had warned me that the vice-president of the milk factory did not like her, but I figured hiring her was harmless. I could always get away with being a "clueless" newcomer to the ways of Manguinhos.*

*On this particular afternoon, I had arranged to meet our native assistant at the D-Sup, as always. We had an interview scheduled with the treasurer of the residents' association of the Veterans' Housing project, and were headed that way when the vice-president of the dairy factory community called me from a parked car. She sat in the passenger seat, and as I approached her open window she asked me in loud whispers what I was doing there with a "fake leader." I did my best to look as confused as I could, as I explained that I had been referred to my assistant by researchers who had long known her. I volunteered that we were on our way to an interview in the Veterans' housing project. She harshly told me to "open my eyes" to "fake leaders." That I was not to go into people's communities without knowledge of their "presidents". She ordered the man in the driver's seat to call the president "of the Veterans' housing project." When he picked up, she explained that I was a university professor, that I had been working "with her" for a year but had misguidedly been on my way to "his" community with a "fake leader." Then she put me on the line. I told him I was doing research for the World Bank about the recent changes in the community, in particular the PAC works. He asked me to wait for him, for he was only ten minutes away, and that he would be happy to lead me into "his" community. But the vice-president of the dairy factory community took back the phone and told him she did not want my assistant to know what was going on. She gave him my phone number and instructed me to walk slowly to the community, for the "president" would meet me there.*

*As we dragged ourselves to the Veterans' Project, my assistant told me that her husband has known the man I had just spoken to on the phone for decades; that they went back to the old labor union days, but made a point of noting that he had not been much of a "leader" back then. Just as we rang the intercom of the building where we had our interview scheduled, my phone rang just as a large expensive silver Honda sedan turned the corner. It was "the president," on the phone and driving the car. The tall strong man wearing five hundred reais sunglasses got out of the car. He was extremely polite and welcoming, but did not hide his suspicion of my interest in the PAC works since, as far as he knew, the project did not include "his" community. Other than that, he performed the role of public relations of the community with the ease of someone used to dealing with researchers and journalists.*

As is the case with most of my fieldnotes from Manguinhos, this excerpt brings together so many issues that can lead into different and contradictory venues of analysis that it is often necessary to take a step back and retrace the connections that make up the context of any interaction in the field.

One first point to make regarding the incident is that the chance encounter with the "vice-president" of the former milk factory could basically only have happened in the D-Sup region. It is the kind of encounter that depends upon the type of sociability brought about by public spaces. Designed, constructed, occupied and appropriated all in the course of the last four years, it has already impacted daily lives and routines. Perhaps not to the extent and scale that its planners may have hoped for, but the PAC-built "central plaza" has, in its own way, fulfilled its planned function as an isle of public space in a region otherwise territorialized by armed force. The D-Sup acts as an anchor of sorts, that renders the idea of Manguinhos as a "complex" more concrete, since this is where public affairs that concern all the communities and their residents now get sorted out. In particular for outsiders, or researchers, it offers a safe haven to set up meetings, encounters or to simply wait without feeling vulnerable to the surveillance of the drug trade. In a field site where countless informants swiftly let one know that "one is not to walk around by oneself," that is, without local guides, the very existence of the D-Sup actually makes research that was otherwise impossible now feasible. Here we could come and go as we pleased, park our car without raising suspicion, and just observe the daily rhythms of the space without calling attention to ourselves. Significantly, it is the only area of Manguinhos – aside from the former dairy factory – that I managed to photograph with some degree of freedom. The concentration of newly inaugurated, highly visible public equipment draws people from all over Manguinhos. Youngsters hang out in the public square after school, or in between activities held at the library. It is by and large, a very different scene from the other areas of Manguinhos.

But the main point I wish to make here is regarding how the very category of "leadership" in Manguinhos has become deeply embattled in the wake of the PAC works. The episode has deep-seated analytical consequences from the perspective of inquiring into how daily life and local politics have been affected by the PAC works. Right when I hired my "native" assistant, one of the first things she called my attention to was a photograph that I had seen reproduced in different places of Manguinhos and in many research materials. It portrayed President Lula's visit to Manguinhos on the occasion of the announcement of the PAC works, in March 2008. It featured Lula, the State Governor Sergio Cabral and the Mayor Eduardo Paes with the presidents of all the residents' associations of Manguinhos. My assistant pointed out to me that by the time Lula and the other authorities returned to Manguinhos to inaugurate the housing project on the D-Sup, many of the community representatives portrayed in the original picture were no longer in office. They had been replaced by new "leaders" – some of them "elected", others just appointed. One of the "new" "leaders" was the president of the association of the Veterans' Project.

Before the PAC, the role of residents' associations in Manguinhos was quite limited. On the one hand, an everyday marked by high levels of violent conflict and an obvious presence of the drug trade presence left little room for any effective political leverage for the associations. Throughout the course of our fieldwork we heard several stories of how NGOs had a difficult time in Manguinhos, how the drug trade attempted to charge them to operate within their territories or downright intimidated them. In the last instance, this context put the personal security of NGO employees at risk, thus further isolating Manguinhos and strengthening the territorial hold of the drug trade. A similar situation can be projected into the possibilities of agency for those running the associations. The role of residents' associations, under these conditions, is reduced to receiving community mail and to occasionally acting as a gateway into the community for public authorities, researchers, and the few residual social programs halfheartedly implemented by the state in recent years.

Thus, the incident of my entry into the Veterans' Project reveals tensions inherent to the relations that govern the disputing sovereignties over the space of the favela, as well as the disparate structures of legitimation underpinning them. My "native" assistant evoked long-standing community and political ties as her credentials for walking me around the communities of Manguinhos freely; the vice-president of the occupation reminded me that I was in the drug trade's territory, and that I should therefore follow a distinct set of social routines – dictated by her, as a mediating presence that guaranteed my safety. While each of these strategies is legitimate in and of itself, the vice-president reprehended me for my "double entry" strategy.

In short, the incident sheds light on how the unprecedented influx of PAC resources into Manguinhos accelerated an ongoing process of substitution of leaders linked to residents' associations left over from previous contexts of social movements linked to labor unions. Many of these historical leaders became involved in short-lived associational movements that flourished right after the democratic opening in the mid-1980s. Most of them withdrew from community politics in the 1990s, and while their trajectories vary considerably, there is a clear pattern of their migration to NGOs or even to the state, where they find some leeway to politically impact daily life in the favela, but that does not place them in direct interactions with the drug trade. The general sense is that from the 1990s onwards, residents' associations lost their legitimacy in the eyes of their alleged constituencies.

However, the fact that residents' associations have become internally discredited does not mean that their strategic role can be undermined in the current political landscape of Rio de Janeiro. Presidents of residents' associations remain the principal mediators in the implementation of public policies in the favelas. This is a role that is increasingly strategic with the continued investments in recent public programs such as the combination of UPP and PAC. And while their legitimacy is considerably undermined in the view of their alleged constituency ("regular" residents), neither the state nor the drug trade can do without such a mediating instance if public policies are to be implemented. This is not to say that all representatives of residents' associations are necessarily submissive or under the influence of the drug trade, for many have been killed or banned from favelas as a result of their insubordination. But in order to play the mediating role, venues of deliberation both in relation to the state and in relation to the drug trade become necessary. As long as this situation of co-dependency endures, the drug trade will make it its business to guarantee some leverage in the routine activities of residents' associations across the city.

The PAC works thus upped the stakes of community associational life, rendering it a strategic activity in favela politics. Not surprisingly, leaders who were not aligned (with the drug trade) were swiftly replaced by new ones who perform the role of mediators between the drug trade and the state. The managerial role of many aspects of the PAC works – in particular in compiling the lists of residents entitled to apartments in the newly built projects, their role in aiding the constitution of records of residents eligible to receive "social rent" checks or to monetary compensations, the allotment of many job posts reserved for local labor, among many other key aspects of the PAC, fell under the daily management of residents' associations. This turn of events has produced a sort of "professionalization" of representatives of residents' associations, with the emergence of new leaders, some of whom do not even live in Manguinhos. On the other hand, they have accumulated experience in dealing with the state and are familiar with the implementation of urbanization and housing policies. They transit well both along the local *bocas* – as the drug sales points are referred to but also a term that names the power structures of the drug trade – and the City Secretariats of Housing, Public Works, or Social Development.

This "new" generation of community "leaders" systematically refers to their role not as presidents of residents' associations, but as presidents of the "communities" themselves. This slippage – "president of community" instead of "association" – is part of the same syntax that refers to what social movements call "occupations" as "invasions." This syntax, of course, dialogues with the language of the constitution of the favelas as territories of the drug trade, that ascribes owners to spaces and sharp boundaries to regular flows of people, things and information. Referring to oneself as president of a community – as opposed to, say, its representative, as "president of an association" – personalizes political power and territorial control. And yet these "presidents" of communities also mimic the motions, procedures and discourses inherent to the language of rights entailed in state interventions like the PAC works.

And this brings me to the final feature of the post-PAC leaders I wish to make regarding this glimpse into daily life in Manguinhos in the wake of the effects of the PAC works. The effects of such arrangements go beyond the restructuring of power relations on the ground. They create a perverse mechanism whereby the implementation of public policies relies on the institutional support of an institution – residents' associations in favelas – that have long lost their political legitimacy, be it as a function of their subjugation to the drug trade, or as a function of their shady relations to some party politics. So the mechanisms of political participation that underpin projects like the PAC remain hostage to local power structures and to the connections of urban informality regimes. In so doing, they foster an acute sense of disconnectedness between what may have been conceived as a legitimate political agenda and the highly shared consensus that recent urbanization projects such as the PAC lack effective mechanisms to ensure citizen participation. As one resident put it, "When I realized it, the PAC was already here … I just saw the holes, the debris, it was the PAC already removing the houses."

## Waiting in the ruins for a conclusion

The PAC works in Manguinhos began in March 2008. The interview just cited was conducted in July 2011, more than one year before I write these lines. For four years now Manguinhos residents have witnessed a great deal of change on a first-hand basis: the PAC has transformed the physical landscape of many communities of Manguinhos; it has displaced thousands of people, many of whom are still awaiting their promised apartment in housing projects under construction. It did so by demolishing hundreds of houses, most of them on river banks or along flood lines, but to make way for public spaces or facilities like schools or day care centers. As I have argued at length elsewhere, house construction and improvement are a central aspect of social life in Rio's consolidated favelas, experienced as a long-term process of turning precarious one-room wooden shacks into larger, multi-floor brick and mortar homes over the course of decades of hard work and diligent savings (Cavalcanti, 2007, 2009). Many long-time Manguinhos residents have been relocated to standardized, 42-sqm apartments in the newly built housing projects. Within a year of inauguration, several buildings were displaying cracks, casting doubt over the durability of the constructions. Cracks also proliferate in houses located in the vicinity of some of the larger PAC construction sites. Frustrated community agents try to get the demands through while knowing that there is no provision in the project for such cases, and that the constant delays in the conclusion of different phases of the works will never allow for such unplanned effects to become a priority.

But cracks in buildings with colorful façades are nothing compared to the ruins of houses that remain full of debris. Particularly along the river banks, the ruined shells of houses become sites for crack cocaine hotspots. They are used as sites for the consumption of the drug, but also for the sexual exchanges that constitute one of the key currencies for addicts to get a hold of crack stones. The accumulated debris and garbage produced by the daily routines of crackheads draw hordes of rats to the ruins. As time passes, the abandoned structures become layered with weeds and vegetation growing amid puddles of putrid water.

Because negotiations over disappropriations seem to follow random patterns, it is often the case that a few houses remain along stretches of demolished ruins. Those who remain amid the ruination tend to accept any sort of compensation in order to escape the derelict landscape surrounding them. Amid the piles of debris, sometimes one can catch a glimpse of the remaining walls of former kitchens, with the carefully placed, decorated tiles once carefully chosen by their former owners and paid for by many hours of work.

Aside from the very clearly limited space of the D-Sup, the construction of public spaces has not translated into a strengthening of public order. The PAC works in Manguinhos evidence some of the great challenges facing urban inter-vention projects in areas where illegality dictates the use of space, and mainly for their actual maintenance. The PAC works simply pushed drug consumption away from the outer sidewalks of the complex into the community's core.

Aside from the D-Sup, the many attempts at constructing public spaces in the core of the communities lay bare the disconnectedness between the utopic projected visions of public space rendered on architects' croquis and the actual logics that govern the uses of space in Manguinhos. Thus children's playgrounds are built on slabs of concrete with no shelter on the banks of foul-smelling rivers, with no protective fences between the decaying and deserted swings that showed signs of rust very early on. Concrete picnic tables with checkers boards printed onto their surface are scattered throughout Manguinhos in what seems a random pattern, for they lack any physical or social connections to the spaces surrounding them; most of the time they just lie there, empty, as the sun heats them to absurd temperatures. Slowly they also become incorporated into the surrounding ruins.

The territorialities of the drug trade – both as structure of authority and as the spaces produced by crack use – seem to creep in upon all PAC interventions. Along the river banks, where the PAC paved a series of roads in what is to become something of a local *rambla* – assuming that the shells of former houses ever get cleared away – an ingenious system of gates has been devised by the drug trade. Installing physical boundaries as a means of blocking the passage of the Military Police Elite Squad armored vehicle has been an old practice of the drug trade. In Manguinhos, however, the new streets paved by the PAC significantly improved inner community mobility, both for residents and for the drug trade. Thus now, at strategic sites throughout the road, there are physical barriers made of steel beams – but they are mobile, and operated by *cracudos* that, surprisingly enough, seem efficient as clockwork, as we found in the few drives within the community we managed to take.

Thus, reality "on the ground" is more complex than the simple "entrance of the state" narrative that tends to legitimize major state investments like the PAC works in the favelas. Major infrastructural works like the PAC favelas affect the distinct territorialities that make up the texture of daily life in the favela, where life unfolds of the militarized drug trade, of crack users, of local power arrangements, of long-term residents who have invested in their homes for decades and found themselves relocated to standardized, 42-sqm apartments in housing projects. The new – physical, social – spaces thus produced are appropriated, disputed and resignified in unexpected ways, and are themselves productive of new forms of political and social mediation between the favela and the state in its many guises.

Manguinhos residents share a tacit sense of waiting for something to happen. Signs of change seem to be closing in on them. As the remote effects of the UPP program entwine with the transformations in the physical landscape of Manguinhos, the sense that a rupture is looming on the horizon colors the imaginations of residents. And yet on a daily level, these changes end up being experienced as an intensification of what is already known. Thus both state-sponsored relocations and occasional reshapings of the physical environment nor modulations in levels of conflict regarding the drug trade are viewed in continuity with past changes that hardly affected the structural conditions under which daily life unfolds. The sense of imminent change itself has, moreover, endured for over three years, thus becoming yet another contradictory part of daily life itself.

Anthropologist Vincent Crapanzano describes a similar structure of feeling in his research among a small, enclosed white community in South Africa at apartheid's twilight. He writes:

> The past gives us security when we are waiting. We know "from experience" that in all likelihood what we are waiting for will or will not come … There is in waiting this backward glance, this seeking security in the experience of the past, this taking solace in history, which devitalizes the here and now. We linger because we know from past experience that we can do nothing. We linger because we know that the "forces of history" will have their way.
> (Crapanzano, 1985: 44)

Between the shining D-Sup and the PAC works that fall into ruins even before their inauguration, Manguinhos residents wait. Amid old and new ruins.

## Post-script

I revise these lines in late October 2012. Just two weeks ago, Manguinhos was taken over by the BOPE, the Army and the Navy. There is little news coverage of what is going on in the alleys and streets of Manguinhos. Brief conversations with residents reveal that the wait wears on, despite the migration of the *cracudos* elsewhere, to inaugurate new *cracolandias* – some of them just across the

Linha Vermelha from Manguinhos. What comes after the occupation may be open-ended, but the sense of waiting in a war zone for forces larger than themselves still seems to set the general mood of Manguinhos.

## Notes

1  Similar processes are underway throughout the old industrial suburbs of the city. Paulo Fontes and I refer to this phenomenon as "factory favelas" (see Cavalcanti and Fontes, 2011; Cavalcanti et al., 2012). See also the documentary film about this particular process: *Factory Favela* (49', 2012).

2  For an account on how individuals move in the interstices of the spaces of the formal and informal, the legal and illegal, the licit and the illicit in the peripheries of São Paulo, see Telles and Cabanes (2006).

3  The "Olympic belt" of favelas with UPPs closely follows the priorities of the next massive favela urbanization program, the Morar Carioca. Its alleged objective is to urbanize all of the city's favelas by 2025. But its priority are those located in the vicinity of areas that are to host events related to the Olympic Games.

4  More than 3,500 police officers are currently part of the program. The state government expects to have units operating in a total of 40 of these territories, reaching a total of 750,000 beneficiaries, and deploying a total of 12,000 police officers, by 2014. UPP Social, the social development phase of the program, designed by the state and municipal governments to coordinate social and urban development interventions in the favelas, is active in all of them. See World Bank (2012). Manguinhos has, since I concluded this research, been occupied but the territorial control of the "pacification forces" here remains weak. There is no estimate as to when Manguinhos is to receive its UPP.

5  This chapter draws on field research conducted in May 2010 and January 2012 in the so-called favela "complex" of Manguinhos, for two different research projects. One was the ethnographic and historical case study of the already-mentioned imploded milk factory turned into a favela. The second research project encompassed the so-called "Manguinhos Complex" as a whole, and was centered on residents' perceptions of the UPPs. Because Manguinhos was included in a larger project, a qualitative analysis of the Favela Pacification program as a control case because it had not been a UPP unit, field research centered on residents' perceptions of the PAC works, and the recent changes in the city at large. See World Bank (2012); Cavalcanti et al. (2012).

6  Like the already mentioned Mangueira project, the urbanization project of Santa Marta undertaken by the State Government of Rio in the late 2000s also emphasized highly visible color schemes next to a large tramline built to connect the highest areas of the favela to the street level. The scenery offered a nice backdrop to the images of the first UPP Unit.

7  See http://g1.globo.com/rio-de-janeiro/noticia/2010/06/passarela-feita-por-niemeyer-para-rocinha-e-inaugurada.html (accessed 2 September 2014).

8  The so-called security complex also encompasses the BOPE headquarters and the Center for Command and Control, that is to host surveillance and intelligence-related police activities, located in downtown Rio.

9  One exception is the urbanistic project of the favela of Mangueira, among the most famous in the city for its traditional samba school. The housing units and new road built in the Mangueira project, designed by architect Paulo Casé – who was also responsible for the simultaneous urbanistic project of Ipanema – is visible from the city's major expressways.

10  Legally, they have the right to the apartments they receive for five years. Only after this period are new homeowners actually allowed to sell their apartments in the

projects. In the case of the housing project built on the site that had formerly housed the EMBRATEL telephone company, the drug trade has taken over certain apartments, and negotiated for them with buyers according to their own rules. In the field we also heard several reports of informal negotiations of apartments. In short, securing housing tenure does seem to have opened up myriad possibilities and schemes of urban informality rather than consolidating a formal housing project housing market.

11   Researcher Kristina Rosales, a Fulbright scholar who had been researching the *cracolandias* of the Complexo do Alemão at the time of its takeover, found that her field site had moved overnight to Manguinhos and Jacarezinho.

# Bibliography

Alsayyed, Nezar (2004) "Urban Informality as a 'New' Way of Life," in Ananya Roy and Nezzar Alsayyed (eds.) *Urban Informality: Transnational Perspectives from the Middle East, Latin America, and South Asia*. Lanham, MD: Lexington Books.

Burgos, Marcelo (in press) "Favela, Conjuntos Habitacionais, Bairros Populares e Outras Formas Urbanas: por uma agenda de luta pela cidade," in *Cidades Saudáveis*. Rio de Janeiro: Editora Fiocruz.

Cavalcanti, Mariana (2007) "Of Shacks, Houses and Fortresses: An Ethnography of Favela Consolidation in Rio de Janeiro," PhD thesis, University of Chicago.

Cavalcanti, Mariana (2009) "Do Barraco à Casa: tempo, espaço e valor(es) em uma favela consolidada," *Revista Brasileira de Ciências Sociais*, 24(69).

Cavalcanti, Mariana and Fontes, Paulo (2011) "Ruínas industriais e memória em uma 'favela fabril' carioca." *História Oral*.

Cavalcanti, Mariana, Fontes, Paulo and Blank,Thais (2011) "CCPL: Favela Fabril," Lincoln Institute of Land Policy Working Paper.

Crapanzano, Vincent (1986) *Waiting: The Whites of South Africa*. New York: Vintage.

Mendonça, Adalton da Mota (2003) "Vazios e ruínas industriais." Ensaio sobre *friches urbaines*. *Arquitextos*. São Paulo.

Rama, Angel (1996) *The Lettered City*. Durham, NC: Duke University Press.

Rosales, Kristina and Barnes, Taylor (2011) "New Jack in Rio: Six Years Ago, Crack Cocaine Was Virtually Unheard of in Brazil. Now It's Out of Control," *Foreign Policy*, September 11. Available at: www.foreignpolicy.com/articles/2011/09/14/new_jack_rio.

Roy, Ananya (2005) "Urban Informality: Toward an Epistemology of Planning," *Journal of the American Planning Association*, 71(2).

Silva, Heitor Ney Mathias (2008) "As ruínas da cidade industrial: resistência e apropriação social do lugar," Master's dissertation for Programa de Pós-Graduação em Planejamento Urbano e Regional da Universidade Federal do Rio de Janeiro.

Silva, Maria Laís Pereira da (2005) *Favelas Cariocas*. Rio de Janeiro: Ed. FGV.

Telles, José (2011) "Favelas, indústrias e subúrbio: história de um Rio esquecido," in *Semana dos Estudantes de História e Ciências Sociais* (SEHCS), CPDOC – FGV.

Telles, Vera and Cabanes, Robert (2006) *Nas Tramas da Cidade*. Paris and São Paulo: IRD/Associação Editorial Humanitas.

Thiago, Cristiane Muniz (2007) "Rio de Janeiro operário: memória dos trabalhadores do bairro do Jacaré," Master's dissertation, Programa de Pós-Graduação em Memória Social da Universidade Federal do Estado do Rio de Janeiro.

Trindade, Cláudia Peçanha (2007) *O Programa de Aceleração do Crescimento: Infraestrutura/Urbanização de Favelas*. Rio de Janeiro.

Trindade, Cláudia Peçanha; Costa, Renato Gama-Rosa and Fernandes, Tânia Maria (2008) *Memória e conflitos sociais no espaço urbano – Manguinhos/Rio de Janeiro*. Rio de Janeiro: XIII Encontro de História Anpuh.

Valladares, Licia (1979) *Passa-se uma Casa: análise do programa de remoções de favelas do Rio de Janeiro*. Rio de Janeiro: Editora Zahar.

Valladares, Licia (2005) *A invenção da favela: do mito de origem a favela.com*. Rio de Janeiro: Editora FGV.

World Bank (2011) *Bringing the State Back into the Favelas of Rio de Janeiro: Understanding Changes in Community Life After a Disarmament and Pacification Process*. Washington, DC: World Bank.

# Chapter 5

# Road 443

## Cementing dispossession, normalizing segregation and disrupting everyday life in Palestine

*Omar Jabary Salamanca*

Those who have read Douglas Adams' book *The Hitchhiker's Guide to the Galaxy* might remember the surreal opening section where Arthur Dent wakes up in his housecoat to confront an army of bulldozers ready to make way for a bypass road over his house. Arthur's initial surprise and anger are quickly interrupted by the prospect of a significantly more dramatic scenario with the appearance of thousands of construction ships hanging motionless in the sky. All of a sudden a god-like voice breaks in:

> This is Prostetnic Vogon Jeltz of the Galactic Hyperspace Planning Council. As you will no doubt be aware, the plans for development of the outlying regions of the Galaxy require the building of a hyperspatial express route through your star system, and regrettably your planet is one of those scheduled for demolition. The process will take slightly less than two of your Earth minutes. Thank you.[1]

As chaos spread on planet Earth, the voice interjected again:

> There's no point in acting all surprised about it. All the planning charts and demolition orders have been on display in your local planning department on Alpha Centauri for fifty of your Earth years, so you've had plenty of time to lodge any formal complaint and it's far too late to start making a fuss about it now.[2]

The Palestinian experience with Israel's road building on the colonial 'frontier' is not as surreal as Adams' account but rather the crude and Kafkaesque reality of a people facing permanent dispossession. The West Bank's southern Ramallah district is a case in point. In the early 1980s, the Israeli government decided to confiscate private land from a Palestinian teachers cooperative in the occupied West Bank for the purpose of building an express route – Road 443. As in Douglas Adams' story, it turns out that the planned road, which had not been previously revealed nor officially approved, was part of a larger highway system that explicitly aimed at annexing the West Bank into Israel – Road Plan 50. The new motorway was to be built virtually in its entirety through occupied territories upgrading a thoroughfare, dating back to the days of the British Mandate, which passed through several Palestinian villages. This highway was meant as a Northeast-to-Southwest corridor that would enable easier and faster settler mobility between the metropolitan region of Tel Aviv and the Israeli colonies scattered along the road and around the Jerusalem area (see Figure 5.1). The plan met resistance from Palestinians who filed a legal petition to halt the construction on the grounds that the road, as a permanent structure, was illegal under international humanitarian law.[3] Ironically, the Israeli High Court of Justice endorsed the project, reasoning that the road could be built, as its primary aim was to serve the local Palestinian population. Two decades later, soon after the outbreak of the second intifada (September, 2000), the Israeli government imposed access restrictions to Road 443. These restrictions, over time, gradually became permanent, resulting in a total ban on Palestinian access to the road. The actual road ban was not published nor made official until Palestinians, once again, took the Israeli government to the High Court in 2007. The legal case lasted several years amidst Palestinian demonstrations and demands for an unconditional, immediate and total removal of the restrictions. Yet in another performance of legal acrobatics, as we shall see, the Court de facto endorsed the ban thus implicitly sanctioning segregation.

At present, while Palestinians remain banned from using Road 443, some 40,000 Israeli commuters use the road daily unobstructed. For many commuters and travelers this thoroughfare is ostensibly as ordinary as any other highway is often assumed to be: a modern motorway with four lanes, intersections, gas

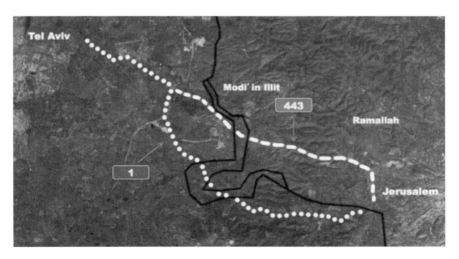

*Figure 5.1*  Road 443 (dashed line) and Highway 1 (dotted line) cutting across the West Bank boundary (dark line)

stations, signs and lighting, as well as an array of background infrastructure such as electricity poles or telecommunication antennas. Few are aware that this road effectively conceals an ongoing colonial history and a crude socio-political reality that lies beneath the mundane asphalt layer and behind the roadblocks, fences, and gates that close access for Palestinians living on the roadsides of this major thoroughfare.

This case raises several questions with regards to the assemblage of road infrastructure in colonial contexts, the processes and actors that are made invisible through their construction, and the impacts on the everyday life of those who are subjected to its violence. More specifically, what are the overlapping discourses of modernization, development, legality and security that constitute the materialities of the road? How do the construction and differential access policies to these transportation networks enforce particular patterns of dispossession and segregation? Similarly how are the everyday lives of Palestinians affected by particular road bureaucracies? Or to what extent can the production of these networks be contested in a context of asymmetric power relations? This chapter seeks to explore these questions in three ways. First, by addressing the role of road infrastructure in the production of settler space in Palestine. This is done in the light of two bodies of scholarship: the burgeoning literature that places Palestine within a settler colonial paradigm, and the recent geography debates on infrastructure networks in postcolonial contexts. Second, by looking at the symbolic and material geographies of roads. Here a detailed study of the genealogy of Road 443 is complemented with a brief description of the origins of road infrastructure in the early stages of Zionist settlement in pre-1967 Palestine. This section posits the case of Road 443 within the context of the larger Israeli road plans for the West Bank, thereby exposing the colonial and political nature of these networks. The third part of the chapter addresses the experiences of those affected by the construction of Road 443 and the different mechanisms and mobility regimes that contribute to normalizing the disruption of everyday life. This section also looks at how these ruptures are contested and at times subverted. Finally, the conclusion considers the implications of the findings.

## Road infrastructure and the production of settler colonial space

Over the course of the twentieth century, roads have shaped the material, political, economic, and socio-cultural landscapes of colonies around the globe. The expansion of roads symbolized progress and modernity as well as crucial forms of colonial and military power. New road networks replaced the tyranny of distance and inaccessibility with a tyranny of proximity that made indigenous populations visible to the colonial state, and their natural resources available for exploitation.[4] These networks defined highly uneven landscapes, bypassing indigenous populations and connecting colonial centers, but they also shaped colonial life and experiences in fundamental ways. As Masquelier argues, the construction of roads was in many ways the first, most enduring and violent aspect of colonialism.[5] Roads are thus complex and far-reaching technologies that are embedded in larger political, economic and socio-cultural frameworks.[6] Despite the importance of these networks, the existing literature has tended to downplay the importance of roads in favor of other infrastructure such as railroads or water projects. A reading of the materiality of roads in relation to the colonial state allows us thus to trace how these networks constitute and transform settler colonial space.

In the Palestinian context, various studies have consistently argued that roads are a defining feature of the colonial and segregationist policies of the state of Israel. In fact, whereas colonial outposts were essential for the early Zionist expansionist endeavor, it was roads that paved the way to the "frontier." As Meron Benvenisti puts it, "the actual 'pioneer' that 'goes before the camp' has been the yellow bulldozer and the lengthening ribbon of asphalt behind it."[7] Back in the mid-1980s, Benvenisti noted how roads in the West Bank facilitated the "creeping annexation" of Palestinian lands into Israel, pointing out the development in practice of two parallel roads systems: one for Jewish settlers and another for Palestinians.[8] This massive infrastructural system effectively constitutes an umbilical cord that enables and feeds the settlement enterprise, connects colonies to each other, and incorporates these "wild" territories as part of the Israeli expansionist state. In this sense, roads, like electricity or water infrastructure, are what Akiva Eldar describes as "the elixir of life for the settlements [and] the secret of their power."[9] Moreover, these grids act as "sunken walls" that give life to Israeli colonial designs, dividing the Palestinian territories into an archipelago of discontinuous enclaves, while simultaneously spatializing the exclusivist and segregationist nature of the settler society.[10] For these networks, as we shall see, are ultimately tantamount to the production of new socio-spatial relations, boundaries and hierarchies. Yet these thoroughfares are not only aimed at annexing and "domesticating" the territory of the Palestinian Other, they also render this "strange" place familiar within the settler imaginary. Eyal Weizman suggests that the visual language of "colonial facts" helps to naturalize infrastructural projects and make them appear as organic parts of the Israeli state.[11] In this way, roads are, as Jeff Halper notes, "massive, permanent structures; they flow, giving the feeling of 'natural' connections with no artificial borders, yet they claim land by their very routes; they are banal and can be made to look inoffensive and even benign and attractive."[12] This potential of abstraction in roads is precisely what makes possible a distortion of the deeply political nature of these networks and how they enable settler narratives of belonging and territorial claims of expansion over their very paths.

While roads enable a sense of settler belonging and territorial possession, this infrastructural assemblage cuts both ways as roads bring vicious destruction through their calculated paths. From the standpoint of the Palestinian population, roadways represent more than bypasses between places: these networks effectively shape native space as they leave behind violent traces of forced removal, dispossession and segregation of the indigenous urban and rural classes. As Samira Shah notes, more than four decades of road construction in the West Bank have resulted in massive land theft, house demolitions, denial of urban growth, towns cut off from each other and from their service centres, and wanton destruction of the landscape. Once laid out, these enduring artefacts alter the status quo of the colonized territories, further undermining the possibility of indigenous sovereignty over their land.[13] At the same time, the traditional Palestinian road network has often been the target of state-led destruction. As Stephen Graham puts it, state-led infrastructure destruction is an attempt at forced de-modernization of the Palestinian society.[14] The rolling out of layers of gravel and asphalt to constitute settler space is thus premised upon a logic of 'destructive creation': one that requires the material and symbolic erasure of indigenous geographies to make way for the new settler society.

The body of work addressing road infrastructure in the Palestinian context has been particularly attentive to geopolitics and violence. Its main concern has been to make visible the political nature of roads while bringing this infrastructure together with notions of power, sovereignty, space and borders. However, two aspects remain largely absent from this literature. First, these studies rarely explore in which ways the development of road infrastructure in the West Bank and Gaza reflect prior patterns and policies of Israeli colonial settlement in pre-1967 Palestine–Israel proper. These rigid spatial and temporal boundaries, which derive mostly from the predominance of the occupation framework, tend to blur the past and present dynamics of Israel's colonial infrastructure. A burgeoning literature that revives the "settler colonial" paradigm for the study of Palestine provides a useful lens to address these spatial and temporal limitations.[15] Locating Palestine – in its entirety—as a site of ongoing settler colonialism, this body of work sees contemporary realities as over-determined by the deep structures that Zionism put into place since its establishment. As John Collins explains, these spatial, social, political and economic structures are the persistent defining characteristic and even the condition of possibility of the contemporary Israeli state.[16] Looking at road networks as signifiers of the evolution in time and space of Israel's settler colonial practice can thus shed some light on the symbolic and material aspects that today inform these urbanizing polities on the West Bank "frontier."

Second, these studies have paid little attention to the myriad of actors and complex processes that define the road and to the ways in which the construction of roads is contested and at times subverted, or how they come to matter to everyday life. To do this, as McFarlane and Rutherford contend, a historized analysis of infrastructure development is crucial to understanding the contested genealogy and political continuities and discontinuities that inform these networks in, nominally, postcolonial contexts.[17] Thus, taking into consideration the social-political dimensions and repercussions of road development helps us to foreground the materiality of infrastructure as it is experienced by those it dispossesses spatially and socially. This attention to bodies, mobility and everyday life, as Joan Long suggests, might contribute to alter the predominance of macro-level debates in Palestine studies, "exposing the intimate biopolitical geographies through which those [Israeli] agendas are pursued and contested."[18]

## "We shall dress you with robes of concrete and cement"

Modern infrastructure and ambitious engineering proposals are central to the symbolic and material geographies of Zionism.[19] Since the earliest nineteenth-century visions of ideologues, surveyors and engineers, the laying of infrastructure over Palestine was understood by the leaders of the Zionist project as a precondition to building a new Jewish settler society. The need to "redeem the empty land" and make "the desert bloom" was necessarily premised upon the perception that infrastructure (as technology) would transform the existing natural conditions.[20] In the process of constructing this symbolic geography, Jewish settlers rendered the Palestinian populations invisible, transforming their habitat into a topographic *tabula rasa* on which to carve their modern and rational infrastructural grid plans. Theodor Herzl, the father of Zionism, projected this infrastructural imaginary onto the future in his manifesto about the Jewish state: "The poorest will go first to cultivate the soil. In accordance with a preconceived plan, they will construct roads, bridges, railways and telegraph installations; regulate rivers; and build their own dwellings; their labour will create trade, trade will create markets and markets will attract new settlers."[21] Herzl, as well as other Zionist ideologues, believed nevertheless that building settler space was as much an effort at "taming" the "wild" nature of the land, as it was to transform Jewish settlers themselves into "new human beings and a better society."[22] Chaim Weizmann, President of the Zionist Organization and first president of the state of Israel, understood that

> A country is acquired in the pain of a struggle against all obstacles. This sort of suffering we have not been permitted to experience in the various lands of our dispersion. In Palestine, we know the pain of drying the swamps, laying the roads, putting up tents and fighting the natural elements. That is why, in relation to us, the world conceives Palestine as something different from New York or Warsaw.[23]

Zionist thinkers believed, as was the case of other settler-national projects,[24] that Jewish pioneers could simultaneously transform themselves as they transformed the land through the construction, in pain and glory, of roads, bridges and other engineering projects.[25] Infrastructure development was thus crucial to achieve the promise of national redemption.

This is perhaps best shown in the case of road construction that, as Tom Selwyn points out, was considered a heroic effort to establish "facts on the ground."[26] Selwyn explains how "road building was accompanied by a whole culture of songs and stories about the brigades which forged the transport infrastructure that made possible the establishment of the state itself."[27] The production of this mythology is best articulated in the Israeli classic *Kalaniyout*, a popular song by Nathan Alterman written in the days leading to the establishment of the State of Israel: "We shall plant and build you, our beloved country, we shall beautify your might; we shall dress you with robes of cement and concrete."[28] Road infrastructure is in this way constitutive of distinctive forms of colonial subjectivity and collective identity formation. Indeed, on the one hand, these emancipatory networks enabled the project of urban modernity that characterizes and differentiates the settler enterprise from the "backward" conditions of the land and peoples to be conquered. And, on the other, it articulated the mythological links between the Jewish people and the "Land of Israel" (Palestine) through a territorialization of sovereignty claims.

The imaginative geographies that underpin road development, however, conceal the actual sites where colonial processes of dispossession and repossession are practiced. Road infrastructure has been crucial to facilitating and sustaining the making of Jewish settler space and simultaneously the unmaking of Palestinian native space. This profound socio-spatial redefinition has its origins in the three decades of the British Mandate (1917–1948), which introduced to Palestine "modern" planning schemes and transportation plans. The British built an extensive and well-developed road network that was used to enhance the export capacity of the colony, to facilitate the movement of troops and police, as well as to extend control over inaccessible and "lawless" areas.[29] Yet the British were not the only ones building roads during the Mandate period. In fact, the Zionist Committee, which advised and helped the British Government to implement and develop infrastructure projects of Jewish interest in Palestine, had its own "Construction and Public works" arm – Solel Boneh. These projects included, among others, the strategic roads from Safed to Tzemah, Haifa to Jaffa, or Jaffa to Jerusalem. In 1948, when the Israeli state was born, the new Government decided to continue the British tradition of road building, which was cheaper and faster to develop than railways. Roads became indeed Israel's preferred tool of expansion and the main means of bringing the periphery within reach of the state.[30] Solel Boneh, in cooperation with several organizations from the Zionist establishment – namely the World Zionist Organization, the Jewish National Fund and Keren Hayesod – were key in preparing the land before settlement; they provided the construction of roads, the supply of water and electricity, and drainage of swamps when necessary. These actors conceived transportation networks as a way to facilitate Jewish settlement through the "frontier" and to extend sovereignty over the expropriated Palestinian lands being annexed in the construction process. In fact, during the first decades of the Israeli state, the layout of roads served to fragment and dispossess the remaining Palestinian population, predominantly in Arab Galilee.[31] It is in this way that road infrastructure makes natural and inevitable the progressive nature of the Zionist undertaking. As Dan Rabinowitz emphasizes, "Transportation and, to a lesser degree, electricity and telephone infrastructure ... shadowed the pattern of [early] settlement instigated by the nationalizing project."[32] Roads serve, as Henri Lefebvre would say, to naturalize power in space, obscuring its very operations and effects.[33]

## The road to Zion: "dunam after dunam"[34]

The philosophy of Zionism to redeem the land and produce settler space is one of pragmatism and flexibility. The territory is conquered one road at a time, as the song goes, "a dunam here and a dunam there."[35] Road building has demonstrated over time the effectiveness of this policy. Today Israel's road network is a comprehensive layout that covers and connects poles of settlement throughout all the territory, from the Jordan River to the Mediterranean Sea. Yet to see this colonial network as a highly planned and consistent project obscures the processes that constitute this infrastructure and both overestimate and underestimate its power. The historiography of Road 443 highlights how the construction of roads is not as coherent as it is sometimes made out to be but rather is a messy and contingent process where different actors modify and learn from one another, but also react and come up with novel solutions to specific problems. In particular, this case provides an illustrative example of the ways in which the materiality and legal/political aspects of road infrastructure constitute one another. And it also shows the intrinsic violence and geographies of dispossession resulting from its development.

The existence of a plan for building Road 443 surfaced in an unusual way in 1980 after a Palestinian teachers cooperative took the military administration to the Israeli High Court of Justice for freezing their permits to build a housing complex in the area of Qalandia, north of Jerusalem.[36] The permits were legally obtained from the military administration through the customary procedures and construction had already begun. The reason given for freezing the permits was that the cooperative had submitted individual permits allegedly hiding their intentions to build an entire neighbourhood.[37] The court initially validated the administration's decision and demanded the cooperative submit a complete plan for the entire project. Eventually, the court revoked the housing permits and the entire master plan. Interestingly the reasons given by the judge for the refusal did not relate to the initial allegations. In fact, the whole project was rejected on the basis that it was too close to the industrial Israeli colony of Atarot and, most importantly, because of the existence of a plan to build a road and a large intersection nearby.[38] It is worth noting that the road plan had not yet received planning approval nor had it been previously published. The court's justification was based both on a 'security' rational and on the 'need' to build a permanent infrastructure for the 'benefit' of the local population. For the teachers cooperative, the ruling meant a legal burial of the housing project. Yet once the details for the new highway were made available, the plan became the subject of a second petition against the confiscation of the cooperative lands for this purpose.

The Israeli proposal, as presented in court, consisted in upgrading a regional road cutting through the West Bank. Road 443, originally paved during the British Mandate, was a major artery passing through and connecting several Palestinian villages in the area to Ramallah and Jerusalem on the East and Jaffa and Tel Aviv in the West. The plan redefined the traditional path of the road in order to bypass the existing Palestinian villages. The military administration in the occupied territories defended the new highway on the grounds that a new road system would address the increasing traffic needs of the Palestinian population providing a rapid link to communities throughout the West Bank. It noted as well that the road would serve not only Palestinians but also Israeli traffic between the West Bank and Israel, benefiting in particular the increasing number of Palestinian commuters working in Israel. Ironically, the State claimed that:

> The military government's role, fifteen years after it was established, cannot be limited to preserving an old and out-dated road system ... [otherwise] it would have been rightly accused of freezing development and preventing the natural development of the Area [West Bank and Gaza] and its population.[39]

Moreover, the new motorway was justified as an attempt to improve the lives of the Palestinian indigenous population and to contribute to meeting the standards of a modern and civilized society.[40] In this way the project was presented as a "cooperation project" between Israel and the West Bank to be co-founded partly by taxes collected from the occupied population and partly by Israel.

The Israeli High Court of Justice endorsed each one of the arguments presented by the military administration recurring to "a long list of seemingly progressive rules whose illusory nature continues to be exposed to this day."[41] Although the judge had his reservations with regards to the order of priorities advanced by the state to justify the road – that is the 'needs' of the occupied population instead of the 'security needs' of the occupiers – he nevertheless argued that "there is no basis for doubting the authenticity of the planning considerations presented by the authorities." The lands of the teachers' cooperative were finally confiscated and, adding insult to injury, the cooperative was obliged to pay the expenses of the trial, including the fees of the military administration. Yet there is one important aspect that the ruling failed to address: the highway was only a section of a larger national highway plan – not disclosed during the process – that eventually would entail a *de facto* incorporation of large sections of the West Bank into Israel. By doing this, the court endorsed the plan, even if implicitly, masking and legalizing the broader catastrophic consequences that its development would have for the Palestinian population.

Indeed, in February 1984, a year after the ruling, it became clear that Road 443 was an intrinsic component of Road Plan 50. The plan encompassed and materialized previous strategic attempts to colonize the Palestinian territories occupied in 1967. It was this plan that the High Court of Justice was referring to in the previous case when resolving that: "Once the commanding officer decided to prepare an all-embracing road-plan, one cannot see this as an illegal act, especially since in the opinion of the court, this was done in the interest of the local population."[42] The Israeli Defense and Housing Ministries and the Military Administration, in cooperation with settler organizations, prepared the plan excluding all Palestinian participation. Its explicit goals were two-fold. On the one hand, it aimed at giving material legibility to the messianic idea that the West Bank – the biblical land of Judea and Samaria in Zionist terminology – was an intrinsic part of the "Land of Israel." And on the other, to legitimize colonial dispossession through an overarching road network that would consolidate settlement expansion, enable the mobility of a Jewish army of suburban pioneers and facilitate the connection of colonies between each other and to Israel. Moreover, it intended to ensure that Palestinian areas "would be isolated and their growth would be hindered by [a] massive road network and non-settler Israeli presence."[43] All facts that obviously run contrary to the allegations repeatedly adopted by the Israeli Government to justify the construction of Road 443 and that expose the expansionist intentions behind the highway system. The plan was disclosed in the West Bank local newspaper: it was presented as a legal undertaking, in accordance with the Jordanian law, to readapt the network to new needs and modernize an aging infrastructure that would benefit the local population. By 1986, 88 kilometers of the plan's roads had already been built over thousands of dunums of Palestinian expropriated land, often without providing the population with the right to submit any objections to the building of these roads.[44]

Road Plan 50 was considered at the time as big a threat as today's Apartheid Wall in terms of land expropriation, economic and environmental impacts, and social fragmentation. A report produced and submitted to the UN by Al-Haq, a Palestinian Human Rights organization, emphasized that

> The proposed system will serve none of the 20 major Palestinian towns and cities in the West Bank, but will skirt around them, cutting them off from municipal land earmarked for development or from land now in agricultural use on which the towns are dependent.[45]

Moreover, the total area of 600 km of roads – in addition to disproportionate widths and unnecessary buffer zones on the sides – was estimated at 37,200 ha; roughly the built-up area of the West Bank at the time which was 43,000 ha. Everything falling under the width and buffer of a planned road could be subjected to building prohibition, confiscation, cease of use and demolition. Al-Haq documented the total value of the destruction in two representative 10 km sections (see Figure 5.2) of the proposed plan at an estimated cost of 15.6 million dinars (39 million dollars at 1984 prices).[46] For Palestinians in the West Bank this meant that land expropriation for building the network would amount to more than a billion dollars. Road 443 provided a vivid example of the consequences of this plan when in 1988 the Israeli authorities began construction. As endorsed

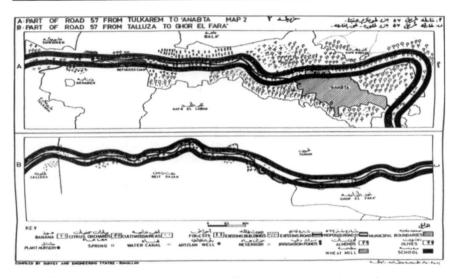

*Figure 5.2* Israeli road sections planned over Palestinian agricultural and urban areas

by the court, the original route was altered to bypass the Palestinian villages of Beit Ur al-Fauka, Beit Ur at-Tahta, and Beit Sira, ensuring that settlers would be prevented from driving through these areas. The construction of the highway meant seizing agricultural lands and uprooting thousands of olive and fruit trees from the nearby villages.

The rationale that derives from this case exposes two important aspects. First, the road is presented as a modernizing and development endeavor effectively concealing the politics invested in such a large infrastructural project, and the territorialization and expansion of the settler state throughout the "frontier." Second, the reification and complicity of a legal apparatus infused in enlightened and benevolent discourse whereby the parameters of customary international law served to justify the permanent – as opposed to "temporary" – nature of settler occupation. Road 443 appears thus not only as a physical object but rather as a hybrid of facts and norms, materiality and legality, and physicality and ideology.[47] The road needs thus to be understood in the context of the legal and political/ideological aspects that constitute its production and enable the enforcement of spatialities of dispossession.

## From dispossession to segregation: experiencing "bureaucracies of evil"

The first Intifada erupted in 1987 as a mass Palestinian uprising across the West Bank and Gaza against decades of Israeli settler colonial policies. The uprising challenged the normalcy of relentless Israeli efforts to annex territory and erase the "green line"[48] physically and symbolically. Suddenly, the illusion of "friction-less" and "enlightened" colonialism was brought to an end and "the icy winds of reality blew through the cosy network of [settler] politics and infrastructure."[49] The early prospects of a "normal life" and the idea of seamless travel, between colonial suburbs in the "frontier" and the urban centers in Israel, turned into settler anxiety. The uprising effectively marked the impossibility of a settler colo-nial formula that could no longer take the land without the people, thus making segregation – à la South African Apartheid – the most viable option to consoli-date and sustain Israel's thirst for land. From this moment on, the idea of *hafradat* (Hebrew for separation), which had guided previous decades of Jewish settle-ment, began to materialize more visibly and forcefully in the spatialities and mobility bureaucracies imposed upon Palestinians. In fact, after the 1993 Oslo Accords, the Israeli government revived the "green line" (or an elastic version of it) as a powerful marker to delimit the West Bank and the Gaza Strip as "hostile" territories. Simultaneously, the Palestinian movement was characterized as a "threat" and associated with settler vulnerability.[50] This, in turn, signified the end of Moshe Dayan's "open bridges" or "free movement" policy, which until then had enabled relative freedom of movement for Palestinians between the West Bank, Gaza and Israel and, in a more restricted way, to the Arab world. For Dayan, the primary architect of occupation, this strategic policy was meant as a way to conceal Israeli efforts at normalizing colonization, canceling the "green line" and, in his own words, to "give them [Palestinians] something to lose."[51] Indeed, the bargaining chip of freedom of movement was the first thing Palestinians lost after rising against their oppressor. As early as 1991, the state of Israel began the enforcement of strict mobility policies on the Palestinian popu-lation, both as access restrictions to Israel and mobility regulations between and within the West Bank and Gaza.[52] The apparatus to segregate the population consisted of a myriad of measures, including personal permits and magnetic cards, the mushrooming of checkpoints across, and on the borders of, the occupied territories, and strict access regulations to virtually all Palestinian roads.

Road 443 provides again a paradigmatic illustration of the normalization over the years of Israel's draconian mobility regulations. Following its construction in 1988, this thoroughfare developed into the major traffic artery in the southern Ramallah district, linking the villages of Beit Sira, Saffa, Beit Liqya, Kharbata al-Misbah, Beit Ur al-Tahta, and Beit Ur al-Fauka to the city of Ramallah. Road 443 also became a popular settler highway connecting suburban colonies in the Jerusalem area and along the way to Tel Aviv, as it is shorter and less busy than the traditional alternative, Highway 1. Yet, in 2002, after the outbreak of the second Intifada, the Israeli army prohibited both pedestrian and vehicular Palestinian travel on the road, including transport of goods and cases of medical and other emergencies. What began in the late 1990s as temporary measures banning access to Road 443, gradually became permanent facts that materialized in roadblocks, fences, gates, checkpoints and military patrols installed on the paths that connect Palestinian villages to this highway. The Israeli army justified this collective punishment as a security measure after Palestinian gunfire killed seven persons on the road in the midst of the Intifada. Gal Hirsh, the Ramallah commander at the time, proudly claimed authorship, as he put it, "I turned Route 443 into a highway for Israelis only … I closed all the exits to the Palestinians."[53] However, as Gershom Gorenenberg notes, "If the highway had really been built for local residents, the army could have taken the opposite tack – ordering Israelis not to use the road, just as it ordered them not to enter West Bank cities."[54] These policies were not exceptional during these years. In fact, as documented by B'Tselem, an Israeli Human Rights organization, the "forbidden roads regime" extended to most parts of the Palestinian network. Today, after restrictions have been relaxed in some West Bank roads, all the access paths connecting the villages to Road 443 still remain blocked.

The harm caused to the affected villages as a result of the closure has had major implications in all aspects of Palestinian life there. Currently the only existing alternative is a narrow, unsafe and tortuous road that crosses under Road 443. More than 30,000 Palestinians are obliged to use this road for access to Ramallah, which is the commercial and business hub for the area, the main provider of various social services – including higher education and medical facilities – and home to relatives of the villagers. Recently, I visited the area and listened to some of the residents. Zaki, a long-time activist from the village of Saffa, accompanied me. When we met, Zaki's first remark, echoing that of many others, was how before the second Intifada it used to take about 15 minutes to reach Ramallah whereas now it takes an hour or more, depending on the presence of Israeli checkpoints.[55] Likewise, he explained how a main concern for the population has been the rise of travel costs, which are a heavy burden for many families. Khaled Sibli, the owner of several mini-buses in the area, notes indeed how prices almost doubled and even tripled as a result of the increase in fuel prices.[56] The mayor of the village of Beit Tur al-Tahta, Naji Arraf, further explained how the highway ban and the consequent increase in travel time and costs have forced students to quit university, workers to move closer to Ramallah, patients to give up necessary medical treatment, and a general decrease in social and family life.[57] Moreover, Naji points out how over the years many Palestinians have died before reaching the Ramallah hospital as a result of the lengthy and difficult alternative road, a situation that did not happen in the past.

This situation has also had an impact on those who do not necessarily need to travel to Ramallah but who are dependent on this road to access schools or agricultural land. The Beit Ur al-Fauqa school, located adjacent to the Beit Horon colony, is a good example. After the closure of Road 443, children from the neighboring village of At-Tira could not be driven to school and now have to walk long distances to get there. In addition, because they are not allowed to pass over the existing road bridge, they are obliged to pass under a rainwater drain conduit under Road 443 to reach school. In rainy seasons this passage becomes full of mud and water (see Figure 5.3). Another major issue, as the mayor of the

*Figure 5.3* Viaduct for school children under Road 443

village of At-Tira emphasizes, is the lack of access to agricultural land as a result of the security buffer zones imposed on both sides of the road, especially for those households dependent on farming.[58] In fact, despite the impact of the closure on the everyday life of the Palestinian population, the main problem for these villages remains the continuous land theft resulting from road construction, security buffer zones, and the ongoing expansion of Israeli colonies.

## Cracks in the pavement? Roads as sites of struggle

Notwithstanding the severity of the dehumanizing policies that deny the population their most fundamental rights – to movement, health, employment, family life and education – Palestinians have relentlessly sought to contest and at times subvert Israeli efforts at dispossession and segregation. In fact, the extensive road ban and mobility restrictions enforced by Israel led instantly to the development of a wide range of Palestinian coping strategies that sway between everyday survival practices and collective struggles. During the early years of the second Intifada, at the height of the siege, the notion of *sumud* or steadfastness was effectively infused with new meaning. What is regarded by Palestinians as a strategy to stay on the land in the face of colonially inflicted hardships and oppression became, additionally, a struggle to continue with daily life: the courage to confront the road as an unpredictable site of frustrations and humiliations. As Rima Hammami maintains "*Sumud* has become about resisting immobility, the locking down of one's community, and refusing the impossibility of reaching one's school or job."[59] Road 443, as many other roads in the West Bank, became in this way a symbolic terrain of contestation to confront an imposed nearly immobile condition and, to a lesser extent, to challenge land theft.

In the early years of movement restrictions on Road 443, the Palestinian vehicular and walking spatial patterns mirrored this steadfastness attitude. Avoiding blocked access routes and military patrols, residents from the affected villages continued to try to use the highway via dirt roads that cut across rural fields and required climbing steep hills. These were the days where Palestinians could be seen strolling through valleys and mountains to avoid Israeli checkpoints located in the alternative back road near the village of Deir Ibzi: mothers and fathers with their kids trying to attend a family gathering or taking their eldest to hospitals, workers with rolled up suit pants hoping to make it in time for their meetings, or teenagers and teachers seeking their way to schools and universities. These are the Palestinian "facts on the ground" that reveal a persistent will to overcome and resist the Israeli policy of disrupting and paralyzing life. As Palestinian artist Khaled Jarrar explains, "It is the hope of being able to cross and reach the other side that gives the trip its meaning and intention."[60] These practices, however, were not always successful, as on many occasions the Israeli army and police would intercept the stream of daring Palestinians. Those caught were regularly subjected to long detention, fines, confiscation of IDs and vehicles, damage to cars, and often to verbal and physical abuse.[61] In fact, since the prohibition on Road 443 was not made official, as is the case for other West Bank roads, the implementation of this forbidden road regime is based solely on verbal orders given to the Israeli forces. According to Ezequiel Lein, researcher at B'Tselem at the time, this unwritten policy was coined as *tsriba toda'atit* (print on consciousness) by Israeli army Chief of Staff Moshe Ya'alon. The idea was indeed to record violent experiences in Palestinian memory. Contesting immobility was turned thus into a continuous game of cat and mouse whereby Palestinians would open ex-novo improvised paths to overcome closure while the Israeli forces would attempt to close and monitor those routes in an attempt to enforce segregation by all possible means. These individualized coping mechanisms are depicted here not as romanticized resistance strategies, but as a real, conscious, and daily struggle, limited as it is, to confront the colonizers within their own oppressive infrastructural geographies. Palestinian determination to overcome the ban on Road 443, however, goes beyond individual practices.

After years subjected to closure, six villages affected by the prohibitions on Road 443 decided to collectively take the case to the Israeli High Court. They approached the Association for Civil Rights in Israel (ACRI). Initially, in 2006, ACRI appealed to the Israeli army demanding the cancellation of all measures prohibiting Palestinian access and movement on the highway. The army, in its response, audaciously denied that it had prevented the movement of Palestinians on the road. A year later ACRI submitted a petition to the Israeli High Court denouncing the state of Israel and the army for the breach of military responsibilities towards the occupied Palestinian population, the sweeping violation of fundamental rights, and the unlawful separation and discrimination based on nationality.[62] The petition was a landmark in so far as it accused the state of Israel, for the first time, of the crime of Apartheid. In August 2007, following the request of the High Court, the army commander in the West Bank signed a written order officially banning Palestinian access to Road 443, allegedly, for security considerations. Shortly after, the Israeli army began to deploy co-optation and intimidation tactics against the petitioners to force them to drop the case. As ACRI's field researcher explains, the army initially held talks with some of the petitioners, offering 80 permits (for more than 30,000 residents) to mayors, businessmen, and transportation companies.[63] When the Palestinians rejected the offer, the Israeli army began to carry out night incursions into the villages and houses of the petitioners, sent threatening letters, and suspended VIP mobility permits of mayors in the area.[64] The Palestinians did not shy away from the harassment, remaining determined to contest the prohibition.

While the legal process was under way, residents in the area initiated popular demonstrations as a means of raising awareness and to pressurize Israel into overturning the ban. Zaki, engaged in demonstrations against the wall since 2003, was one of the main organizers of this initiative. In 2007, he and other individuals affected by the closure began enlisting friends, family and activists to hold weekly protests on the roadsides of Road 443. Some of these protests took place with the help and support of villages such as Al-Masarah or Bil'in and organizations like the International Solidarity Movement or Anarchists Against the Wall. Yet, despite the success of some particular actions in momentarily attracting attention to the injustice of the road ban, the weekly protests did not manage to gather a critical mass or to sustain sufficient media attention. Zaki related the difficulties of organizing and maintaining momentum as connected to the fact that many Palestinians in the area were reluctant to participate in the protests for fear of losing their work permits in Israel or in the colonies across the West Bank: mostly those with jobs in Ramallah or other locations in the West Bank would stand on the front lines, even if facing the risk of being imprisoned.

Moreover, as Zaki underlined, the "death and prison threats by the Israeli army to anyone daring to get close to the Road 443 during the protests" hampered the capacity to mobilize an already weakened population, especially as the international media, which often functions as a 'shield' for protesters, was frequently absent. The lack of support from the Palestinian Authority did not help either; in fact they only facilitated hospital access to those injured during demonstrations. In March 2008, the High Court inflicted another blow to Palestinian efforts as it implicitly endorsed segregation by approving an army proposal to build a separate road for Palestinians through improved tunnels under Road 443 while sustaining the traffic prohibition. This alternative "fabric of life"[65] road would, according to the army, minimize the damage caused. A month later there was a collective decision by Palestinian organizers from the affected villages to stop the demonstrations. The strategy became thus to maximize visibility for actions in other areas and wait for the final verdict of the Court. Zaki nevertheless remained convinced that "if the resolution does not suit our interests and access and land are not given back, then we will struggle again", as he says, "the third intifada will take place on the roads."[66]

Eventually the Palestinian efforts bore fruit insofar as they increasingly lent visibility – locally and internationally – to the racist nature of the road ban, casting a shadow over the High Court's troubling endorsement of Israel's apartheid policies. The pressure led the Court, in December 2009, to finally issue a ruling on the case, ordering the state to open the road to Palestinian traffic after eight years of closure. The decision was initially perceived by some international media pundits as a victory for the rule of law and human rights and proof of "Israel's liberal and democratic spirit."[67] However, as ACRI pointed out "the ruling contained an untenable gap between lofty principles and concrete instructions for the military."[68] In fact, the army was allowed to make do with a ruling that in principle opposed the road ban but that in practice enabled them to pursue its continuation by disingenuous methods. In April 2010, the army announced its plan, which consisted of two new entry points into Road 443 monitored by checkpoints in which Palestinian drivers would be searched and questioned before accessing the road. Yet only a section of 4 km, out of 28, was made available and the roads leading to Ramallah and Jerusalem remained closed for Palestinians (see Figure 5.4). After the "opening," the few Palestinians who accessed the road quickly understood that having access to 4 km did not change a thing and that the particularly long waits and dehumanizing experience at these checkpoints were a sign of Israel's army and government determination to keep this road closed. When the army was criticized for maintaining a de facto

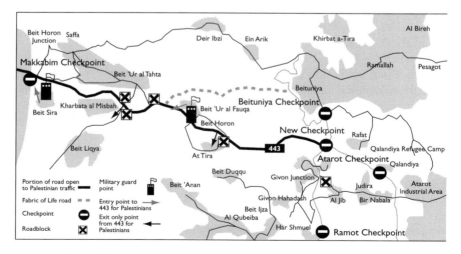

*Figure 5.4* Road 443 after the ruling of the Israeli High Court of Justice

closure, their response was that "their mandate [according to the ruling] was merely to allow local Palestinian traffic on Route 443, not to turn it into a thoroughfare to Ramallah."[69] The months leading to the "opening" saw a fierce debate in Israel and a surge of fear mongering among Israeli ministries and organizations. The Israeli Ministry of Transport, for example, exposed its real concerns when it warned that if Road 443 were opened, this would destroy the alternative, and less convenient, Israeli motorway between Tel Aviv and Jerusalem – Highway 1. Today, after what ACRI has described as the "human rights travesty" of the High Court, Road 443 remains virtually banned to Palestinians. The Israeli High Court ruling is an instance of what Ronen Shamir calls "landmark cases." The significance of these verdicts, Shamir argues, is primarily symbolic rather than substantive, for they legitimize government policies (at least in the eyes of most Israelis) precisely because these decisions become symbols of democracy in action. For Palestinians, fully aware of the limits of going to the High Court, the ruling constituted another step in exposing the hypocrisy that infuses the Israeli legal system and the tyranny and consequences of using liberal humanitarian law in an illiberal settler context.

## Seeing through (road) infrastructure

Assessing the seemingly mundane nature of road networks exposes the significance of this urban infrastructure and the injustice and violence that often accompany its development in colonial contexts. This chapter has presented the road as a tool of analysis but also as an "archive" of Israel's settler colonial practice which, when unpacked, makes visible the layered assemblage of colonial discourses, practices, actors and experiences that justify, enable and characterize this infrastructure. A historicized analysis of roads in Palestine shows how these networks are constituted in past and present colonial discourses of modernity, development, legality, and security in an attempt to make natural, legitimate and inevitable the production of Israel's settler space. The construction of roads, however, not only entails discourses supporting the rationalities of infrastructure development, but also a physical and violent reworking of Palestinian space that materializes the colonial nature of the state. Thus, as this chapter suggests, road infrastructure is an outcome and a means of the project of colonial settlement and modernization, but also a mirror of the social and political form of the settler state. Another significant aspect that emerges from this chapter is the relevance of the law not only as a tool to normalize and justify the dispossession resulting from road building, but also as an active agent involved in the production of space and the segregation of the indigenous population. Finally, by paying particular attention to the everyday life experiences of the Palestinians, I have stressed how roads effectively obscure a larger story of struggle against conquest, dispossession, exploitation, and destruction. The building and experiencing of roads enable the formation of colonial subjectivities that are meant to normalize claims over stolen land and produce settlers as modern and mobile subjects. For the indigenous population, in contrast, road infrastructure and draconian access restrictions signify a continuing history of dispossession and a condition of limited mobility. In this sense, the road appears as a contested terrain that rests fundamentally on a dialectical production of socio-spatial relations, for the colonized population are able to deploy individual and collective strategies that expose, challenge, and force to readapt, even if in discrete ways, the colonizer's racialized policies and geographies.

## Acknowledgments

Many thanks to Stephen Graham and Colin McFarlane for their helpful readings of an earlier draft. I am also grateful for the insightful comments and suggestions of Christopher Harker, Kareem Rabie, Mezna Qato, Punam Khosla, Nicola Perugini, Barbara Van Dyck, Christopher Parker and Sami Zemni. Finally, I would like to thank the Flemish Interuniversity Council (VLIR) for funding the research on which this chapter is based. The usual disclaimers apply.

## Notes

1   Douglas Adams, *The Hitchhiker's Guide to the Galaxy* (New York: Del Rey, 2002), p. 25.
2   Ibid.
3   Under International Humanitarian Law, Israel, as an occupier force, does not have the authority to make far-reaching changes in the territories as, in principle, any occupation is supposed to be temporary.
4   See Penny Edwards, "The Tyranny of Proximity: Power and Mobility in Colonial Cambodia, 1863–1954," *Journal of Southeast Asian Studies*, 37(2006): 421–443, 427 and James C. Scott, *Seeing Like a State* (New Haven, CT: Yale University Press, 1999).
5   Adeline Masquelier, "Road Mythographies: Space, Mobility, and the Historical Imagination in Postcolonial Niger," *American Ethnologist*, 29 (2002): 829–856, 829.
6   Libbie Freed, "Networks of (Colonial) Power: Roads in French Central Africa after World War I," *History and Technology*, 26(3) (2010): 203–223, 205.
7   Meron Benvenisti, *Son of the Cypresses* (Berkeley, CA: University of California Press, 2007), p. 36.
8   Meron Benvenisti and Shlomo Khayat, *The West Bank and Gaza Atlas* (Jerusalem: West Bank Data Project, 1988), pp. 35–36.
9   Idith Zertal and Akiva Eldar, *Lords of the Land* (New York: Nation Books, 2007), p. xv.
10  See Eyal Weizman, *Hollow Land* (London: Verso, 2007).
11  Ibid, p. 26.
12  Jeff Halper, "The Road to Apartheid," ICAHD, May 15, 2000. Available at: www.icahd.org/?p=4474 (accessed September 2011).
13  Samira Shah, "On the Road to Apartheid: The Bypass Road Network in the West Bank," *Columbia Human Rights Law Review*, 29 (1997–98): 252–260.
14  Stephen Graham, "Lessons in Urbicide," *New Left Review* 19 (2003): 63–77.
15  See Gershon Shafir, *Land, Labor and the Origins of the Israeli-Palestinian Conflict, 1882–1914* (Berkeley, CA: University of California Press, 1996); Lorenzo Veracini, *Israel and Settler Society* (London: Pluto Press, 2006); or Omar Jabary Salamanca *et al.* "Past Is Present: Settler Colonialism in Palestine," *Settler Colonial Studies*, 2(1) (2012).

16  John Collins, "Beyond Conflict: Palestine and the Deep Structures of Global Colonization," *Politica y Sociedad*, 48 (2011): 139–154.
17  Colin McFarlane and Jonathan Rutherford, "Political Infrastructures: Governing and Experiencing the Fabric of the City," *International Journal of Urban and Regional Research*, 32(2) (2008): 363–374.
18  Joanna Long, "Geographies of Palestine-Israel," *Geography Compass*, 5(5) (2011): 268. See also Christopher Harker, "Geopolitics and Family in Palestine," *Geoforum*, 42(3) (2011): 306–315.
19  See Alon Tal, "Enduring Technological Optimism: Zionism's Environmental Ethic and Its Influence on Israel's Environmental History," *Environmental History*, 13(2) (2008): 275–235 and Noah Efron, "Zionism and the Eros of Science and Technology," *Journal of Religion and Science*, 46(2) (2011): 413–428.
20  This is what Veracini calls the "anticipatory geographies" of settler colonialism. See Lorenzo Veracini, "The Imagined Geographies of Settler Colonialism" in Tracey Banivanua-Mar and Penelope Edmonds (eds.) *Making Settler Colonial Space* (Basingstoke: Palgrave, 2010), p. 182.
21  Theodore Herzl, *The Jewish State* (New York: Dover, 1988), p. 26.
22  Joseph Massad, "The Persistence of the Palestinian Questions," *Cultural Critique*, 59 (2005): 4.
23  Laurence Krane, "Chaim Weizmann, Builder of Israel," *Jewish Magazine*, October, 2002. Available at: www.jewishmag.com/60mag/ weizmann/weizmann.htm (accessed September 2011).
24  See Penny Edwards, "On Home Ground: Settling Land and Domesticating Difference in the 'Non-Settler' Colonies of Burma and Cambodia," *Journal of Colonialism and Colonial History*, 4(3) (2003).
25  For a similar example on identity construction through swamp draining, see Sandra Marlene Sufian, *Healing the Land and the Nation: Malaria and the Zionist Project in Palestine* (Chicago: University of Chicago Press, 2007).
26  Tom Selwyn, "Landscapes of Separation: Reflections on the Symbolism of By-pass Roads in Palestine," in Barbara Bender and Margot Winer (eds.), *Contested Landscapes: Movement, Exile and Place* (Oxford: Berg, 2001), p. 230.
27  Ibid.
28  Rachel Werczberger, "Memory, Land, and Identity: Visions of the Past and the Land in the Jewish Spiritual Renewal in Israel," *Journal of Contemporary Religion*, 26(2) (2011): 283.
29  The British expanded the paved road network built during the Ottoman Empire from 230 km to 2,600 km in 1945. See J.V.W. Shaw (ed.) *A Survey of Palestine*, Vol. II (Washington, DC: Institute of Palestine Studies, 1991), p. 859 and Yair Aharoni, *The Israeli Economy: Dreams and Realities* (London: Routledge, 1991), p. 67.
30  Dan Rabinowitz, "Disentangling Nationalizing Projects and Sustainable Development: Can the Case of Israel and Palestine Provide a Model?" Paper presented at the Palestinian and Israeli Environmental Narratives Conference, Toronto, December 5–8, 2004, pp. 12–13.
31  Elia T. Zureik, "Benvenisti's Palestine Project," *Journal of Palestine Studies*, 4(1) (1984): 99, see also Elia T. Zureik, *The Palestinians in Israel: A Study in Internal Colonialism* (London: Routledge, 2000).
32  Ibid., p. 33.
33  See Henri Lefebvre, *The Production of Space* (London: Blackwell, 1991).
34  Turkish measure still used in Palestine/Israel that is equal to 1000 square meters.
35  See Ury Avnery, "Dunam after Dunam," *Coldtype*, February 5, 2005. Available at: www.coldtype.net/Assets.05/Avnery/Avi.06.05.pdf (accessed September 2011).
36  Israeli Supreme Court (verdict HCJ 393/82), "Jam'iat Iscan Al-Ma'almoun v. Commander of the IDF Forces in the Area of Judea and Samaria," December 12,

1983. Available at: www.hamoked.org/items/160_eng.pdf (accessed September 2011).

37   Yossi Wolfson, "Expropriation of Private Palestinian Land for the Purpose of Building a Road for Israelis: Jam'iat Iscan Al-Ma'almoun v. Commander of the IDF Forces in the Area of Judea and Samaria," HAMOKED, September, 2009. Available at: www.hamoked.org/Document.aspx?dID=Documents1050 (accessed September 2011).

38   Ibid.

39   Israeli Supreme Court (verdict HCJ 393/82) "Jam'iat Iscan Al-Ma'almoun v. Commander of the IDF Forces in the Area of Judea and Samaria", op. cit.

40   Ibid.

41   Wolfson, "Expropriation of Private Palestinian Land for the Purpose of Building a Road for Israelis," op. cit.

42   Shehadeh, A. et al., Israeli Proposed Road Plan for the West Bank: A Question for the International Court of Justice (Ramallah: Al-Haq, 1984), p. 2.

43   Samira Shah, "On the Road to Apartheid: The Bypass Road Network in the West Bank," Columbia Human Rights Law Review, 29 (1997–98): 252–260.

44   Shehadeh, et al., Israeli Proposed Road Plan, op. cit.

45   Ibid.

46   A.G. Coon, "Development Plans in the West Bank," Geojournal, 21(4) (1990): 368.

47   For a similar discussion on the Wall, see Yishai Blank, "Legalizing the Barrier: The Legality and Materiality of the Israel/Palestine Separation Barrier," Texas International Law Journal, 46 (2011): 309–343.

48   The "green line" is the 1949 armistice line that "separates" Israel from the occupied Palestinian territories, that is the West Bank, Gaza and East Jerusalem.

49   Peter Shaw-Smith, "The Israeli Settler Movement Post-Oslo," Journal of Palestine Studies, 23(3) (1994): 1.

50   Selwyn, "Landscapes of Separation," p. 233.

51   Avram S. Bornstein, Crossing the Green Line (Philadelphia, PA: Pennsylvania University Press, 2002), p. 42.

52   Amira Hass, "Israel's Closure Policy: An Ineffective Strategy of Containment and Repression," Journal of Palestine Studies, 31(3) (2002): 5–20.

53   HCJ 2150/07 (petition) Abu Safiya et al. v. Minister of Defense et al. Available at: www.acri.org.il/pdf/road443petition.pdf (accessed September 2011).

54   Gershom Gorenberg, "The Road to Injustice," The American Prospect, May 28, 2010. Available at: http://prospect.org/cs/articles?article=the_road_to_injustice (accessed September 2011).

55   Zaki (this name has been changed). Interview by author, Ramallah, August 25, 2008.

56   Khaled Sibli. Interview by author, Ramallah, September 1, 2010.

57   Naji Araf. Interview by author, Beit Tur al-Tahta, August 30, 2008.

58   Taysir. Interview by author, At-Tira, August 30, 2008.

59   Rima Hammami, "On the Importance of Thugs: The Moral Economy of a Checkpoint," Jerusalem Quarterly, 22(23) (2005): 18.

60   Marie Medina, "Passages de Khaled Jarrar à la galerie AlHoash," Babelmed, August 19, 2008. Available at: www.babelmed.net/Pais/M%C3%A9diterran%C3%A9e/passages_de.php?c=3508&m=34&l=fr (accessed September 2011).

61   B'Tselem, Forbidden Roads: Israel's Discriminatory Road Regime in the West Bank (Jerusalem: B'Tselem, 2004).

62   HCJ 2150/07 (petition) Abu Safiya et al. v. Minister of Defense et al. Available at: www.acri.org.il/pdf/road443petition.pdf (accessed September, 2011).

63   Fairaz Alami (2008) Interview by author, Jerusalem, September 15, 2008.

64   Ibid.

65   "Fabric of life" is the term given by the Israeli army to describe the construction of an

alternative and dedicated road system for Palestinians that effectively separates them from Israeli traffic in particular sections of the network.

66  Zaki. Interview by author, Ramallah, August 25, 2008.
67  Julian Kossoff, "The Opening of Route 443 Proves Israel's Liberal and Democratic Spirit," *The Telegraph*, May 28, 2010. Available at: http://blogs.telegraph.co.uk/news/juliankossoff/100041337/the-opening-of-route-443-proves-israels-liberal-and-democratic-spirit/ (accessed September 2011).
68  ACRI, "Route 443: Fact Sheet and Timeline," May 25, 2010. Available at: www.acri.org.il/en/?p=726 (accessed September 2011).
69  Tovah Lazaroff, "Route 443 Opens to Palestinians," *Jerusalem Post*, May 28, 2010. Available at: www.jpost.com/Israel/Article.aspx?ID=176692&utm_source= twitterfeed&utm_medium=twitter (accessed September 2011).

# Part III

# Waste, process, infrastructure

# Chapter 6

# The uncanny materialities of the everyday

## Domesticated nature as the invisible 'other'

*Maria Kaika*

> This is the true nature of home – it is the place of peace: the shelter not only from all injury, but from all terror, doubt and division. In so far as it is not this, it is not home; so far as the anxieties of the outer life penetrate into it, and the ... unloved, or hostile society of the outer world is allowed ... to cross the threshold, it ceases to be a home; it is then only a part of the outer world, which you have roofed over and lighted fire in.
> (John Ruskin 1891, 'Sesame and Lilies', 136–37, cited in Sennett 1990: 20)

Using the domestication of water as a vehicle, the chapter analyses the process through which nature became scripted as 'the other' to the bourgeois home and explains the contribution of this separation to the conceptual construction of the home as a distinct and autonomous 'space envelope' supposedly untouched by socio-natural processes. Using the domestication of water as a vehicle, the chapter identifies an inherent contradiction: though the complex set of socio-natural networks, pipes and cables that carry clean, commodified nature inside the modern home and pump bad metabolised nature outside remain visually excluded, it is these same visually excluded socio-natural networks that constitute the material basis upon which the familiarity of the home is constructed. Thus, in a simultaneous act of need and denial, the bourgeois home remains the host of the elements that it tries to exclude. This contradiction surfaces at moments of crisis (such as power cuts, burst mains, water shortages, etc.) when familiar objects acquire uncanny properties. At such moments, the continuity of the social and material processes that produce the domestic space is unexpectedly foregrounded, bringing the dweller face to face with his/her alienation, within his/her most familiar environment.

## Scripting natural processes as 'the other': *good* versus *bad* nature

> Modernity emerges from the belief that man is fundamentally a clean body.
> (Lahiji and Friedman 1997)

Attempts to re-conceptualise the nature/society relationship have focused on the production of objects which are neither purely natural nor purely human constructions. The notions of the 'hybrid' introduced by Donna Haraway (1991), or the 'quasi object', introduced by Bruno Latour (1993), offered insightful ways to go beyond the nature/society dualism. Water provides an excellent example of such a 'quasi-object' that, unlike cloned sheep or genetically modified organisms, we encounter in our everyday life. Like other natural elements (gas, petrol, etc.), water is produced, purified, standardised and commodified. As it is abstracted, dammed, channelled, stored, distilled, and chlorinated, its physical and social qualities change. It becomes a 'hybrid': neither purely 'natural' nor purely a 'human product' (Swyngedouw and Kaika 2000). The modern city and the modern home cannot function without adequate supply of this modern produced quasi object: drinking, bathing, cleaning draining, are all subject to its continuous flow inside the city and inside one's home. Ironically, however, as nature in the form of commodified water, gas, electricity, etc. became essential for the construction of the modern city and the modern home, it simultaneously became *discursively* constructed as separate, as 'the other' to the private space of home, as it appears in Ruskin's opening quote.

Indeed, traditionally water was searched for outside the house, often outside the settlement area, and brought into the house through painstaking efforts, predominantly carried out on the part of women, practices still found in non-western societies (Curtis 1986; Cleaver and Elson 1995). However, through a historically and geographically specific process of domestication and commodification, access to water in the western world has been made as easy and simple as turning a tap inside the private space of one's home. The domestication of water changed the traditional places where this element can be found. As water travels through a myriad of intricate physical socio-spatial networks (channels, reservoirs, pipes, taps) from spaces of production (dams, wells, reservoirs, pumping stations, purifying stations,) to spaces of consumption/reproduction (city, home), it is not only its physical and social qualities that change, but also its relationship to space. Water's dwelling space shifts geographically from the countryside (rivers, lakes, boreholes) to the city (public ornamental and drinking fountains) and finally to the house (taps, baths, private swimming pools, private ornamental fountains, ponds). During the nineteenth and early twentieth century the increasing incorporation of water into the economic and social life of expanding urban areas, combined with the discovery of the link between water and epidemics, generated a science, economy and practice of treating and purifying water. This practice led to the material production of purified drinking water as a new modern hybrid; and to the discursive construction of two distinct 'types' of water: *good water* (clean, processed, controlled, commodified) and *bad water* (dirty, grey, metabolised, non-processed, non-commodified). The first category includes water for drinking, bathing, swimming, baptising, etc. while the second comprises untreated metabolised water, to be found in city rivers, lakes, rainwater, sewerage, etc. It was therefore established that before water is allowed to make contact with the human body, it has to be controlled and mastered, processed and produced, like almost every other form of nature (Foucault 1977). While contact with *bad* water was considered to be harmful to the human body, *good* water became the cleansing, purifying, healthy element.

These changes in the physical and social character of water went hand in glove with the creation and allocation of specific spaces for the use of *good* and *bad* water. Getting in touch with water in the form of bathing in a bathtub, swimming in the newly devised and constructed temples for swimming, or purifying mind and body in the middle-class's favourite spas was considered to be a safe and sanitizing activity. By contrast, getting in touch with water flowing in an uncontrolled and unregulated manner – swimming in rivers and lakes, getting wet in the rain, or drinking untreated water – became a negative and potentially harmful activity.

While free flowing water in the city became a source of threat, and thus something to be controlled or eradicated from the cityscape, controlled water running in one's house became exactly the opposite: the ultimate purifying, cleansing element. The *hydrophobia* developed towards the uncontrolled waters of the public (urban) domain, was paralleled by a *hydrophilia* towards the controlled waters of the private space of one's home (Chappells Shove and Selby 1999). By the late nineteenth century bourgeois homes included designated 'wet rooms' (i.e. bathroom and kitchen) as indicators of social status (Lupton and Miller 1996), while 'bathing institutions' sprouted in popular quarters of western cities.

However, as the availability of and access to commodified water increased in the domestic sphere, availability of *good* (e.g. drinking) water in the public sphere became confined to the past in the western world. Whilst in the Islamic world public water is still an integral part of the urban landscape, corresponding to the Islamic law that defines it as a right of people and animals alike (Wescoat 1995), in the western world public fountains or taps have disappeared from the urban domain, and publicly available free of charge clean drinking water is a rare species, corresponding to the re-conceptualisation of water as a commodity. On many European flights one cannot get a glass of water unless one pays for it, while until recently, nightclub owners in London would block the cold taps in the bathrooms to prevent patrons from drinking 'free' water.

Along with publicly available *good* drinking water, uncontrolled, dirty *bad* water was also slowly but steadily eradicated from the visible urban domain. In London during the nineteenth century,[1] for example, over a dozen rivers were covered by streets in an effort to rationalise urban space and to eliminate the threat of epidemics (Halliday 1999). All European and most North American cities experienced a similar process (see Keil 1998; Latour and Hernant 1998). By eliminating clean water from the public sphere, the bourgeois home became the 'natural' space to look for 'freely' flowing *good* water and a separation was generated between the urban as the place where *bad* water dwells, and the protected space of the home where *good* water emerges in its commodified form. This double process of casting processed nature outside the modern home, while allowing controlled commodified nature inside, reinforced the ideological construction of the private sphere as the utopia of the autonomous and the protected, and of the modern private individual as clean, pure, and free of fear and anxiety.

The conceptual distinction between *good* and *bad* water also perpetuated (and in many ways accentuated) the gender distinction related to its handling. From washing the floor to cleaning the dead (Illich 1986), handling water in the domestic sphere (Shiva 1997; Hill, 1972) has traditionally been the task of women, whilst handling water outside the domestic sphere (from field irrigation to dam construction and the conquest of the sea) has traditionally been the task of men (Kendie 1996). However, when water became domesticated in the western world, the traditional gender distinction around handling water did not change: it was again the 'wet rooms' of the bourgeois home that became the place of women in the domestic spatial arrangements that accompanied the social division of labour, thus endorsing further the confinement of women to the domestic sphere (Seager 1997).

> Never before had a woman worshiped [cleaned] her home the way I worshiped [cleaned] mine ... I ... threw away the mop pole and fell on my knees to mop the floor with my own palms, with devotion. And while mopping I was caressing it [the floor] ... the way a mother would caress her ill child.
>
> (Maria Iordanidou, *The Twirling of the Circle*, 1987, p. 36;
> author's translation)

In the above passage from the semi-autobiographical novel set in post-war Athens, the narrator, a woman who works hard to support her family, takes both pride and pleasure in making time to clean her home. In an almost perverse manner, cleaning her home becomes an act of worship as it becomes identified with caring for her family. The 'elevated status of housekeeping' (Rose 1993:121) expressed in the identification of an act of worship with that of cleaning one's home has even permeated the language. In the original Greek text, the word 'λατρεύω' signifies both 'to worship' and 'to clean'. Thus, the act of worshiping one's home (and family) collapses linguistically with that of cleaning one's home, indicating the extent to which the role of women as home cleaners and water handlers is socially and culturally embedded (Pollock 1988; Young 1990).

By contrast, the process of taming *bad* water as well as that of producing *good* water – the construction of dams, wells, aqueducts, the irrigation of fields, etc. – still remains predominantly the task of men (McDowell, 1983; Rose 1993). In short, the gender division between places and activities of production and reproduction (Hayford 1974) was itself reproduced through the process of domestication of water in the western world.

The control of nature's water also contributed to the production of the new set of marks of social distinction that could be embodied by the modern individual. As Swyngedouw (1997) contends, the olfactorial segregation between class and gender (rich smelling clean/poor smelling foul; women smelling of roses/men smelling of tobacco) was made easier with the domestication of water (see also Pratt 1990). The dwelling places of modernity embody the material connections that make the social construction of bodies possible, by first materially constructing 'others', in the form of natural or social processes, and then keeping them outside.

## Keeping 'the other' outside: exclusion as an act of creating space

In the opening quote of this chapter, Ruskin defines the 'true nature of home' as 'a shelter from anomie and division'. Dirt, fear, and anxiety stemming from social and natural processes are supposed to have been 'exiled' from the isolated private space of the home and instead confined (if not relegated) to the urban sphere or to nature. Thus, excluding socio-natural processes as 'the other' becomes a *prerequisite* for the construction of the familiar space of the home. The inside becomes safe, familiar, and independent not only by excluding rain, cold, and pollution, but also by keeping fear, anxiety, social upheaval, and inequality outside.

Of course, the practice of keeping *natural elements* outside the home is not particularly new. The whole purpose of building a home throughout human history has been precisely to establish a level of control over the interaction between the edifice and its environment; to construct an inside in opposition to an outside. However, what distinguishes the modern home from earlier forms of 'dwellings' is that modernist planning design and engineering established practices and technologies of unprecedented control of both produced nature and social relations. Laying down a sophisticated set of networks for the flow of socio-natural processes (water, sewage, electricity, gas, etc.), was complemented by the laying down of a set of rules for the flow of socio-economic processes (zoning of urban functions and land use, movement of pedestrians and vehicles, distinction between places of production, reproduction and recreation, etc.). Technological advancement (plumbing, central heating, air conditioning, etc.) made the exclusion and control of natural elements more efficient and sophisticated than ever before. Unwelcome social and natural elements (from sewage to homelessness) were also exiled underneath or outside the modern home, below the streets and inside the walls, eliminated into underground passages, sent to a domain separate to that of the dwelling places of the modern individual. These practices of modernist planning failed to deliver the modernist promise to 'open up' space for everybody; instead, they rendered the line that separates the inside from the outside, the public from the private, more solid than ever before, virtually impenetrable.

However, when we move from the discursive/representational level to the material/spatial foundations of the separation between public/private, nature/home, it can be argued that this same act of exclusion that separates and demarcates the inside from the outside, in fact puts these two supposed 'opposites' in a dialectical relationship of interdependence to each other, within which they are both sustained and continue to function. Whilst the inside (the familiar) needs the outside (the unfamiliar) to construct and define itself as a distinct space, the excluded outside in turn functions by following the logic of the inside. In doing so, the outside always remains in a certain way inside, subject to the rules and the logic dictated by the inside (Faust *et al.* 1992): there can be no homelessness without an economic, political, and social process that produces 'the home' as a commodity; no refugees without practices of exile from a 'country of origin'; no margin without a centre; no periphery without a core. The very act of trying to keep social and natural processes outside inevitably puts the home into a dialectical relationship of *dependence on/autonomy from* the very processes that it tries to exclude.

## The selective porosity of the modern home: a simultaneous act of need and denial of 'the other'

As we have seen, natural elements are not in fact kept altogether outside the modern home; instead, they are *selectively* allowed to enter after they have undergone significant material and social transformations, after they have been produced, purified, and commodified. Polluted air and recycled water, for example, have to undergo a complex chemical and social process of purification before they are allowed to enter the domestic sphere of consumption. In fact, the more human activities transform nature, the more the intervention of technology (e.g. water purifiers, air conditioning, ionisers) becomes necessary in order to 'cancel' the effects of this transformation and to render nature *good* again before it is allowed to enter the private home in the form of a commodity. Thus, although excluded ideologically, natural processes (just like social processes) remain connected materially to the inside of the home, constituting an integral part of its material production and its smooth function.

Moreover, despite the ideological and visual exclusion of *bad* nature from the modern home, this ostracised *bad* nature is largely the by-product of the metabolism of the *good* nature that is allowed inside the home: sewage is the by-product of domestic water consumption; urban smog is the result of the need to produce warmth inside one's home and to commute for miles in order to inhabit the suburban domestic paradises (Swyngedouw and Kaika 2000). Viewed in this light, the socially constructed categories of *good* and *bad* nature become blurred. The purified water that flows into the modern home is as much the product of the interaction between the physical environment and human beings as the water that flows out of the modern home in the form of sewage. However, the material and social networks involved in the production of *good* nature and in the metabolism of *bad* nature remain invisible, hidden outside and underneath the modern home, and are kept away from the eyes of the home dweller, buried inside the walls of the modern home or underneath the modern city. Thus, the function of the modern home as safe and autonomous is predicated not only upon the exclusion of *bad* nature from its premises, but also upon the *visual* exclusion of the networks and social relations that produce and transport *good* nature into the domestic and pump *bad* nature back into the urban domain (Graham and Marvin 1996). This way, the networks of production of the socio-natural hybrids that enter into and are expelled from the modern home, also constitute the 'other', the 'outside' to this modern institution. Although visually excluded, these networks of socio-natural transformation lie at the core of the production of the functionality of the modern city and at the heart of the production of the safety and familiarity of the modern home.

For example, while the home dweller experiences the familiarity and comfort of his/her domestic tap, bathtub, or swimming pool, the intricate set of networks that produce this bliss remains invisible to him/her, hidden underneath and outside the house. It is precisely this visual exclusion of production networks, of metabolised nature and of social power relations, that contributes to the production of a sense of the familiar inside one's home. In a deceitful way, remaining unfamiliar with the above socio-natural networks is a prerequisite for feeling familiar within one's own home.

Thus, although the modern home is ideologically constructed as independent and *disconnected* from natural processes, its function is heavily dependent upon its material *connections* to these very processes which are mediated through a series of networks and social power relations. The 'other' in the form of natural processes or social relations of production is simultaneously inside yet outside, domestic yet unfamiliar, homely yet unhomely.

In the light of the above argument, Heidegger's metaphorical description of the divide between the inside and the outside of the home as a 'line' becomes rather too rigid to express the complex dialectical relation that exists between these two spaces and to capture the ever shifting boundaries between the inside and the outside of the domestic sphere. Perhaps a more pertinent way to describe this line would be to compare it to a *porous membrane*, a membrane which separates the two spaces, yet still allows significant but controlled interaction between them. This membrane works as a filter which allows certain elements in, while excluding others. Walter Benjamin refers to *porosity* as 'the lack of clear boundaries between phenomena, a permeation of one thing by another, a merger of, for example old and new, public and private, sacred and profane' (Gilloch 1996: 25). By keeping out the undesired (most of the time non-commodified) natural and social 'things' and processes, and by welcoming the desirable ones (filtered, produced and commodified), the modern home has acquired a *selective porosity*, by maintaining a set of invisible connections that enable it to function in its supposedly autonomous manner.

Representative of modernity's inherent contradictions, the modern home in a simultaneous act of need and denial, hosts in its guts everything it tries to keep outside. It is its connection to everything it tries to disconnect from, to the invisible material and social relations that lie underneath its visible counterparts, that makes the modern home appear to be functioning in an autonomous way. In a subversive manner, remaining unfamiliar with the socio-natural networks that produce and maintain it is a prerequisite for feeling familiar within one's own home.

## The threatening geographies of the familiar: the invisible 'other' as the domestic uncanny

I have argued that the construction of the familiarity of the domestic sphere as the place of peace, free from division and anomie, but also as the epitome of the familiar is predicated upon keeping the social and material elements that constitute 'the other' invisible, hidden outside. Yet at times of crisis, hidden elements can surface unexpectedly, and familiar objects can behave in unusual ways. Blackouts, when the flick of a switch no longer results in the instant provision of light, or water shortages when a tap goes dry, prompt us to think of the intricate system of networks, pipes, and social relations of production that make the modern home tick, yet remain invisible.

Such incidents expose the limits of domestic bliss, and reveal its dependency on social relations of production. By doing so, they generate a feeling of 'not being at home in one's own home' (Vidler 1992: 4). This *unhomely* feeling within the *homely* was termed by Sigmund Freud as 'The Uncanny' [*Unheimlich*]. In his essay with the same title Freud notes that the German word *'heimlich'* which signifies the homely, the familiar, can also mean 'the concealed, what is kept from sight, withheld from others' (Freud [1919] 1990: 342–344). The linguistic opposite of *'heimlich'*, the word *'unheimlich'* signifies the thing that 'ought to have remained secret and hidden but has come to light' (ibid: 345). It is precisely the familiar character of the *heimlich* (homely), which produces the *unheimlich* (*unhomely*) effect when the former behaves in ways outside the ordinary, when things that ought to have remained hidden come to light. Freud investigated epileptic fits or manifestations of insanity, as instances of the 'uncanny' effect produced when the predictable nature of the familiar acts in unpredictable ways (ibid.: 347).

In spatial terms, the haunted house is the most cited expression of the uncanny, a manifestation of the unfamiliar within what is supposed to be the most familiar space. However, a building showing its 'guts', the networks that support its function, can produce a similar uncanny effect. Renzo Piano's and Richard Rogers' Pompidou Centre in Paris (1972–1976) is a good example of the uncanny effect produced by turning a building inside-out. The pipes, lines, and cables of this building seemed to be 'out of place' when they unexpectedly appeared on its façade in 1976 (Silver 1994). This appearance of typically hidden elements, although widely praised by 'informed' scholars and architects, was not originally equally appreciated by the Parisian public that remained perplexed for a while at the bold revelation of the building's guts.[2] Closer to the experience of the 'everyday', a disrupted domestic routine like a dry tap, a dripping tap, a burst pipe, or piled up refuse, can produce a similar feeling of discomfort and anxiety, whereby 'one no longer feels at home in his most familiar environment' (Heidegger, cited in Wigley 1996: 109). The surfacing of things that ought to remain hidden also undermines the air of familiarity that a home is supposed to exhale.

One of the reasons why anxiety and discomfort are produced by a 'domestic network' crisis is precisely because it forces us to reflect on the existence of things and social and economic relations to which the home is connected and which, when disrupted, render the 'normal' function of our lives anomalous and reveal that the familiarity based on the supposed autonomy of the private space is itself a form of alienation. It is for this reason that Heidegger urges us to interrogate the familiar, since 'the familiar carries an air of harmlessness and ease, which causes us to pass lightly over what really deserves to be questioned' (Heidegger, cited in Wigley 1996: 109). Familiarity can veil the complex fabric of social and spatial relations involved in its own production. The familiarity of the domestic space conceals the 'violence' (in the form of social power relations) dwelling in this institution. Being unaware of this 'violence', being trapped in a constructed domestic familiarity, we remain 'alienated' in the very space which is supposed to be the most familiar to us. The bourgeois home operates as a blissful private shelter insofar as it is selectively sealed from the world outside. One can be lost forever inside one's own painstakingly created familiarity, insofar as one is confined inside it. By eliminating (visually, perceptually, and discursively-ideologically) the material connections and social relations that make its existence possible, the modern 'home' acquires the properties of both a refuge and a prison (Bachelard 1948). The innocence of the familiar, if not interrogated, 'alienates by masking a more fundamental alienation: the obviousness and self-assurance of the average ways in which things have been interpreted as such' (Wigley 1996: 109).

This form of alienation not only makes us prisoners of our own fears and needs, but also facilitates practices of exclusion. The supposedly undisputed imperative of maintaining public order and domestic bliss is often used as the main justification for political practices of exclusion: from the emergence of North American gated communities to the South African Apartheid regime, such practices are performed is the name of keeping *social processes* under control. But, in a stunningly similar manner, practices of social exclusion and political hegemony occur also in the name of keeping *natural processes* under control. The process of burying urban rivers underground in the name of keeping *bad* nature away has been invariably connected to the clearance of the slums along the banks of urban rivers, and was, more often than not, hailed by the authorities as an 'inevitable' side effect of the necessary process of sanitising urban space (Boyer 1983; Gandy 1999). When the Seine (Zenne), in Brussels was covered during the nineteenth century, the settlements around its banks were swept away, giving way to what now constitutes the 'centre ville', and to emblematic examples of nineteenth-century bourgeois architecture. In the same way, the embankment of the Thames in London was part of the glorification of the British Empire, while also contributing to what Oliver (2000: 229) refers to as 'cultural amnesia': a process which goes beyond changing the public's ideas of what a 'natural' river should look like.

Although these examples are drawn from the early period of rationalisation of urban space in the western world, similar practices are still with us. Swyngedouw (2003) explores how in present-day Guayaquil, Ecuador, mechanisms of social exclusion ensure that water flows abundantly into private pools and water fountains inside the secluded, policed, private bourgeois homes, while 36 per cent of the city's population lacks access to piped potable water. Gandy (1997) interprets the introduction of environmental management technologies in New York, as a means of creating new investment opportunities for surplus capital. Nevarez (1996) investigates Southern California, where public anxiety induced by the possibility of an imminent water crisis became a major political and economic tool for a consent-building exercise in favour of importing additional water to the area. Elsewhere (Kaika 2003), I document similar practices in early 1990s Athens, when due to a prolonged drought period taps inside people's homes refused to provide their services and became a form of domestic uncanny: familiar objects which behaved in unfamiliar ways. From being invisible and unproblematised, the connections between the house, the city, and nature's water became the number one topic of media coverage and public awareness, a source of public anxiety and a threat to domestic bliss.

The above examples illustrate how the anxiety produced by the uncanny can be used as a political tool for the manipulation of public opinion. As Sibley (1992: 245–246) contends, anxiety can be deepened by the creation of a false sense of security. If this holds true, then it would appear that the modernist enterprise to create binary distinctions and boundaries in order to do away with fear and anxiety, actually served to deepen the very same problem it tried to eradicate. However, as we shall explore in the final part of this chapter, the unexpected surfacing of typically hidden elements which brings to the foreground a recognition of the condition of alienation within the most familiar of environments, can also become a source of knowledge and emancipation.

## Interrogating the familiar: from anxiety to emancipation?

> We are nomads born, haptic creatures, and we spend our lives forgetting it. ... We pile up stones feverishly in an attempt to reproduce the container, the vessel ... We, like Sisyphus, never reach the goal because the impossibility of so doing is programmed into the rules of the game.
>
> (Bloomer 1993: 32)

Bloomer's assertion of the impossibility of constructing a familiar environment appears to be standing at the antipode of Ruskin's century older declaration of the feasibility of such an enterprise. Insofar as Ruskin's declaration echoes the optimism of the Enlightenment with respect to the possibility of doing away with human fear and alienation, Bloomer's quote echoes the post-modernist denial of the possibility of doing so and the acceptance of the condition of human alienation as an inevitable way of being. However, these two viewpoints share more in common than might appear at first glance. For, although Bloomer appears to disagree with Ruskin about the possibility of achieving *materially* the 'vessel' in the form of the familiar 'home', she nevertheless subscribes fully, along with Ruskin, to the sacredness of the platonic *ideal-type* of 'the home' as the sublime, 'the vessel', 'the container', and to the importance of trying to reproduce it. What Bloomer and Ruskin have in common is that they portray alienation and fear as the result of failing to produce *materially* this ideal-type, which remains sacred.

Somewhere between Enlightenment's optimism and post-modernist pessimism lies modernity's contradictory efforts to construct a disconnected modern home and a disconnected modern individual within a world that becomes increasingly connected; the contradiction between the ideology of the disconnected home as a sacred principle, and the impossibility of producing it materially. Reflecting this contradiction, the modern home became simultaneously both the *par excellence* cultural sign of sublime modern living and its antipode: the *par excellence* cultural sign of the uncanny, of the alienation of the modern individual within his/her most familiar environment (Vidler 1992). Indeed, in literature, art, media, film, etc. the home functions as the representation of the celebrated modernist dream of sublime western living, but it also functions as the paradigmatic cultural sign of the antipode: of fear and anxiety. From Edgar Allan Poe's (1809–1849) short stories, to Kafka's (1883–1924) *Metamorphosis*, to Harold Pinter's (1930–2008) *Homecoming* the home moves away from its role as a signifier of familiarity and bliss and becomes instead the emblematic representation of the uncanny. By putting one small detail of the familiar environment 'out of place' – yet still within the familiar domestic sphere – by revealing the contradictions and the *uncanny* qualities of modern living, nothing remains the same; the sublime, normalised character of modern dwelling is upset. In a similar manner, the unashamedly modernist movements of dadaïsm and surrealism also disputed the sacredness and the sublime character of modern living and used the *uncanny* to replicate the individual's alienation within his/her own private space. Duchamp's ready-made objects included re-branding *urinoirs* as 'fountains' and displaying them on a pedestal as works of art. In a similar vein, Magritte's series of paintings entitled *The Treachery of the Images* (*La Trahison des images*) features everyday objects in great representational detail, yet, a title above the object informs us that they are not what they seem: '*ceci n'est pas une pomme*', '*ceci n'est pas une pipe*', etc. These works produce an effect of feeling unfamiliar and ill at ease with the most familiar objects, words, concepts, and spaces. The subversive use of the uncanny in these movements aims at bringing the viewer/reader face to face with their alienation experienced within their most familiar environment and with their most familiar objects.

However, the modern home does not function only as a *sign* or a *representation* of the uncanny (Vidler 1992: 12). Once stripped of its well-constructed familiarity, or during moments of crisis, the home is revealed as the spatial manifestation of the alienation of the dweller that inhabits it. In a simultaneous act of need and denial, the home guards in its guts and its underbelly everything it tries to keep outside: sewerage, pipelines, dirt, rats, pests, crime, disease, the homeless, the crisis, etc.

Thus, questioning the familiarity of our most familiar environments can be a subversive act, not only because it reveals our alienation, but also because it undermines the belief in the possibility of producing a space that is totally disconnected from both social and natural processes. Questioning this belief becomes particularly important at a time when excess individualism has, at large, replaced civil action, and when the belief that 'no-one any longer has any alternatives to capitalism' (Giddens 1998: 24, 43) has substituted imaginings of possibilities for human emancipation and of spaces where these possibilities can be fought for. Exposing the dysfunctionality of the private spaces where blind individualism can be practised in isolation, calls for a reflection on alternative ways of engaging with the world. As Mary Douglas suggested, exploring the margins is important since it opens both destructive and creative possibilities (Douglas 1970). Exploring the uncanny materiality of 'the other' in the form of the invisible metabolised nature or technology networks reveals 'the individual', 'the social' and 'the natural' as a socio-natural continuum that disrupts the boundaries between the above socially constructed categories. Demonstrating the ideological construction of private spaces as autonomous and disconnected and insisting on their material and social connections calls for an end to individualisation, fragmentation, and disconnectedness that are searched for within the bliss of one's home. It calls for engaging in political and social action, which is, invariably, decidedly public.

## Acknowledgements

This article is an abridged version of Kaika, M. (2004) 'Interrogating the Geographies of the Familiar: Domesticating Nature and Constructing the Autonomy of the Modern Home', *International Journal of Urban and Regional Research*, 28: 265–286.

## Notes

1   Although for two of them, the Walbrook and the Fleet, the covering began much earlier, in 1463 and 1732 respectively (Halliday, 1999).
2   The political cultural process of 'normalisation' of the original uncanny character of this building is beyond the scope of this chapter. For a 'biography' of the Pompidou centre, see Silver (1994).

# Bibliography

Bloomer, J. (1993) *Architecture and the Text: The (S)crypts of Joyce and Piranesi*. New Haven, CT: Yale University Press.

Boyer, C. (1983) *Dreaming the Rational City*. Cambridge, MA: MIT Press.

Chappells, H., Shove, E. and Selby, J. (1999) 'Reservoirs, Pipes and Taps: A Sociology of Water, Control and Flow', paper presented at a conference on Sustainability, Risk and Nature: The Political Ecology of Water in Advanced Societies, School of Geography, University of Oxford, March.

Cleaver, F. and Elson, D. (1995) *Women and Water Resources: Continued Marginalisation and New Policies*. London: International Institute for Environment and Development.

Curtis, V. (1986) *Women and the Transport of Water*. London: Intermediate Technologies Publications.

Douglas, M. (1970) *Purity and Danger: An Analysis of Concepts of Pollution and Taboo*. Harmondsworth: Penguin.

Faust, D., Leitner, H., Nagar, M. B. R., Sheppard, E., Van Drasek, B. and Zhou, Y. (1992) 'Collective Response: Social Justice, Difference, and the City', *Environment and Planning D: Society and Space*, 10: 589–595.

Foucault, M. (1977) *Discipline and Punish: The Birth of the Prison*. Harmondsworth: Penguin.

Freud, S. ([1919]1990) *Art and Literature*. vol. 14. London: Penguin.

Gandy, M. (1997) 'The Making of a Regulatory Crisis: Restructuring New York City's Water Supply', *Transactions; Institute of British Geographers*, 22: 338–358.

Gandy, M. (1999) 'The Paris Sewers and the Rationalization of Urban Space', *Transactions of the Institute of British Geographers*, 24: 23–44.

Giddens, A. (1998) *The Third Way*. Cambridge: Polity.

Gilloch, G. (1996) *Myth and Metropolis*. Cambridge: Polity.

Graham, S. and Marvin, S. (1996) *Telecommunications and the City*. London: Routledge.

Halliday, S. (1999) *The Great Stink of London: Sir Joseph Bazalgette and the Cleansing of the Victorian Metropolis*. Stroud: Sutton.

Haraway, D. (1991) *Simians, Cyborgs and Women: The Reinvention of Nature*. London: Free Association Books.

Hayford, A. (1974) 'The Geography of Women: An Historical Introduction', *Antipode*, 6: 1–19.

Heidegger, M. (1962) *Being and Time*. Oxford: Blackwell.

Hill, P. (1972) *Rural Hausa: A Village and a Setting*. Cambridge: Cambridge University Press.

Iordanidou, M. (1987) *The Twirling of the Circle [Στου κύκλου τα γυρίσματα]*. Athens: Hestia.

Kaika, M. (2003) 'Constructing Scarcity and Sensationalising Water Politics: 170 Days That Shook Athens', *Antipode*, 35: 919–954.

Kaika, M. (2004) 'Interrogating the Geographies of the Familiar: Domesticating Nature and Constructing the Autonomy of the Modern Home', *International Journal of Urban and Regional Research*, 28: 265–286.

Keil, R. (1998) *Los Angeles: Globalization, Urbanization, and Social Struggles*. New York: John Wiley & Son Ltd.

Kendie, S.B. (1996) 'Some Factors Influencing Effective Utilization of Drinking Water', *Environmental Management*, 20(1): 10.

Lahiji, N. and Friedman, D.S. (1997) *Plumbing: Sounding Modern Architecture*. New York: Princeton Architectural Press.

Latour, B. (1993) *We Have Never Been Modern*. Trans. C. Porter. London: Harvester Wheatsheaf.

Latour, B. and Hermant, E. (1998) *Paris Ville Invisible*. Paris: La Decouverte.

Nevarez, L. (1996) 'Just Wait Until There's a Drought: Mediating Environmental Crises for Urban Growth', *Antipode*, 28: 246–272.

Oliver, S. (2000) 'The Thames Embankment and the Disciplining of Nature in Modernity', *The Geographical Journal*, 166: 227–238.

Pollock, G. (1988) *Vision and Difference: Femininity, Feminism and the Histories of Art*. London: Routledge.

Pratt, G. (1990) 'Feminist Analyses of the Restructuring of Urban Life', *Urban Geography*, 11: 594–605.

Rose, G. (1993) *Feminism and Geography: The Limits of Geographical Knowledge*. Cambridge: Polity Press.

Seager, J. (1997) 'The Earth Is Not Your Mother', in L. McDowell and J. P. Sharp (eds) *Space, Gender, Knowledge: Feminist Readings*. London: Arnold.

Sennett, R. (1990) *The Conscience of the Eye: The Design and Social Life of Cities*. New York: Knopf.

Shiva, V. (1997) 'Women in Nature', in L. McDowell and J. P. Sharp (eds) *Space, Gender, Knowledge: Feminist Readings*. London: Arnold.

Sibley, D. (1992) 'The Binary City', *Urban Studies*, 38: 239–250.

Silver, N. (1994) *The Making of Beaubourg: A Building Biography of the Centre Pompidou, Paris*. Cambridge, MA: MIT Press.

Swyngedouw, E. (1997) 'Power, Nature and the City', *Environment and Planning A*, 29: 311–332.

Swyngedouw, E. (2003) *Flows of Power*. Oxford: Oxford University Press.

Swyngedouw, E. and Kaika, M. (2000) 'The Environment of the City or ... The Urbanisation of Nature', in G. Bridge and S. Watson (eds) *A Companion to the City*. Oxford: Blackwell, pp. 567–580.

Vidler, A. (1992) *The Architectural Uncanny: Essays in the Modern Unhomely*. Cambridge, MA: MIT Press.

Wescoat, J.L. (1995) 'The "Right of Thirst" for Animals in Islamic Law: A Comparative Approach', *Environment and Planning D: Society and Space*, 13: 637–654.

Wigley, M. (1996) *The Architecture of Deconstruction: Derrida's Haunt*. Cambridge, MA: The MIT Press.

Young, I. M. (1990) *Throwing Like a Girl and Other Essays in Feminist Philosophy and Social Theory*. Bloomington, IN: University of Indiana Press.

# Chapter 7

# Kampala's sanitary regime
## Whose toilet is it anyway?

*Stephanie Terreni Brown*

## Introduction

This chapter explores the sanitary regime of the capital city of Uganda, Kampala. It looks at the ways in which shit matters by exploring how sanitation infrastructures work, how they are understood, and how they are performed. The chapter focuses on the sanitary contestations that are apparent within the city's wetlands along the Nakivubo Channel, by looking at the debates and controversies over toileting provision that are being waged in the informal settlement of Namuwongo, where approximately 12,000 people share access to eighteen toilet stalls.[1] The stories detailed by residents during ethnographic fieldwork in 2010/11 elucidate structures of power, and reveal attempts and struggles to participate in urban life.

This chapter draws inspiration from both postcolonial urban critiques (Roy 2004, 2005; Simone 2004; Robinson 2006; Myers 2011) and discussants of the right to the city (Lefebvre 1996; Dikeç 2002, 2007; Purcell 2002; Staeheli, Mitchell et al. 2002) to argue that sanitation projects in Kampala are entrenched within hierarchies of power and privilege that conceal and legitimise urban inequalities. Jennifer Robinson (2006) argues against definitions and categorisations of cities in hierarchical ways, and posits that this creates a bifurcation between cities of the Global North and South based on ideas about modernity and development(alism). Robinson shows that such classification privileges some cities over others, and creates a system that encourages the emulation of modernity through development practices, thus favouring flows of global capital over the demands of city residents. Furthermore, hierarchies of power intensively operate *within* cities, privileging the demands of some urban residents over others (Isin 2002), with consequence for how socioeconomic inequality is produced across space, and for the poorest urban residents and their ability to participate in decisions that affect them (Purcell 2002). Hierarchies *of* and *within* cities, then, serve to exemplify modernity and urbanity, with the former framing the city itself as problematic, and the latter positing certain areas within the city as the epitome of urban crisis, most often identified as a crisis of 'slum'. This 'spatialisation of the Other' (Dikeç 2002: 93) increases unevenness and inequality, and divests urban residents of their ability to fully participate in city life. Thus, in Kampala, the structural dynamics of the urban social imaginary contains and limits the space and the people within, with Namuwongo emerging as the 'proper' place for slum residents within the order of the city. Those in positions of power affect demands for sanitation provision in the city in very different ways precisely because of this imagined urban hierarchy, enacting the socio-spatial dialectic (Soja 1980; Dikeç 2002, 2007).

The consequences of this spatial fix of poverty and impoverished opportunities for sanitation provision in the city are profound – certain spaces and residents, such as Namuwongo, are limited in accessing sanitation and in the ability to participate in dialogue about Kampala. And it is this ability to participate in urban decision-making that is crucial to Lefebvre's understanding of the right to the city, which he in part describes as fostering the interests 'of all those who *inhabit*' (Lefebvre 1996: 158). The right to the city opens up the possibility of including the most marginalised residents of Kampala in what happens in and to the city, and points to both an analytical purpose and a moral imperative to disaggregate the categories that saturate individuals' lives in informal settlements such as Namuwongo in order to understand how this spatialisation of power both transforms and reinforces marginality, while concurrently, and more optimistically, unveiling possibilities for a different way of thinking about, planning, and living in the city.

The following section introduces the reader to Kampala, before discussing the relationship between informality and the sanitary regime. The chapter then places this in relation to the ethnographic fieldwork exploring everyday toileting practices. Through a discussion of toileting performances, I show how residents' knowledges of bodily waste and sanitation infrastructure challenge the orthodoxy of the slum metonym, and indicate alternative readings for urban infrastructural practices.

## Shit inequalities

Kampala, the capital of Uganda, is the country's largest urban area, yet in contrast to popular depictions of African cities (see Davis 2006; Hobkinson 2011), it is not a sprawling megacity of tens of millions of people. Its population is estimated to be approximately 1.7 million people, with an annual growth rate of 5 per cent (UBOS 2011), and while the city's population is purported to be higher than this estimate, it is clear that the city's sewerage infrastructure reaches only a small proportion of residents (Kyambadde 2005). The National Water and Sewerage Corporation estimate that its main sewer network reaches less than 10 per cent of the city, with the rest of the population relying on a variety of on-site sanitation solutions (NWSC 2004). The current sewerage treatment works (STW), the Bugolobi STW, was originally constructed in the 1940s to service a city of up to a million people, but a lack of investment and technology upgrades means that much of the plant is not in use, and what is in working order is hugely over capacity, often leading to an overflow of sewage into the Nakivubo Channel, and into Lake Victoria's Inner Murchison Bay (Kansiime and Nalubega 1999). For residents not connected to the sewerage system, a combination of septic tanks, long drops, buckets and plastic bags have to be used to manage and eliminate their bodily waste. These different toileting methods and performances are largely dependent on differing socio-economic circumstances, and as such are integral components of the sanitary regime.

The concept of the sanitary regime takes inspiration from Collier and Lakoff's (2005) idea of 'regimes of living', which they describe, in part, as a methodological tool that 'refer[s] to a tentative and situated configuration of normative, technical, and political elements that are brought into alignment in situations that present ethical problems – that is, situations in which the question of how to live is at stake' (ibid.: 23). For the sanitary regime, then, ethical problems of toileting are bound up with questions of health, civility, aesthetics and modernity, and I argue that this operates in distinctly spatial ways. To understand Kampala's sanitary regime requires deciphering how the city is produced, valued, and managed, and yet many of the terms and concepts that have been deployed to describe cities like Kampala obscure the interconnections between different places and different lives. Annaya Roy persuasively argues for studies of urbanism of the Global South to challenge its familiar metonyms ('slum', 'megacity'), in a bid to go beyond analyses of bounded spaces of poverty (Roy and Alsayyad 2004; Roy 2011). Roy challenges ontologies of Global South urbanism, one of the most ubiquitous of which is urban informality. Informality is, she contends, a 'mode of the production of space' that does not serve to divide formality from informality, as is often assumed, but rather operates in a variety of forms throughout city space (Roy 2011). Informality is, then, not reduced to the preserve of the slum, but is productive throughout the city, 'as much the purview of wealthy urbanites as it is of slum dwellers' (ibid.: 233). Thus, by conceptualising the processes and relations that constitute how the city is produced, it is possible to elucidate how domination, power and oppression function (Young 1990).

Informality, as an expression of power, is critical to understanding the sanitation regime in Kampala, as it effects imaginations and developments of service provision and infrastructure, as well as determining that which is formal, legitimate, and felonious. Furthermore, imaginations of informality influence the very performance and materiality of toileting, with certain toileting behaviours and tools rendered improper, thus providing justification for the interpretation of space, activities and people as illegal. Urbanity and propriety are important for an understanding of the sanitary regime, as 'cityness' often delineates modernity and civility. And, as studies detailing relationships between sanitation and civility attest, perceptions of bodily waste and dirt inform socio-spatial coding practices of order and status (Douglas 1966; Corbin 1986; Laporte 2002). Within the sanitary regime, then, it is not just the acts of toileting, or the excrement produced, that contribute to such imaginations of spatial limits and disgust, as the 'big' infrastructure is equally important. The flush toilet is the epitome of urban, personal, sanitary propriety, and the sewage treatment plant is its equivalent for the manifold toileting waste produced by a city. Both adhere to certain 'civilised' principles: that they contain waste, and minimise both visual and olfactory contact with bodily waste. This sensory sanitary aesthetic speaks to Asher Ghertner's work in Delhi, where he suggests there is an 'aesthetic mode of governing' that influences infrastructure developments in cities attempting to become 'world-class' (Ghertner 2011: 280). The aesthetics of things (people, objects, buildings, performances, spaces) provides a codifying, and therefore a justifying, logic that determines propriety within the rubric of city-making worlding practices; and, more than being simply about toileting decorum, sanitary aesthetics influence ideas about who has a right to take part in debates about city life.

Sanitation inequality in Kampala is legitimised, then, as particular spaces and practices are characterised as being unsanitary, unhealthy and poverty-ridden slum spaces in direct contrast to what a modern city *should* be (Flood 2002; Ghertner 2011). Discussions of sanitation, urban space and power thus echo broader debates about marginalisation in urban contexts. Imaginaries of the slum, and of slum residents, lend weight to the conviction that particular individuals or groups are not part of the city, and do not share the characteristics to make them effective in participating in debates about the city and its developments (see Staeheli, Mitchell *et al.* 2010).

The slum imaginary posits the behaviours and practices of the residents of Namuwongo as uncivil and unacceptable, excluding them from debates about the use of the wetlands, while also serving to legitimise the lack of sanitation provision in the area. Sanitation is a critical component sustaining urban imaginaries of difference, and is a way of analysing how such forces manifest themselves in Kampala. Community members in Namuwongo utilise a variety of techniques to combat the near absence of sanitation infrastructure, as well as using it as an advocating mechanism to fight for better services in the area. I would like to suggest that informal methods of toileting, such as the 'wrap and throw' method of shitting into a plastic bag and throwing it away (Black and Fawcett 2008: 209), is a vernacular form of toileting. Such vernacular toileting is used in areas of Kampala where there is a lack of sanitary infrastructure, such as in Namuwongo. It is known as 'flying toilets'. This act of throwing bags full of shit, where people act as infrastructure in its absence, is not one that is a defilement of public space. This is not, as Ayona Datta argues about open defecation in Delhi squatter settlements, 'a resistance against a bourgeois order', but is rather 'a mundane politics of everyday survival' (Datta 2012: 118). To interpret vernacular toileting as uncivilised and 'dirty' is therefore to ignore the inherent logic of the flying toilet as a system to manage the containment and expulsion of bodily waste, which is exactly what the flying toilet does. You shit into a plastic bag and wrap it up. This conceals the faeces and limits further emanation of its smell. You then throw it away; the shit is no longer in your home. Throwing it away into some space outside of the home does not necessarily mean defiling public space, but is rather transferring it to 'that which is not inside' (ibid.: 117).

The dominant interpretation of Kampala, however, sees flying toilets as dirty, disordered, and illogical. The limited conception of, and lack of a willingness to understand, the logics of vernacular toileting practices have an impact upon development projects that seek to improve sanitation infrastructures in informal areas. My research suggests that inhabitants of Kampala's informal areas are divested of full participation in these projects because they are assumed to lack knowledge of what they want and need. Further, not recognising the logics of vernacular toileting and adhering to the principle that this is 'dirty' promotes intervention to 'develop' informal areas. This has the potential to further marginalise the existing inhabitants from urban life through processes of gentrification and revanchism (Smith 1990; Wacquant 2008; McFarlane 2012).

To understand how this takes places and comes to matter requires, I believe, a methodological commitment to follow 'the everyday' (Lees 2003; Hart 2004; Dyck 2005), and indeed to recognise the 'multiple sites of agency in the world beyond the human' (Hawkins 2009: 188). To inquire about sanitation is, certainly, to inquire about its infrastructure, but it is also very much about the routine acts of toileting, performativity and materiality. This approach brings together Lefebvre's (1991) concern with the importance of the politics of everyday trivialities with Robinson's (2006) call to challenge the received wisdoms about cityness, to look to the political associations imbued within the sanitary materiality of urban life. While there is a burgeoning literature on urban infrastructures, much of it tends to shy away from the 'down and dirty' performativities of everyday toileting; indeed, the focus has tended towards the trope of catastrophe and infrastructural politics (Gandy 2006a, 2008; Kooy and Bakker 2008; McFarlane 2008; McFarlane and Rutherford 2008; Graham 2010), and upon shit's more palatable sanitation partners, water and rubbish (Fredericks 2006; Gandy 2006b; Kimani-Murage and Ngindu 2007; Fredericks 2008; Swyngedouw 2012).

A focus on the everyday aspects of sanitation, then, places an emphasis upon the politics of urban materialities that often follow different trajectories to city planning and its concurrent (mega)projects. There is a politics to shit, and the act of shitting, that does more than speak to Robinson's (2006) call to disrupt the hierarchies of urban analysis; rather, the performativity and materiality of defecation offer a way of thinking through the struggles, negotiations and emotions inherent in iterative, everyday acts (Scott 1985; Holloway and Hubbard 2001; Simone 2010). How the sanitation regime operates in the everyday enables a focus upon the very messiness of urban life, and the inherent (and productive) struggles therein; it fosters ways of thinking that grapple with the practicalities of 'how urban life takes place and gets done' (Swanton 2011: 345). This allows discussions about infrastructure and 'things' to be unfastened from the lens of accumulation, allowing other interrelated interpretive trajectories of performativity (Butler 1990; Gregson, Crang et al. 2010; Gregson, Watkins et al. 2010; Gregson 2011), materiality (Hawkins 2006, 2009; Whatmore 2006) and potentiality (Simone 2004, 2010; Pieterse 2006) of everyday urban life. One of the ways in which toileting performativities comes to matter in the imagination of socio-spatial difference in Kampala is through the use of flying toilets. The following section explores the use of flying toilets in Namuwongo.

## Flying toilets

Namuwongo is in the east of Kampala, sandwiched between the Industrial Area, middle-class residential areas and the Nakivubo wetlands. Its proximity to the centre of town, and to the city's industry, has meant that the number of middle income houses has increased substantially since the 1990s as the city entered a period of still on-going rapid population growth (Nyakaana, Sengendo et al. 2007). The north-eastern edge of Namuwongo lies astride the Nakivubo Channel, an open drainage canal that cuts through the city and empties into nearby Lake Victoria, and it is along a 2-kilometre stretch between this channel and the Namuwongo Road that approximately 12,000 residents live in informal settlements. This particular area of Namuwongo is popularly defined as a slum, and for the sake of brevity and in accordance with the naming colloquialisms of Kampala is defined from hereon as simply Namuwongo.[2]

Namuwongo has existed as a residential area along this stretch of land for over 50 years, but such longevity does not mean that the residents have protection or rights to remain living there. Namuwongo is a gazetted environmental area, with conservational wetland status, and is protected against construction (KCC 1994); this move simultaneously makes existing residences illegal, and prohibits the construction of new buildings. The population of the area has, however, continued to increase since the area's gazetting.

That the residents' homes are constructed on a wetland area, and are therefore considered illegal by the city authorities, lends itself to legitimising non-action with respect to service provision. Toilets cannot be built, it is argued, because 'the people are living there illegally should go' (interview with Kampala Capital City Authority [KCCA] Town Planner, 25 March 2011).[3] Thus, some of the 12,000 residents of Namuwongo must wait in line for hours during the dawn rush to use one of the 18 toilet stalls that cater for the whole area. Others use plastic bottles for their morning urination, and empty out buckets of faeces and urine into the nearby Nakivubo. Some school-going children will hold their bowel movements until they get to the school loos; others will go and toilet in the grass near the Channel, and many more will use *kaveera* (plastic bags) to defecate in. The *kaveera*, full with shit, are then thrown away, out of the household space (hence 'flying toilets').

The flying toilet is arguably the defining feature of Kampala's slums. It marks the informal settlement as more than unregulated urban space; it is the act that renders the space filthy and uncivilised, and is perceived as inhumane in its disgustingness. The flying toilet is the ultimate example of non-urbanity, relegating both the area and the people that inhabit it as un-urban, and unfit to participate in city life. The absence of flush toilets is also seen as a marker of non-urbanity. In the Ugandan urban imagination, latrines are intimately linked with rural life and their usage should be limited to 'up-country'.[4] The presence of latrines and flying toilets within the city, then, compromises the ability of Kampala to be thought of as a modern city; moreover, individuals using latrines and flying toilets are affected by what Pierre Bourdieu (1999) calls 'site/place effects' whereby inhabitants themselves become stigmatised from place association.

Such imaginations are shaped by the geopolitics of knowledge production about what cities are and what they should be, privileging Western affluent urban space and relegating those which are not (Grosfoguel 2002; Robinson 2006). This narrative privileges modernity and established types of cities (Robinson 2004; Ong 2011) and for Kampala, this places a great onus on it – as the sole city in Uganda, it is *the* representative space of urbanism and thus modernity in the country. Its occupants must, therefore, live and act in a way that is suitable to the collective modern urban project. The existence of 'up-country' toileting behaviours and practices contravenes this urban imagination, and threatens aspirations of modernisation; such areas must therefore be contained as best possible so as not to contaminate the rest of the city.[5] The following section explores some of the effects of this marginalisation, and details how some of the area's residents cope with the inadequate sanitation.

## Tactical toileting

Elizabeth, like many of her neighbours, rises early. She needs to wash, dress and eat, and get her five grandchildren ready for the day ahead. This would be a simple enough task if the amenities needed were nearby, available and free of charge to use. For Elizabeth, however, her mornings are a series of physically demanding challenges that see her navigating the uneven muddy ground to the Nakivubo Channel to empty last night's buckets of waste, filling up the jerry cans with water for drinking and washing, and roasting the yams for the day's sustenance. The children help with the chores, but she says, require constant chiding and prompting to do as she wishes and she constantly worries that their lack of energy is because they are hungry or sick.[6]

The children's health is a relentless concern for Elizabeth. Their mother, her daughter, died from HIV/AIDS, and she is unsure whether the children are infected too. Diarrhoea is a frequent occurrence for the whole family, and is one of the reasons Elizabeth gives for being so fastidious about emptying the buckets into the Channel, away from the house. Of the bucket and its contents, she says, 'It is disease, all [of its contents]. I do not want it here' (interview with Elizabeth, 31 January 2011). She tells me that the children have sometimes knocked over the bucket when it is placed outside in the communal washing area behind the house, so she would much rather get rid of the waste quickly than keep it festering and smelling for some time.

The buckets are required for toileting in as the family do not have their own latrine and cannot afford the two hundred shillings it costs per visit to the public ones nearby.[7] Elizabeth relies on the children's plastic collecting for some of the household income, and her daily income, she estimates, rarely exceeds UGSH 2500. She feels that using this money on the public toilets is wrong, she feels, saying:

> Their mother is passed. I am their one [carer] and we are poor. My money is my money. It is not for these things [toilets]. This is for government. Why do they not give us these things?
>
> (Interview with Elizabeth, 31 January 2011)

Elizabeth's sentiments echo what many residents in Namuwongo were expressing; that there is a need for government agencies to provide services in areas such as Namuwongo that are felt to be overlooked and ignored. Such opinions were expressed not just for toileting, but also for other public services and infrastructure such as garbage collection, water provision and road tarmacking.[8] Jeremiah, a 24-year-old man who subsidises his income through 'picking' (recycling found objects, or opportunistic petty thieving), agrees with Elizabeth. He states,

> This [toilets] is needed! We need to live. I can build a house from small small things but it is too too difficult to make the latrine ... But it is how they want it, the Big Men, the Untouchables. They do not want to help with this, even if Museveni said he would provide, we haven't seen anything.
>
> (Interview with Jeremiah, 3 February 2011)

Jeremiah is angry with the number of broken promises from those in power; here, he is referring to President Museveni's election campaign that included a pledge to build more toilets in the city (Mukasa and Mulondo 2010). Thus far, toilet construction has not commenced. This furthers a profound sense of being left out of decision-making and exacerbates sentiments of being marginalised from participating in Kampalan life, except for when politicians are in need of votes (Muhumuza 2011).

For Jeremiah, like so many of his neighbours, the lack of toilets in Namuwongo means employing a variety of tactics to circumvent this everyday inconvenience. Jeremiah has more disposable income than Elizabeth and he is more able to utilise other toilets in the city, including those that are cheaper than the UGSH200 ones in Namuwongo. It enables him to diminish his reliance on *kaveera*, bottles and buckets to toilet in, and for Jeremiah, this is empowering. Despite this, he, like Elizabeth, is angry that socio-economic status and place of residence limit urban participatory capacities. Vernacular toileting methods are a way to manage the daily effects of marginalisation, and are used simply to get by in situations where few other sanitary options exist.

As mentioned above, one of the methods that residents use to navigate the lack of toilets is to make use of flying toilets. Rather than the full bags being tossed anywhere, however, residents describe being strategic in the way they get rid of their waste. Unlike recent events in Cape Town in South Africa, where human excrement was thrown at political leaders in emotive and visceral demonstrations about the city's sanitary inequalities (Torchia 2013), the shit of Kampala's flying toilets is not thrown into public spaces in such overt, or organised, political ways.

The majority of participants living in Namuwongo described throwing their flying toilets into the drainage channels nearest their homes, or walking to the larger Nakivubo to dispose of their waste. Figure 7.1 is a photograph of the Nakivubo Channel nearby the settlement, and clearly shows its congestion.[9] The

*Figure 7.1* Congested Nakivubo Channel at Namuwongo

waste in the channel is by no means constituted entirely by the nearby inhabitants, as my interviews and fieldwork revealed the dumping of solid waste (rubbish) and bodily waste by nearby factories, private sanitary contractors, and the city abattoirs.

Inhabitants, though, state its congestion as a justifying reason for throwing their bodily waste there. The Nakivubo is a public space that is not well looked after by the city authorities, and is a space that is not home. Informal inhabitants maintain the private space of home as sanitary and ordered, demonstrating the internalisation of modernist discourses of dirt. To leave bodily waste within the space of the home would indeed be 'matter out of place' (Douglas 1966). Yet to throw flying toilets into the Nakivubo is not seen as defilement of a public space, which is how it is read within the dominant discourse of the city's shitscape. Participants stated that they could not get rid of their bodily waste in private, as middle- and upper-class residents can, and that accessing public conveniences was problematic because they were expensive and had limited opening times. Flying toilets offer a degree of privacy in that the act can be done at home, and provide containment of shit and its smell. To get rid of the shit by tossing it into any open space was described as problematic for a variety of reasons, including health concerns and taboos about faeces (see section below). The Nakivubo was not conceptualised by Namuwongo participants as public space in the same way that the swamps around it were. The swamps are used by many residents as a space of peri-urban agriculture and provide an income for many. The Channel, however, was seen as the responsibility of KCC, and because the authorities fail to maintain it, it is the area that is least problematic to throw flying toilets into. Participants did not, then, throw their waste anywhere. The use and tossing of flying toilets are a tactical toileting performance in very constrained socio-economic and infrastructural circumstances.

A limited number of participants did, however, describe throwing their flying toilets in spaces that were seen as demonstrative of inequality. Six of the residents interviewed admitted throwing flying toilets onto particular rooftops. Jacob, an energetic man in his late teens, describes his flying toilet practice, stating that he can, 'just throw it up there and they will not know. They ... don't have to use the *kaveera*, so I think they can have mine!' (interview with Jacob, 15 February 2011).

His friend Evans details saving his full *kaveera* for his early morning walk to the taxi park, where he works selling newspapers. He says he will throw his bags in one of three places, either into or nearby the Nakivubo Channel, onto the roof of a small plastic-recycling company, or on the ground near the railway tracks (interview with Evans, 15 February 2011). The Nakivubo Channel and the railway tracks are not of the residents; both are seen as unproblematic spaces to throw faeces and plastic bags in and onto. The rooftops belong to those who are in various ways different from the average Namuwongo resident, and I think it is correct to interpret this as a sign of disrespect and anger at urban inequalities; but because my research suggests that this is restricted to a small number of individuals and is not a commonplace way of getting rid of flying toilets, I do not think it is correct to label throwing flying toilets as a politicised or emotive act.

Contrary to the opinions of some Kampalan residents and commentators, no participant in Namuwongo replied that they used *kaveera* to shit in because they did not know how to use a toilet; indeed, such an idea was laughed at, and derided for being derogatory. The Namuwongo participants are acutely aware of the insecurity of their tenure, and would much rather manage their everyday affairs without the involvement of the city authorities to limit their chances of being removed from their homes, something that Ayona Datta writes is common-place in illegal settlements in Delhi (Datta 2012). The Namuwongo participants' residence within the informal city limits their ability to protest against sanitation services because of the precarious situation they survive within; their acts of toileting that make use of everyday objects such as plastic bags and buckets are not depraved acts, or ones that seek to make profound political statements, but rather are routine performances brought about by the need to manage everyday bodily requirements.

Participants who used flying toilets described this method as the best and most cost-effective way that they had to manage the sight and smell of their excrement. As such, the use of flying toilets mirrors that of the flush toilet: that is, to confine bodily fluid as much as possible from sight and smell, and to expel the product from its proximity to the self. The flying toilet is a ritualistic way of managing uncleanliness, limiting shit's potential as 'matter out of place' (Douglas 1966). It is a different system, a way of maintaining sanitary order, by a margin-alised urban population. This is not to deny the occurrence of open defecation, which does happen in Namuwongo and other informal areas of Kampala, but this research found that the majority of participants would rather use a shared latrine or *kaveera* than defecate in public.[10] This echoes the results in another sanitation study in Kampala (Katukiza *et al.* 2010), but seems contrary to much research about toileting in other urban areas, particularly those in South Asia, which suggest that open defecation is a common form of toileting in places without private access (Thompson and Khan 2003; Buttenheim 2008; Datta 2012).

Colonial reports from Uganda describe customary beliefs that go some way to explaining why open defecation is not more common than it is currently. These records suggest that shit was associated with complex taboos that limit the mixing of people's waste, and constrain the extent to which other people can access one's excreta for fear of being cursed (Gillanders 1939). Thus, people would have specific, often gendered, demarcated spaces within which to openly defecate, and the use of latrines was only acceptable if the pits were deep enough that faeces could not easily be accessed. Such practices may, however, have been restricted in urban areas simply because space is more limited; yet, this research found that such defecation customary practices are still very much part of everyday life, contrary to the views of many of the sanitation experts interviewed, and are evident in distinct ways in Namuwongo. How such taboos are formulated and why they are so powerful is not well understood (Jewitt 2011), but as Douglas' (1966) work on dirt has shown, taboos surrounding waste are pervasive and rooted in differing spatio-temporal cultural interpretations. The colonial accounts of faecal prohibitions can be read, as per Douglas' thesis (1966), as efforts to order matter out of place, and flying toilets are a contemporary manifestation of these taboos. The practice of defecating into *kaveera* is a way of managing what would otherwise be seen as disorderly; hence open defecation in Kampala is minimal.

That the full bags are disposed of promptly and in particular places intimate particular coding practices and ordering of space. There is need for more research, however, to determine to what extent the throwing of *kaveera* is a signal of dissatisfaction and anger, as suggested by Jacob's testimony, or whether the disposal of flying toilets is less political and more pragmatic, as the majority of participants in this study who use this toileting method suggest. However, flying toilets could, contrary to the dominant view within Kampala, be interpreted as a desire for modern urban aesthetics because the flying toilet satisfies the basic principles of modern sanitation in much the same way that the flush toilets does – shit is quickly contained and eliminated, and faecal odour is limited. Flush toilets may be the ultimate way in which to demonstrate success (Jemsby 2008: 6), but in their absence, the inhabitants of Kampala's informal settlements have found another way to manage the sights and smells of their bodily waste.

It is important not to romanticise this practice, though. The users of flying toilets do not shit into plastic bags because they like it, or throw them at objects and symbols of power and inequality in grand gestures of protest. Despite some users stating that they threw their full *kaveera* in particular places as deliberate and understated acts of defiance, the subtlety of their everyday usage, and of the disposal, suggests that this practice of defecation should be understood as the only option in limited circumstances. This is very much a mundane politics brought about by everyday marginalisation.

The dominant interpretation of Kampala's shitscape, however, sees flying toilets as dirty, disordered, and illogical. The limited conception of, and lack of a willingness to understand, the logics of vernacular toileting practices also have an impact upon development projects that seek to improve sanitation infrastructures in informal areas, even upon projects that claim to be 'participatory' and 'local'. My research suggests that inhabitants of Kampala's informal areas are divested of full participation in these projects because they are assumed to lack knowledge of what they want and need. For example, the Kampala Sanitation Master Plan (KSMP) states that there is a need in low-income areas of Kampala for 'social marketing and hygiene promotion ... in order *to encourage households to want improved sanitation facilities and to use them correctly* so that the health benefits actually materialise' (NWSC 2004: 35, emphasis mine). There is a conflation here between lack of toilets and a lack of toileting knowledge, and an assumption that low-income households do not desire better sanitation facilities. This is, according to the KSMP, because there is an 'unwillingness of households to commit more funds to this sector, due to the low priority accorded to sanitation in the household budget' (ibid.: 15).

There is no recognition in the report that low-income households, like that of Elizabeth, might not want to 'commit more funds' to improving sanitation facilities because every shilling she earns is already accounted for. For Elizabeth, there is, quite simply, no expenditure to spare, regardless of how much she would like not to have to use *kaveera* and buckets for toileting. Paying for sanitation is, therefore, most definitely accorded a low priority for Elizabeth's household for the same reason: the income of the household is required to survive. Bodily waste is managed in such a way that minimises financial commitment, but it is managed nonetheless. Flying toilets, and the use of buckets and bottles, are the best possible toileting practice in a difficult situation, and one that makes creative use out of readily available materials.

The management of excreta by plastic bags and bottles is not, however, regarded by sanitation and development experts as a good or healthy way to manage bodily waste. And while I do not wish to sentimentalise the use of such materials by trying to suggest that flying toilets are a 'healthy' alternative to latrines or flush toilets, I strongly believe that dismissing these practices outright ignores the logics of their usage and risks discounting local sensibilities. This is not only a disservice to the inhabitants of informal areas, but jeopardises the success of future sanitation projects by failing to understand local responses to, and knowledges of, sanitation materials and infrastructure.

This is demonstrated in Namuwongo where a sanitation project has been implemented and subsequently rejected by the residents. A community-led sanitation advocacy project was felt to have been 'hijacked' by the involvement of an NGO and has led to a new toilet block not being used by the community.

## Whose toilet is it anyway?

In 2005, keen to try and improve sanitation services in Namuwongo, a group of residents came together to form NCBO, a Namuwongo community-based organisation. NCBO sought to align themselves with organisations that could offer financial and practical support and, drawing on (primarily church-based) networks that its members were already part of, they managed to secure support from a UK-based charity that promotes the use of simple low-cost technological solutions to housing and sanitation problems in the developing world. The charity, referred to here as Green NGO, advocates using 'appropriate technologies', including ecological sanitation (ECOSAN) toileting systems that utilise waste material, composting it so that it can be used as fertiliser. Green NGO agreed to construct two toilet blocks in addition to the two KCC-owned blocks in Namuwongo. The new NGO ones are designed to have four stands in each block. Florence, a resident of Namuwongo, describes her reaction to the news of the new toilet blocks:

> We were so happy! We were celebrating! … But then some time passed and we seen that in fact we would be having some strange ones, not like how we

are used [to] or flush ones like how some people have in the smart [areas]. This was ah! [Throws her hands up]. It was in fact because these toilets … they are not like latrines, they keep the faeces and it is then used by farming. But these people they came and they sensitised us about it [ECOSAN] and said how it is so good for places like here. So now it's this toilets we have.

(Interview with Florence, 29 January 2011)

NCBO members recall feeling elated when they heard they were going to get support from a foreign organisation. They felt this would mean greater success in managing to get the toilets constructed and hoped it would also mean financial support to keep the toilets operational in the long term. Despite not knowing about ECOSAN toilets beforehand, the 'sensitisation' was effective in persuading the members it would be a good solution to their problem, but as NCBO-founder Freddie remarks,

NCBO said to them we need toilets and this is what we now have. First, we didn't understand [the ECOSAN system] and [Green NGO] said it would be OK. God gave us this gift, we could not say no, even if some of us were not so happy with it.

(Interview with Freddie, 28 April 2011)

NCBO felt they were in a position where they were unable to negotiate how the toilet blocks were to be constructed; Green NGO were unequivocal about both the method of construction (using their technologies rather than local brick-making methods) and the type of toilets that were to be built. The reasons for this, according to Green NGO, were to encourage sustainability and limit deforestation, as local brick-making practices require considerable amounts of wood. Participants, however, felt this was an imposition of foreignness that ignored Namuwongo residents' tradition and expertise. There was also a deep sense of unfairness about the type of toilets on offer in Namuwongo. Participants described the ECOSAN toilets suspiciously, and as an inferior system of toileting. The act of constructing new toilets that are not flushing ones was seen as a snub, and furthered the participants' sense of marginalisation.

Furthermore, once constructed, the ECOSAN toilets caused considerable consternation because of the way in which they store and use faeces, and have become a focal point of residents' worries about being cursed. An ECOSAN toilet requires the separation of urine from faeces in order that the liquids and solids can be composted and subsequently used or sold as fertiliser; this, however, contravenes a belief held by participants' that the handling of faeces should be limited, and once it is stored that it should remain in place. Contravention of this could lead to the faeces being used for cursing by the 'night witches'. These beliefs limit the number of people who use the ECOSAN toilets, and restrict the number of times that people who do use them visit to defecate. Freddie describes how the relationship between taboos and the toilets manifests itself:

The night dancers, here, the night witches, have you heard about them? Maybe I should call them wizards, you would understand this, I think. They dance around naked and they use faeces to put it on people's doors and it can mean a curse … these are some of the things people attach to the ECOSAN, so how can you use ECOSAN?

(Interview with Freddie, 28 April 2011)

The shit that is deposited into the ECOSAN toilets is thus viewed as suspicious, as are the people who use them. Faecal mysticism renders shit powerful, and it is never seen as making the transition to fertiliser. Geoffrey, a Namuwongo resident who also expressed deep misgivings about the ECOSAN toilets, said that he 'will not put faeces in it'. Further, he stated that he 'will not use ECOSAN faeces to put on the land' as 'what grows, it can be cursed' (interview with Geoffrey, 3 May 2011). Contemporary fears about the ECOSAN toilets are, however, not limited to curses by the night witches. Rose, a young woman who has lived in Namuwongo for two years, says using the ECOSAN toilets will cause her to become infertile. Rose believes that many women have similar concerns, and will continue to use *kaveera* and buckets to defecate in (interview with Rose, 3 May 2011).

NCBO members say they explained the existence of such taboos and fears to their donor. Green NGO, however, reassured the group that they would carry out community-wide sensitisation in order to assuage fears about how the faeces and urine are used. NCBO maintain that with the exception of their specific training, no other community education took place. Green NGO also encouraged NCBO to attempt to sell the fertiliser outside of the immediate area, to find markets elsewhere; NCBO, however, say that the high cost of fuel makes it impossible for them to travel to sell the fertiliser far from Namuwongo.

The fear and distrust of ECOSAN toilets mean that they are not being utilised by as many people as NCBO wished; moreover, the lack of success at selling the fertiliser has stunted the economic sustainability of the two new toilet blocks, prompting NCBO to charge money to cover the costs of maintenance. The ECOSAN toilets now cost one hundred shillings per use, with children under 12 years old exempt from payment. The overwhelming response from participants was that the ECOSAN toilets might look more impressive than the KCC ones, and may be cleaner too, but they are too strongly associated with taboo to be used in the manner the Green NGO had assumed they would be. Florence, one of the founding members of NCBO, is stoic but angry at what she sees as a further example of injustice. Reflecting on NCBO's first experience of working with an NGO partner, she states:

It is true that some [toilets] are better than having what, what we did. But we don't have the … It is too hard for us to get the help to write these reports [for funding]. We are not Big Men. So [to have] these people [Green NGO] with us, it makes it so we can do something … But I think, these people,

they don't listen, they don't really listen to us, they just think we are poor
and we will take whatever, live like whatever. And so we have these things
that are not how we want.

(Interview with Florence, 28 January 2011)

Florence is frustrated by what she sees as the conditionality of sanitation assistance that is premised upon principles about urban sustainability that fail either
to take into account, or to take seriously, the fears and taboos of the community
that the excreta-management system is meant to benefit (Jewitt 2011). In
Namuwongo, informality and poverty give licence to the imposition of ideas and
projects by those in positions of power: the informality of the residents' homes
means that KCC will not provide public toilets; landlords feel they can legiti-
mately ignore planning standards and residents' requests for sanitation; and the
slum status of Namuwongo legitimises the NGO's toileting diagnosis and intervention. The cumulative effect reinforces Namuwongo as a space that is
not-quite-city, an anti-modern space that does not belong in the future of
Kampala.

## Conclusion

The implications for infrastructure – how it is understood, interpreted and implemented – are significant. The ECOSAN project in Namuwongo suggests that
solutions to a lack of sanitation infrastructure in informal areas cannot simply be
solved through innovative technologies alone. Everyday practices and materialities of toileting reveal meanings attached to sanitation infrastructure that
challenges normative understandings of infrastructure as a waste disposal mechanism. The material aspirations of the people whom development projects seek
to serve must be taken into account, as must already existing knowledges about
sanitation, health, and order.

This dominant discourse, however, posits certain areas as not-quite-city,
producing spaces of difference and inequality. This powerful spatial imaginary
ignores the structural forces that create urban inequality, and is instrumental in
situating the slum as the perpetrator of difference (Wacquant 2008). The emphasis, for planners of sanitation projects at a variety of scales, is placed upon the
space and its inhabitants to change; in Kampala, this involves 'sensitising' the
population of Namuwongo and encouraging NGO involvement in developing
sanitation infrastructure in the absence of the municipal authorities. These
development projects are attempts to rationalise the city; there is little to no
evident attempt by the implementers and designers of sanitation projects to
promote livelihoods and political capacities in the areas designated as requiring
upgrading (Roy 2005: 150).

For many residents of Namuwongo, representations of slum render the space
as undeserving of urban status. This legitimises the city authorities' lack of
engagement with the residents of Namuwongo, and circumvents any require-

ment for dialogue about toilet provision. The perceived sanitary ignorance of the Namuwongo community denigrates the residents, disenfranchising both the space and its inhabitants from urban decision-making. Such imaginations are embedded within hierarchies of knowledge and expertise, thereby providing justification for sanitary development interventions that lead practitioners to assume poverty means grateful acceptance of infrastructure without debate. Yet by attempting to understand the everyday performativity of defecation, subaltern political and aesthetic practices are revealed, challenging the assumptions implicit in the slum imaginary. This analysis of the city's sanitary regime, then, explicates the processes of urban social inequalities, and allows for a reading of infrastructure practices that is mindful of the creativity, aspirations, and politics of all urban residents. To not recognise the potentialities of the everyday is to '[keep] life from being worse than it reasonably should be' (Simone 2010: 261). Recognition of how power realises itself in and through the city is, then, not enough to challenge how sanitation projects are diagnosed, planned and implemented. To implement a more ethical and just form of urban transformation, expertise of the residents must be acknowledged and made equal (Roy 2005; Robinson 2006) in order to foster urban governance that truly works for the city and its inhabitants.

## Notes

1    An ethnographic study was carried out during 2010/11 as part of a wider PhD research project. Fieldwork was carried out between July 2010 and June 2011. Some 48 interviews were conducted with Kampala residents, in addition to three focus groups, and 31 interviews with elite stakeholders in urban planning and sanitation in the city.
2    Namuwongo may also refer to the area surrounding the International Hospital of Kampala, which houses mainly middle-class residents. It seems, however, that middle-class residents in this area regularly refer to themselves as living 'near the IHK' or in Tank Hill, rather than defining the area as Namuwongo. In addition, some maps of Kampala will label the area directly to the south-east of Namuwongo as 'Kasanvu Slum' or 'Kanyogoga Slum'; the researcher, however, did not find these names were widely used in the city. Thus, for the sake of clarity, and in line with the naming idioms identified during the research, the informal settlement of the case study here is referred to as Namuwongo.
3    The city's municipal authority, Kampala Capital City Authority (KCCA), replaced its former entity, the Kampala City Council (KCC) in March 2011.
4    'Up-country' is a common Ugandan term referring to anywhere other than Kampala.
5    This kind of urban territorialisation is an extension of colonial attempts to separate difference within the city, and whereas some of the reasoning and language used to justify difference and geographical separation has changed, the rhetoric remains couched within ideas around urbanity, civility and health.
6    Two of Elizabeth's children are sponsored by a UK-based charity to attend primary school. They receive breakfast and lunch during the school terms.
7    At the time of writing, 3700 Ugandan Shillings equals one British pound. Elizabeth is reluctant to urinate or defecate in public as some of the men and children do.
8    A feature of these responses that is particularly interesting in light of the emphasis

and efforts by UN Habitat is that adequate housing provision was *not* high on participants' agendas of needs or wants. Rather, participants were adamant that getting
access to land was difficult, and being granted land tenure was even more so, causing
significant stress due to the constant threat of eviction. The fact that many houses in
Namuwongo are self-built was seen as a symbol of pride in the ability of both individuals and the community to construct things that have significant use and
emotional value.

9    Shortly before this photograph was taken (31 January 2011), one participant
     confided that one of their cows had drowned in the Nakivubo Channel because the
     animal had thought the channel was in fact land.

10   Of the 27 participants who identified themselves as living in an informal area of the
     city, 22 said they did not defecate in the open. Four people expressed that they have
     done so only in emergencies, and one stated that they practised open defecation on
     a regular (but reluctant) basis.

## Bibliography

Black, M. and Fawcett, B. (2008) *The Last Taboo: Opening the Door on the Global Sanitation Crisis*. London: Earthscan.

Bourdieu, P. (1999) 'Site effects', in P. Bourdieu (ed.) *The Weight of the World: Suffering in Contemporary Society*. Stanford, CA: Stanford University Press.

Butler, J. (1990) *Gender Trouble: Feminism and the Subversion of Identity*. New York: Routledge.

Buttenheim, A. M. (2008) 'The sanitation environment in urban slums: implications for child health', *Population and Environment*, 30(1–2): 26–47.

Collier, S. J. and Lakoff, A. (2005) 'On regimes of living', in A. Ong and S. J. Collier (eds) *Global Assemblages: Technology, Politics and Ethics*. Oxford: Blackwell, pp. 22–39.

Corbin, A. (1986) *The Foul and the Fragrant: Odor and the French Social Imagination*. Cambridge, MA: Harvard University Press.

Datta, A. (2012) *The Illegal City: Space, Law and Gender in a Delhi Squatter Settlement*. Farnham: Ashgate.

Davis, M. (2006) *Planet of Slums*. London: Verso.

Dikeç, M. (2002) 'Police, politics and the right to the city', *GeoJournal*, 58(2–3): 91–98.

Dikeç, M. (2007) *Badlands of the Republic: Space, Politics and Urban Policy*. Oxford: Blackwell.

Douglas, M. (1966) *Purity and Danger: An Analysis of the Concept of Pollution and Taboo*. London: Routledge.

Dyck, I. (2005) 'Feminist geography, the "everyday", and local–global relations: hidden spaces of place-making', *Canadian Geographer/Le Géographe canadien* 49(3): 233–43.

Flood, J. (2002) 'Secure tenure: global definition and measurement', paper presented at European Housing Network Conference. Vienna.

Fredericks, R. (2006) 'Participatory cities? The cultural politics of community-based waste management in Dakar, Senegal', paper presented at Breslauer Graduate Symposium, 'The Right to the City and the Politics of Space'. University of California, Berkeley.

Fredericks, R. (2008) 'Gender and the politics of trash in Dakar, Senegal: participation, labor and the "undisciplined" woman', Thinking Gender Papers, UCLA Center for the Study of Women, UC, Los Angeles.

Gandy, M. (2006a) 'Planning, anti-planning and the infrastructure crisis facing metropolitan Lagos', *Urban Studies*, 43(2): 371–396.

Gandy, M. (2006b) 'Rethinking urban metabolism: water, space and the modern city', *City*, 8(3): 363–379.

Gandy, M. (2008) 'Landscapes of disaster: water, modernity, and urban fragmentation in Mumbai', *Environment and Planning A*, 40(1): 108–130.

Ghertner, D. A. (2011) 'World-class city making in Delhi', in A. Roy and A. Ong (eds) *Worlding Cities: Asian Experiments in the Art of Being Global*. Chichester: Wiley-Blackwell, pp. 279–306.

Gillanders, G. (1939) 'Rural housing', *The Journal of the Royal Society for the Promotion of Health*, 60(6): 230–240.

Graham, S. (2010) 'When infrastructures fail', in S. Graham (ed.) *Disrupted Cities: When Infrastructure Fails*. New York: Routledge.

Gregson, N. (2011) 'Performativity, corporeality and the politics of ship building', *Journal of Cultural Economy* 4(2): 137–156.

Gregson, N., Crang, M. *et al.* (2010) 'Following things of rubbish value: end-of-life ships, "chock-chocky" furniture and the Bangladeshi middle class consumer', *Geoforum* 41(6): 846–854.

Gregson, N., Watkins, H. *et al.* (2010) 'Inextinguishable fibres: demolition and the vital materialisms of asbestos', *Environment and Planning A*, 42(5): 1065–1083.

Grosfoguel, R. (2002) 'Colonial difference, geopolitics of knowledge, and global coloniality in the modern/colonial capitalist world-system', *Review (Fernand Braudel Center)*, 25(3): 203–224.

Hart, G. (2004) 'Geography and development: critical ethnographies', *Progress in Human Geography*, 28(1): 91–100.

Hawkins, G. (2006) *The Ethics of Waste: How We Relate to Rubbish*. Oxford: Rowman and Littlefield.

Hawkins, G. (2009) 'The politics of bottled water', *Journal of Cultural Economy* 2(1): 183–195.

Hobkinson, S. (2011) *Andrew Marr's Megacities*. UK, Acorn Media UK: 217 mins.

Holloway, L. and Hubbard, P. (2001) *People and Place: The Extraordinary Geographies of Everyday Life*. Harlow: Pearson Education.

Isin, F. (2002) *Being Political: Genealogies of Citizenship*, Minneapolis, MN: University of Minnesota Press.

Jemsby, C. (2008) 'The most famous toilet in Uganda', *Sanitation Now*, Stockholm Environment Institute: 4–7.

Jewitt, S. (2011) 'Geographies of shit: spatial and temporal variations in attitudes towards human waste', *Progress in Human Geography*, 35(5): 608–662.

Kansiime, F. and Nalubega, M. (1999) *Wastewater Treatment by a Natural Wetland: The Nakivubo Swamp, Uganda. Processes and Implications*. Rotterdam: A.A. Balkema.

Katukiza, A. Y., Ronteltap, M. *et al.* (2010) 'Selection of sustainable sanitation technologies for urban slums: a case of Bwaise III in Kampala, Uganda', *Science of the Total Environment*, 409(1): 52–62.

KCC (1994) *Kampala Development Plan And Structure Report*. KampalaCityCouncil. Kampala: Kampala City Council.

Kimani-Murage, E. W. and Ngindu, A. M. (2007) 'Quality of water the slum dwellers use: the case of a Kenyan slum', *Journal of Urban Health Bulletin of the New York Academy of Medicine*, 84(6): 829–838.

Kooy, M. and Bakker, K. (2008) 'Technologies of government: constituting subjectivities, spaces, and infrastructures in colonial and contemporary Jakarta', *International Journal of Urban and Regional Research*, 32(2): 375–391.

Kyambadde, J. (2005) 'Optimizing processes for biological nitrogen removal in Nakivubo wetland, Uganda', PhD thesis, KTH Biotechnology, Stockholm, University of Stockholm.

Laporte, D. (2002) *A History of Shit*. Cambridge, MA: The MIT Press.

Lees, L. (2003) 'Urban geography: "New" urban geography and the ethnographic void', *Progress in Human Geography*, 27(1): 107–113.

Lefebvre, H. (1991) *The Production of Space*. London: Wiley-Blackwell.

Lefebvre, H. (1996) *Writings on Cities*. Oxford: Blackwell Publishing.

McFarlane, C. (2008) 'Governing the contaminated city: infrastructure and sanitation in colonial and post-colonial Bombay', *International Journal of Urban and Regional Research*, 32(2): 415–435.

McFarlane, C. (2010) 'Infrastructure, interruption and inequality: urban life in the global south', in S. Graham (ed.) *Disrupted Cities: When Infrastructure Fails*. London: Routledge.

McFarlane, C. (2012) 'From sanitation inequality to malevolent urbanism: the normalisation of suffering in Mumbai', *Geoforum*, 43(6): 1287–1290.

McFarlane, C. and Rutherford, J. (2008) 'Political infrastructures: governing and experiencing the fabric of the city', *International Journal of Urban and Regional Research*, 32(2): 363–374.

Muhumuza, R. (2011) 'Museveni woos rural voters', *Think Africa Press*. London: Think Africa Press.

Mukasa, H. and Mulondo, M. (2010) 'Kampala city to get 300 free toilets', *The New Vision*. Kampala.

Myers, G. (2011) *African Cities: Alternative Visions of Urban Theory and Practice*. London: Zed Books.

NWSC (2004) *Kampala Sanitation Master Plan*. N. W. a. S. Corporation. Kampala: Government of Uganda.

Nyakaana, J. B., Sengendo, H. *et al.* (2007) 'Population, urban development and the environment in Uganda: the case of Kampala City and its environs', PRIPODE Workshop on Urban Population, Development and Environment Dynamics, Nairobi, Kenya.

Ong, A. (2011) 'Introduction: worlding cities, or the art of being global', in A. Ong and A. Roy (eds) *Worlding Cities: Asian Experiments in the Art of Being Global*. Chichester: Wiley-Blackwell.

Pieterse, E. (2006) 'Blurring boundaries: fragments of an urban research agenda', *Urban Forum*, 17(4): 398–412.

Purcell, M. (2002) 'Excavating Lefebvre: the right to the city and its urban politics of the inhabitant', *GeoJournal*, 58(2–3): 99–108.

Robinson, J. (2004) 'In the tracks of comparative urbanism: difference, urban modernity and the primitive', *Urban Geography*, 25(8): 49–66.

Robinson, J. (2006) *Ordinary Cities: Between Modernity and Development*, London: Routledge.

Roy, A. (2004) 'Transnational tresspassings: the geopolitics of urban informality', in A. Roy and N. Alsayyad (eds) *Urban Informality: Transnational Perspectives from the Middle East, South Asia and Latin America*. Lanham, MD: Lexington Books.

Roy, A. (2005) 'Urban informality: toward an epistemology of planning', *Journal of the American Planning Association*, 71(2): 147–158.

Roy, A. (2011) 'Slumdog cities: rethinking subaltern urbanism', *International Journal of Urban and Regional Research*, 35(2): 223–238.

Roy, A. and Alsayyad, N. (2004) *Urban Informality: Transnational Perspectives from the Middle East, South Asia and Latin America*. Lanham, MD: Lexington Books.

Scott, J. C. (1985) *Weapons of the Weak: Everyday Forms of Peasant Resistance*. New Haven, CT: Yale University Press.

Simone, A. (2004) *For the City Yet to Come: Changing African Life in Four Cities*. Durham, NC: Duke University Press.

Simone, A. (2010) *City Life from Jakarta to Dakar: Movements at the Crossroads*. New York: Routledge.

Smith, N. (1990) *Uneven Development: Nature, Capital and the Production of Space*. Oxford: Blackwell.

Soja, E. (1980) 'The socio-spatial dialectic', *The Annals of the Association of American Geographers*, 70(2): 207–225.

Staeheli, L., Mitchell, D. *et al.* (2002) 'Conflicting rights to the city in New York's community gardens', *GeoJournal*, 58: 197–205.

Staeheli, L., Mitchell, D. *et al.* (2010) 'Disorderly democracy', in *PSA Conference Proceedings*, 1–13.

Swanton, D. (2011) 'Assemblage and critical urban praxis: part two: introduction', *City*, 15(3–4): 344–346.

Swyngedouw, E. (2012) 'Privatizing water: governance failure and the world's urban water crisis', *Annals of the Association of American Geographers*, 102(1): 245–247.

Thompson, T. and Khan, S. (2003) 'Situation analysis and epidemiology of infectious disease transmission: a South-East Asian regional perspective', *International Journal of Environmental Health Research*, 13: S29–S36.

Torchia, C. (2013) 'In South Africa, toilet talk turns political', *Associated Press*. Johannesburg, AP.

UBOS (2011) *TP5: 2010 Mid-Year Projected Population for Town Councils*. Kampala: Uganda Bureau of Statistics, Government of Uganda.

Wacquant, L. (2008) *Urban Outcasts: A Comparative Sociology of Advanced Marginality*. Cambridge: Polity Press.

Whatmore, S. (2006) 'Materialist returns: practising cultural geography in and for a more-than-human world', *Cultural Geographies*, 13(4): 600–609.

Young, I. M. (1990) *Justice and the Politics of Difference*. Princeton, NJ: Princeton University Press.

# Chapter 8

# Cleaning up the streets

## Newcastle-upon-Tyne's night-time neighbourhood services team

*Rob Shaw*

## Introduction

The streets of Britain's city centres are busy at night: taxi drivers, 'revellers', fast food sellers, bouncers, policemen, street pastors, leafleteers and more take to the streets to promote, produce or consume the night-time economy. 'Night-time economy studies' has catalogued this vast range of activities associated with consumption in city centres at night, particularly within a British context. Roberts and Eldridge's comprehensive overview of research across social science on the night-time economy provides examples of research into many of these groups, and more. In revealing such a wide and mature academic field, however, research relating to infrastructural maintenance at night is conspicuous in its absence, despite an awareness of the importance of the night as a time for maintenance (Roberts and Eldridge, 2009: 26). Separately from this research into the night-time economy, a growing literature has begun to emphasise the need for social scientists to look at repair and maintenance of cities (Graham and Marvin, 2001; Herod and Aguiar, 2006; Graham and Thrift, 2007). In urban geography, as this edited collection shows, this increase in attention paid to repair and maintenance has begun to reveal that, far from a 'back stage' of the city (Goffman, 1959), infrastructure takes on a central role in everyday, and everynight, urban experience. Furthermore, rather than just a tool, resource, opportunity or hindrance, infrastructure presents itself as constitutive of urban life (Pieterse, 2008) and, by extension, the urban subjectivities which emerge from this. Once again, however, the night as a specific site of repair and maintenance is often overlooked as unproblematically a time of 'out-of-the-way' repair, which has little direct impact on the urban other than in hiding some of the dirtiest jobs that constitute a city (Herod and Aguiar, 2006).

Missing from the list of actants in the night-time city are two related elements: first, litter and other discarded materials; and second, street-cleaners. Most local authorities in the UK employ a night-shift of street-cleaners, who may also have some responsibility for gritting roads and other regular maintenance jobs around the city. As Murray Melbin suggests in his 1987 book, *Night as Frontier*:

The timetable [of the city] shows a tendency to gather rejuvenating tasks in the once-dormant phase. The new order of the day is to rely on the night-time to restore the community's well-being. Many of its projects represent a service connection between one day and the next, functions that overhaul and revive ... a good-sized portion of the activity is cleaning, repairing, waste removal and maintenance.

(Melbin, 1987: 83–84)

Crudely, a parallel can be made between the need for humans to rest, restore and recuperate at night, and the need for the cities that we have created to do the same thing. In this chapter, however, I intend to show the ways in which this activity of cleaning at night is more than simply a task of overhaul and revival, and more than a 'connection' between days. This chapter therefore contributes to the ongoing attempts to use an 'everyday' or practice-based approach to focus on the encounter between infrastructure and other processes in society, specifically at the moments of becoming in which a diverse range of objects is transformed into 'waste'. In doing so, it focuses on the range of actants and moments which have not traditionally been considered infrastructural, which nonetheless form part of the process of making infrastructure. This then populates our understanding of infrastructure with a diverse range of things – people, objects, animals, encounters, affects, laws, structures, emotions. Of course, a focus on just one moment will inevitably provide just part of the picture: behind practice lies planning, legislation, structure and wider processes which are only seen in fleeting, distant translations on the street. Furthermore, the objects which become waste do not completely lose their heterogeneity once they become part of this mass category (Bennett, 2004): some objects are split off into new groups through recycling, others leech out of the category as pollutants, while others might be eaten by animals or are simply blown away by the wind. As such, this process of becoming is not a complete removal of agency or power from the objects which are becoming-waste; nevertheless, it is a significant moment in the formation of networks of infrastructure.

This chapter's argument is broken down into three parts. First, I will show how night-time street-cleaning must take place in and alongside the late night alcohol and leisure industry – that which is typically labelled the 'night-time economy' in academia and policy – and that this results in a very visible form of infrastructural work, in contrast to the invisibility of much infrastructural work in the Global North. Due to the incongruity of street-cleaners among the 'playscape' of the urban night, they have a specific form of visibility that they must negotiate. Second, then, I want to explore the position of this night-time street-cleaning within practices of regulation and management that produce the subjectivities of the urban night. In doing so, I do not want to show that night-time street-cleaning somehow determines or is singularly vital for the formation of subjectivities at night; rather, that it is one of many vectors of subjectification which are 'relatively autonomous in relation to [each] other, and, if need be, in open conflict' but which nonetheless come together to establish subjectivity in individuals (Guattari, 2000: 25). Third, I will then use a series of photographs taken by a research participant in a night-time street-cleaning team in Newcastle-upon-Tyne, a city in Northern England with a well-developed 'night-time economy' (Chatterton and Hollands, 2001) to illustrate that the practices of repair and maintenance of infrastructure in the urban night form the first stages of the 'waste assemblage' (McFarlane, 2009). In doing so, I arrive at these moments of formation of the category of waste (Crang and Gregson, 2010), as discarded materials become litter and then begin to interact with the workers and objects of infrastructure (Bennett, 2004).

## Infrastructural work in the urban night

Since the 'Manchester School' of cultural studies and urban planners first persuaded local authorities in their city to conduct an experiment into extended opening hours of city centre retail, recreational and cultural facilities (Comedia, 1991; Lovatt, 1993), there has been a significant field of research which has looked at the development of the night-time alcohol and leisure industry in British cities in particular, and to a lesser extent globally (Roberts and Eldridge, 2009; Jayne et al., 2011). This area of research was initially led by urban planning and was concerned with the promotion of the urban night as a possible panacea for empty city centres, a tool for creating a leisure-based consumption economy (Vall, 2007), which would have the dual benefits of 'doubling the city's economy' (Bianchini, 1995: 124) while simultaneously making it more liveable, urbane and cosmopolitan (Landry and Bianchini, 1995).

As a programme for urban regeneration, developing a night-time economy sought to right the wrongs of 1980s urban developments, in which a business-led focus had resulted in single use districts developing in cities, consisting of office blocks without any other function, shopping centres and malls that relied on the automobility of citizens to be connected to the rest of the city, and modern residential developments in which there were no communal or leisure spaces. Discourses of a 'cosmopolitan' or 'European lifestyle' (Bianchini and Parkinson, 1993) were developed in which an idealised version of Mediterranean culture – with city centre living, wine consumption and cafés with outdoor seating – was contrasted with a beer-laden British culture, isolated in small and dingy pubs (Jayne et al., 2008). As Jayne et al. suggest, such a distinction had little basis in reality, but it chimed with both policy-makers and the public so that the 'European-café culture' moved more centrally into the domain of policy. Tony Blair's Labour government, which came to power in 1997, incorporated licensing law relaxations into its aims and this became one of the central manifesto promises when it was re-elected in 2001 (Hadfield, 2006).

The leisure- and alcohol-based economy of the urban night has thus become a key part of the reinvention of city centres as sites of consumption and entertainment (Vall, 2007; Jayne et al., 2011). In this context, Newcastle-upon-Tyne is emblematic of British cities. Following a decline in the traditional industries of coal mining, shipbuilding and other engineering, Newcastle has rediscovered its working-class drinking culture as one of its major resources in an era of inter-urban competitiveness in which a strong urban brand is vital to success (Pike, 2011). As Vall suggests, 'The local state [in Newcastle] has attempted to capitalise upon the city's vibrant consumer culture, or more particularly, the night-time economy, in pursuit of urban regeneration' (2007: 25). Thus the provision of leisure venues was central to the redevelopment of Newcastle's Quayside, while The Gate, an indoor leisure and entertainment complex with multiple bars and restaurants, was opened in 2004 in Newcastle and provided a new anchor for the city's nightlife. In 2007, the city council was able to proclaim that 'our night time-economy is the envy of the rest of the country and a major tourist attractor' (Newcastle City Council, 2007: 119). In popular representations of the city, the heavy drinking and party culture is also prominent. From the regular awards or accolades that the nightlife is granted in travel media – such as the number one attraction in the UK title from the 2006 Rough Guide, or its regular appearance in 'best party city' lists – through to the media controversy surrounding the 2011 MTV television programme *Geordie Shore*, in which the city's residents were represented as heavy drinking hedonists, Newcastle is a city commonly represented at night.

This active nightlife means that night-time cleaning cannot be simply a task of late-night renewal while the city sleeps. Yet this night-time cleaning has typically been conceived only in these terms. In Tomic *et al.*'s (2006) research in Chilean shopping malls, the night is a relatively empty period in which the more visible and obtrusive aspects of cleaning can be hidden, in order to maintain the fiction of modernity. For Rowbotham as well, it is the invisibility of night cleaning which is problematic, in relation to the attempts of women night cleaners to unionise in the 1970s (Rowbotham, 2006). Undoubtedly, the night does provide a convenient time to hide the messy side of modernity so that governments can claim success in providing clean and efficient cities; from a less insidious perspective, night-time cleaning is simply a practical solution to the demands created by 'incessancy', that is, the need for activities cities to be timetabled across both day and night (Melbin, 1987). In such a context, and in industries which tend to rely heavily on immigrant or casual employment, the resultant invisibility of workers is a major issue, and is one of the ethical imperatives for academic engagement in such topics.

However, in the nightlife of Newcastle-upon-Tyne, which I experienced during ethnographic research with the city's night-time 'neighbourhood services team', that is, the night-time street-cleaners, the role of cleaning presents itself very differently. Rather than an invisible practice cleaning up the mess of the day, it is instead an active practice of managing and controlling a spiralling flow of materials in a context of complex and constantly negotiated visuality. There are three aspects to this relationship which are of particular interest.

First, street-cleaners in these spaces are clearly very visible and present. Figure 8.1 shows people having to walk around the 'swingo' cleaning vehicle. This

*Figure 8.1* The swingo machine in action

vehicle is used to clean pavements, and the site in the image is a public space which is located in front of The Gate, a large entertainment complex of bars, restaurants, clubs, a casino and a cinema. The high number of leaflets indicates the amount of cleaning which needs to take place in this busy location. During my ethnographic work with the street-cleaners, I was able to take a half-hour journey sitting in the cab of a swingo. We received repeated attention from people in the street: slapping the cabin windows; jumping in front of the vehicle; jumping away from the vehicle; dropping litter in front of the vehicle for collection; asking for lifts up the road; and refusing to move from the pavement. During their shifts, then, the drivers must constantly negotiate the difficulties created by the very obvious visibility of their sweeping vehicles.

Similarly, the workers who sweep the streets with brooms are presented with a different range of challenges in the urban night. As Figure 8.2 suggests, cleaners need constantly to negotiate their visibility. Unlike most actants on the night-time street, their presence is not necessarily expected: they are not 'revellers' or drinkers in the urban night, and nor are they one of the limited range of regularly represented professions that are associated with the urban night – bouncers, taxi drivers, dancers, leafleteers and fast food sellers. Furthermore, the nature of their work means that they are obliged to move in

*Figure 8.2* Street-cleaner at work

and around the drinking crowd. Of course, as Jayne *et al.* note, drinkers form a heterogeneous group, with 'diverse practices and experiences' (2011: 21), and so there is not a singular route to avoiding interaction – and nor need there be, as the majority of drinkers do not cause trouble for the street-cleaners.

Nevertheless, while wandering through the crowds, the mantra of these work-ers is 'don't make eye contact'. They walk in a very submissive stance, with their face on the task in hand, that is, the floor. The cleaners are able to remove litter from the middle of a drunken, chatting group, ducking between bodies which provide them almost no attention. At times, however, their brooms do contact people's feet, or their eyes do meet those around them. When they are engaged in conversation, they do so in a manner which is extremely polite, friendly, and happy. Here, the unofficial practice of putting only men on the night-shift, and generally those over 35, allows the workers to position themselves in a certain way. Younger workers would be more likely to meet friends, or be seen as poten-tially targets for violence. Women, meanwhile, continue to receive regular unwanted sexual attention in the urban night (Leyshon, 2008; Holloway *et al.*,

2009) and so managers perceive that they would be more at risk of assault in this environment. Brought together, all this means that the workers draw from a series of learnt behaviours, to manage very carefully the interactions with drunken people who, while unlikely to be violent, can be unpredictable in their actions.

These two images also show the amount of waste which is created in the process of the urban night. In Figure 8.1 there is about 40 minutes' worth of waste accumulation, while Figure 8.2 shows the amount collected in about 10 minutes' worth of sweeping done by one worker at one site. A variety of materials, then – flyers, bottles, food packets and more – begin to become waste during the urban night, as will be discussed later in the chapter. This waste would simply build up if left uncleaned, dramatically changing the image of Newcastle at night. Thus, this cleaning cannot be solely conceptualised as simply a process of clearing up after the day, of repairing the city as it sleeps (Melbin, 1987). Rather, it is a practice of active management, of identifying the busiest sites and the build-up of litter. Learnt behaviours allow the staff to operate within this time and space, negotiating their visibility. It is undoubtedly true that the night-time cleaners remain invisible to many including, perhaps crucially, senior members of the city council's executive body and other parts of the local authority, yet during the night itself they must constantly work to create invisibility. While more diverse than a group with a single purpose (Roberts, 2006), the users of the night-time city are not as heterogeneous as the day and so those actants which are not directly involved in the drinking and leisure economy can and do stand out. The unyielding materiality of the swingo machine or the embeddedness of the workers with brooms means that the cleaners must constantly negate their rupturing visuality. Yet the sheer amount of litter generated in the night-time economy means that their job and presence are inherently necessary: they are not maintenance workers in a sleeping city, but a response team managing an ever increasing flow of materials. In studying the 'night-time economy', we must also remember then that it is the 'people who clean the floors, distribute tickets, cook the food, wash the glasses and make the coffee' (Brabazon and Mallinder, 2007:168) who allow this assemblage to function.

## Emergent subjectivities and the role of street-cleaning

If the initial academic research into the alcohol and leisure industry at night was led by cultural studies and urban planners, this had changed by the time that the Licensing Act was passed in 2003, permitting licensed premises to apply for unlimited opening times and removing the power of judges to appeal against the granting of licences on the grounds of over-saturation (Hadfield, 2006). A series of critical studies from urban geography, sociology and criminology in particular began to show the problems that were associated with this liberalisation of legislation associated with the urban night. Broadly, they critiqued what Chatterton and Hollands described as the conversion of city centres into neoliberal playscapes (Chatterton and Hollands, 2001, 2002). As the ability to prevent licences being granted was slowly eroded, city centres became filled with chain bars run by 'pubcos', that is, large multi-bar companies. These bars were often themed in a variety of ways, simultaneously expanding and fragmenting the market (Hadfield *et al.*, 2001). Such increased competition resulted in discounting of alcohol prices and a myriad of '2 for 1' offers on drinks. Academics argued that such practices resulted in the increased consumption of alcohol, while simultaneously legislation prevented authorities from restricting the activities of those producers who had encouraged this increased consumption. Law enforcers, unable to restrict the activity of producers, instead turned to 'those most thoroughly seduced of consumers, to the tune of a dozen lagers, who are most inclined to be targeted by swarming police units, teams of bouncers and couplets of street wardens' (Hobbs *et al.*, 2003: 273). Having lost their ability to act to prevent excessive sale of cheap alcohol in the urban night, the only way to enforce behavioural norms was through legislative responses which controlled consumers.

In addition to this punitive control from authorities, Hadfield's research in bars revealed a world in which a variety of techniques had been learnt by various actants to control and manage behaviour in the urban night. As he suggested, 'The ability to exert control over the behaviour of one's customers is essential to the successful operation of licensed premises' (Hadfield, 2006: 81). Management, bouncers and disc jockeys all attempt to manipulate the mood of their premises, in order to create the right environment. Leyshon extends this official control from practices to the infrastructural, as 'the shape, objects and textures of pubs contour movement and regulate performances' (2008: 282). In fact, what is key in controlling the mood of a bar is the relationship between practices and infrastructural or institutional features. Such a claim is not necessarily new. In his 1946 essay 'The Moon Under Water' about his ideal (fictional) public house, George Orwell recognises that: 'If you are asked why you favour a particular public-house, it would seem natural to put the beer first, but the thing that most appeals to me about the Moon Under Water is what people call its "atmosphere"' (Orwell, 1946). He goes on to list a variety of features that contribute to this atmosphere, including the noise levels and style of music, the architecture, the furnishings (which should have 'the solid, comfortable ugliness of the 19th century'), the food and beer sold, regulatory practices such as whether children are allowed in the bar, and its geographical position in relation to bus stops and pedestrian thoroughfares. Indeed, Orwell's essay has been stated as an inspiration for the JD Wetherspoon's chain of pubs, which have become one of the most successful 'chameleon bars' in the UK. Chameleon bars are premises which manipulate their layout, menu, music, prices, regulations and lighting over the course of a day so that they can act as cafés during the daytime, restaurants in the evening, and pubs, bars or clubs at night (Kubacki *et al.*, 2007). In doing so, they epitomise a form of experience capitalism in which manipulation of subjectivities to encourage consumption is central.

With all this in mind, Jayne *et al.* note that many researchers have concluded that in the urban night there are 'a number of contradictory tendencies towards both deregulation and (re) regulation, and the twin imperatives of fun and disorder' (2011: 19). Certainly, there would seem to be a tension between, on the one hand, governmental practices which attempt to cut down on alcohol consumption in order to prevent 'anti-social behaviour', and other legislative changes and practices which encourage increased consumption behaviour. However, I argue that these trends are not inherently contradictory or, rather, that if they appear to have contradictory tendencies, then this contradiction should be seen neither as some sort of hypocrisy nor as particularly unexpected. Rather, as I will show through my discussion of street-cleaning at night, such practices of manipulation of 'mood' can be better understood as part of the machinic assemblages of the production of subjectivity.

Subjectivity is taken here to mean the behaviour, experiences and identity of an individual-as-assemblage. It is an assemblage which recognises itself and other selves as actants and attributes agency to both itself and other selves (Bateson, 1973: 315). The 'subject' of the subjectivity is 'immanent to the larger system – man [sic] plus environment' (ibid.: 317), as it emerges as a process from the world. Guattari adapts Bateson's thinking into a more post-structuralist account of subjectivity by recognising it not as a closed system, but as the result of 'a multitude of *machinic* systems' (Guattari, 1996b: 95, emphasis added) which interact with one another. These machines are 'machines of meaning, of sensation, abstract machines ... that can standardize individual and collective subjectivity' (Guattari, 1993: 143–144). While they are autonomous and often conflictual (Guattari, 2000), these machinic systems nonetheless do come together to produce subjectivities. In other words, subjectivity is the subject-as-process, a constantly manipulated and created assemblage. In the urban night, as at all times, subjectivity is emerging from the changing experience and behaviour of the self. Re-reading Hadfield and Orwell's accounts above, then, the manipulation of mood or the sensation of atmosphere can be understood as a recognition of the sensation of this emergence, in which practices, infrastructures and institutions come together to produce subjectivities.

A growing subsection of the literature on infrastructures and urbanism has focused on the constitutive role of infrastructure in subjectivities. Such work has emerged from a concern with 'the ways in which the construction of difference through processes of segregation and exclusion has both spatial and discursive dimensions' (Kooy and Bakker, 2008: 377) and in particular the material aspects of this. Kooy and Bakker's research into Jakarta reveals, for example, the ways in which access to certain forms of infrastructure shapes and is shaped by discourses of which subjects should and should not have access to 'modernity'. Infrastructures thus jointly represent access to, but dependency on, networks of various forms. As Graham and Thrift (2007) suggest, attention to the continual work required to repair and maintain these connections can help reveal the dependent nature of urban subjectivities on infrastructures, particularly in the Global North. Such dependency is further revealed, according to Coward, by the targeting of critical urban infrastructure in contemporary war and terrorism. Rather than traditional urban warfare, which has sought to decimate and destabilise populations or destroy key infrastructural nodes, urban warfare now seeks to 'disrupt urbanity through the destruction of that substrate which is central to contemporary cities: critical infrastructure' (Coward, 2009: 402).

In the context of these approaches, a study of street-cleaning at night can further add to our understanding of the relationship between urban infrastructure and subjectivity. Street-cleaning at night plays a big role in bracketing off the city centre at night as a time of difference or exception, by controlling the excess of material flows which are created. As Szmigin *et al.* suggest, the urban night creates a place for 'planned letting go which balances out the constrained behaviour they are subject to in the formal structures of everyday life in school, work and family' (2008: 363). This time-space has been labelled the night-time high street or urban playscape (Chatterton and Hollands, 2002), in which a limited amount of hedonism and release is encouraged, in order to ensure that desire for experimentation of subjectivity is met, without threatening the cohesion of the self. One of the techniques of release which is used in the urban night is the relatively reckless attitude towards the built environment, the classic example of which might be the student prank of stealing traffic cones. Street-cleaners tidy up after this recklessness, doing minor repairs to street furniture which is damaged at night, or at least securing it or tidying up the mess created. As experimentation with subjectivity in the urban night is centred around bodily consumption of various products – principally alcohol – waste is also created by this process, as shown in the next section. This excess amount of waste materialises the affective excesses of the urban night, and by cleaning this up, the street-cleaners absorb this excess. Crucially, the necessary act of cleaning up after this mess results in a city centre which is clean and undamaged the following day, largely removing the evidence of the previous night.

In practice, the day city and the night city are not separate discrete periods in which normal, responsible citizens become abnormal, irresponsible drinkers. Rather, the British cities at night contain processes of intensification of flows of materials through and around bodies: flows such as music, alcohol, images, food and sounds. In other words, the urban night is a space in which excess emerges; night-time street-cleaning, and other forms of monitoring and control which attempt to constrain this intensification of corporeal flows, absorb this excess. This allows for the creation of hedonistic subjectivities without threatening the 'normal' being of the day. By looking at the work which is done to maintain this appearance of separation between night and day, we can further explore the relationship between the night-time city and wider urban processes.

## Becoming-waste

In the previous two sections of this chapter, I have been concerned with the relationship between infrastructural work – night-time street-cleaning – and the night-time alcohol and leisure industry. In this section, I look at the relationship between this work and the wider infrastructures into which it feeds. As Crang and Gregson suggest, research into waste has tended to focus on waste management, that is, on the movement and treatment of waste as part of wider techno-scientific or policy-oriented studies into the management of resources. A result of this is that waste has been remarkably fixed as a concept within academia, a feature of modernity which 'just is: [waste] is the stuff that is being governed, or that which is the outcome of policy' (Crang and Gregson, 2010: 1027). While this focus is understandable, it means that there have been few attempts to rethink or trouble the category of waste. A deeper exploration into the ontologies of waste, whether through studies of its moments of formation, termination, disruption or spillage, can show the work of assemblage which goes into the creation of 'waste' and, in doing so, indicates the dynamism and contingency of the waste-category. With the management and control of waste contested on a variety of ecological, economic, legal and social grounds, explorations into the practice of waste creation can help to show the potential for doing waste differently and, if so, then creating less waste.

Recent studies into waste which have attempted to engage with this problem have typically taken on two approaches. The first has been to show the materiality or agency of the objects which are typically bundled into the category of waste (Bennett, 2004; Hawkins, 2011), revealing the ways first in which they remain separate objects and second in which they can act or disrupt waste management processes. As Edensor (2005) suggests, such studies can also reveal an aesthetics of the world, in which pollution and spillage are written out in favour of narratives of clean, waste management. A second set of responses, to which this paper is allied, seeks to engage with the moments at which waste is present in unexpected sites or ways, often at its moments of formation or change. In these studies, there has been a recognition of the power of imagery of waste and litter (Crang, 2010). Crang, following Deleuze, conceives of images of waste-creation as showing a 'time-image', that is, a moment at which a transition between different times takes place: a 'moment of recognition of linkages, and of disturbance, where disjunctural states are shown to connect' (Crang, 2010: 1085). His study of images of ships being dismantled shows that the power of these images is in the presence of these disjunctural states. The ship, an object of mobility, globalisation and transportation, is shown as becoming-waste, being dismantled in dangerous ways.

Within this chapter, I use participant photographs, of which two have already appeared, to show similar moments of the formation of the waste assemblage. These photographs were taken by a member of Newcastle's neighbourhood services team in the course of his work. As such, they focus on the labour and tools which are added to deposited materials to create waste. The assemblage of cleaners, nightlife, alcohol, bodily fluids, leaflets, brooms, bins, pavements, water, etc., can be understood as a 'waste-machine'. As previously discussed, the machine is being used in the sense developed by Guattari and explored also in his collaborative work with Deleuze, in which what is important is the machine's 'singular power of enunciation: what [Guattari] calls its specific enunciative consistency' (Guattari, 1995: 33). The enunciative consistency of a machine is its power to enunciate, that is, to produce both new meaning and form. In the caste of the waste-machine, the enunciative power comes from the ability of the various components to together produce 'waste'. Before waste can begin, then, materials are first deposited onto the city streets.

Perhaps the most commonly discarded materials in the city at night are advertising leaflets and fast-food packaging, as seen in Figures 8.3 and 8.4. Night shift workers estimate that there are over 50,000 flyers distributed on a typical night in Newcastle, and that this figure may be over 100,000 at certain times. Though in theory regulated through a licensing system, there is little interest from police in monitoring this distribution, due to the range of pressures made on policing in the urban night. Shift managers of the neighbourhood services team occasionally approach and challenge unlicensed leafleteers, but this does little to reduce the overall flow of materials. Fast food consumption at night is high, which is linked both to its convenience, and also the high levels of fat and sugar which help keep the body warm. This warmth is important where people who are dressed to be

*Figure 8.3* Discarded advertising leaflets and fast food packaging

*Figure 8.4* Some of the 50,000 on average nightly discarded leaflets

inside warm, sweaty clubs move around city streets. Furthermore, as nights-out can often be long processes which involve movement from pubs, to bars, to clubs (Hollands, 1995), individuals can often be very hungry by the time that 2 a.m. comes around. As such large quantities of fast food packaging are used up during the night, and these can build up as waste around fast food shops and vans, as in Figure 8.4. In particular, this sort of waste also builds up in large public spaces which can form a significant period of the night out as people queue, smoke, or simply hang around in the night-time city.

But the litter on the city streets at night does not just consist of discarded materials. Night-time streets are, we are told, 'splattered with blood, vomit, urine and the sodden remains of take-aways' (Hadfield *et al.*, 2001: 300) and indeed there are a range of bodily fluids which are regularly deposited onto the streets of Newcastle. Certain alleyways and corners become public urinals, though pissing also occurs in more public locations as well: Figure 8.5 shows urine stains beside one of the exits to The Gate entertainment complex. Indeed, The Gate has suffered at the hands of the activity of urine, as seen in Figure 8.6. Here, the acid of repeated urination is beginning to corrode the brickwork of a building which opened in 2004. This reveals an agency of urine in the city centre and indicates

*Figure 8.5* Urination damage

*Figure 8.6* The Gate has suffered urination damage

*Figure 8.7* Urine traces

that the issue of public urination goes beyond one of bodily norms or anxieties over public behaviour (Eldridge, 2010). These images are also from relatively public places, showing that urination is not just a back alley activity, but a central part of the waste that is created in the night-time city.

As well as bodily waste and litter, other materials appear on the streets at night. Smashed glass and other alcohol containers are (perhaps surprisingly) rare, as drinking in public is prohibited under bylaws and is quickly stopped by police or bouncers. The grease from fast food restaurants, on the other hand, spreads out over the city streets, creating paths that are slippy and dangerous. In Figure 8.8, the shining grease outside of a McDonald's is a potential safety hazard if not cleaned quickly, whilst in Figure 8.9 grease has come into contact with other materials, such as leaflets, holding them and sticking them to the ground: these are only removable with a power wash. Different materials thus continue to have some agency, interacting on the ground so that they become more difficult to remove. Weather conditions will also affect this: in rain, heat, and cold, the chemicals of the various materials will respond differently, requiring new tools and techniques on behalf of the cleaners.

From materials in heterogeneous forms, these objects become litter on the streets. As litter, two sets of practices and objects are then added to create waste.

*Figure 8.8* Grease on the pavement outside McDonald's

*Figure 8.9* Leaflets stuck to the ground with grease

First, there is the manual labour and learned behaviours which were previously discussed in this chapter. This labour, however, is intimately tied to the second set of objects required to create waste, and that is the infrastructure and tools of cleaning. In the interaction with this infrastructure, the material changes from individual cigarette butts, fast food packaging, leaflets, vomit, etc, to become the mass of 'waste'. As such, the process of becoming waste is not simply a linguistic division in which objects are renamed, but rather a qualitative change in the being of the material. This process of becoming is part of the wider waste-management assemblage. Waste management thus begins with gathering. These photos draw attention to, as McFarlane puts it, 'the labour of assembling and re-assembling sociomaterial practices that are diffuse, tangled and contingent' (McFarlane, 2009). As an assemblage is a dynamic object, however, it is always being changed and altered: parts can be literally plucked out of it at any time.

Figure 8.10 thus shows one of the many sea-birds which come to the streets after the closure of clubs and till the early morning, removing some of the material from the streets before it can become part of the waste management system. Most of the waste, however, comes into contact with the tools of litter removal. The most obvious of these tools is the bin, though as Figure 8.10 indicates, the work that these can do is limited. In Figure 8.11, the litter in the bin is being pulled into the waste assemblage. Materials on the street are swept together using the brooms, becoming a mass. These are then siphoned into kerbs, so that sweeping vehicles can easily collect them off the floor (Figure 8.12). This is an ongoing process through the night, in which a constant stream of materials are input into the waste assemblage through the combined actions of those depositing the materials on the streets, the cleaners who collect it together, and sweeping machines which gather it off the floor. As such the materials, workers and tools form a single waste-production-machinic-assemblage.

This process of becoming waste, however, is often disrupted. One example of this comes from the recent ban on smoking in licensed premises in the UK. Many bars and pubs have opened 'smoking areas' outside, often separated from the pavement using temporary metal fencing. This fencing encroaches onto the pavement and makes the job of negotiating this space with sweeping vehicles particularly difficult. The presence of more smokers outside of pubs and bars depositing cigarette butts has also increased the work of street-cleaners, who now have to make more effort to move in and out of doorways and alcoves.

So in Figure 8.13 we see a summary of many of the arguments made in this chapter. A street-sweeping vehicle is moving towards one of the public squares in Newcastle, which is quickly filling with litter. Its presence fills the narrow pavement, thanks in part to the smoking area at the adjacent bar, which is already taking up half of the available space. In this area, more litter is being created in the form of disposed cigarettes. To the right, ongoing roadworks compound these problems with no space for people to move round the vehicle. Legislative, corporeal, infrastructural and affective practices thus feed in together to create this image of a moment in which the necessity but difficulty of

*Figure 8.10* A seagull scavenger

*Figure 8.11* The overflowing litter bin: input into the waste assemblage

*Figure 8.12* Waste in the kerb awaiting pick-up

*Figure 8.13* The range of actants in the urban night streetscape

night-time cleaning is revealed. This picture shows some of the wide range of actants, both human and non-human, which can contribute to the urban night streetscape and which go beyond the limited range of binge drinkers, dancers, police and bouncers that are often studied in social science.

## Conclusion

This chapter does not seek to argue that the night-time city is as diverse a time and space as the day-time city. Certainly, at night, a number of rhythms come to rest or to a stand-still; recuperation and repair take place with little activity ongoing. The absence of many actants creates a somewhat contradictory trend in which the night is both a space for those who wish to express difference or explore subjectivity to act (Melbin, 1987; Malbon, 1999), but also a generally less diverse population, in which there is a greater danger of violence towards those who stand out as different (Valentine, 1989; Whitzman, 2007). Nevertheless, the visible 'hoards' of night-time drinkers quickly become less homogeneous when explored in greater depth (Jayne et al., 2011). The existence of these subjectivities are dependent upon a much wider range of diverse actants and practices, which are necessary to support the night-time economy but which are not immediately imagined as part of the night's streetscape. Contradictory and 'hypocritical' elements of these assemblages are to be expected, as forces act in antagonistic ways to create complex and dynamic subjectivities. By understanding better the range of different contributors to the machinic-assemblage of the urban night, we might better also understand the subjectivities which are produced from this assemblage.

In this chapter, we have followed the process of the formation of litter, and then waste. After this, the waste is transported off to a site in Heaton, where it enters the process of waste management, as a formal part of infrastructure networks. This process, as we have seen, is different at night compared to the day, with the specific actants of the night-time economy creating their own problems, such as violence and on-street urination, but also opportunities, such as their absence from shopping streets. Perhaps, then, we might place greater focus on these different rhythms of infrastructure in the city. Night plays a variety of different roles in infrastructure: it can be a time for running low priority but complex tasks, such as particular computer programmes, or rail network maintenance; it can be an opportunity for poorer actants to access networks, such as cheaper public transport journeys or electricity; and in other forms of infrastructure, such as hotels and accommodation, it can be the times of busiest activity. A focus on the everyday reveals these patterns, and the politics of infrastructural use, access and visibility which accompany them.

For the night-shift workers of Newcastle's neighbourhood services team, this street-cleaning does not exhaust their work. Among other things, they must respond to road traffic accidents, clean graffiti, clear street flooding and, in winter months, grit city pavements and roads. These images do, however, show one of their main roles and show that they are both embedded within the urban night and necessary to its operation. While supporting the night-time economy, the street-cleaners are also necessary to the process of waste management. To put it simply, for the management and control of waste materials, objects must first be deposited and collected together. The images of the third section of this chapter show, first, materials as they become litter, in a position of disjuncture: lying on the floor, mixing with each other or overflowing bins, these materials are all out of their proper place. As such, these images can be understood as time-images (Crang, 2010), that is, images which freeze moments of becoming and between-states. Second, then, these images show the work that goes into removing these out of place materials and turning them into the category of 'waste'. By coming into contact with the cleaners, and their various machines, these materials are treated in ways that turn them into waste: processes of sweeping, blasting with water, or sucking of the street by machines, all add to the materials to make them waste. As such, waste in an assemblage both in the sense of something which has been arranged, or assembled (McFarlane, 2009), and also in the sense of something which consists of a heterogeneity of components, including embodied practices of work, machines, weather, materials, and more (Guattari, 1996a: 154).

## Bibliography

Bateson, G. (1973) *Steps to an Ecology of Mind: Collected Essays in Anthropology, Psychiatry, Evolution, and Epistemology*. St Albans, Australia: Paladin.
Bennett, J. (2004) 'The Force of Things: Steps Towards an Ecology of Matter', *Political Theory*, 32(3): 347–372.
Bianchini, F. (1995) 'Night Cultures, Night Economies', *Planning Practice and Research*, 10(2): 121–126.
Bianchini, F. and Parkinson, M. (eds) (1993) *Cultural Policy and Urban Regeneration: The West European Experience*. Manchester: Manchester University Press.
Brabazon, T. and Mallinder, S. (2007) 'Into the Night-Time Economy: Work, Leisure, Urbanity and the Creative Industries', *Nebula*, 4(3): 161–178.
Chatterton, P. and Hollands, R. (2001) *Changing Our 'Toon': Youth, Nightlife and Urban Change in Newcastle*. Newcastle upon Tyne: University of Newcastle upon Tyne.
Chatterton, P. and Hollands, R. (2002) 'Theorising Urban Playscapes: Producing, Regulating and Consuming Youthful Nightlife City Spaces', *Urban Studies*, 39(1): 95–116.
Comedia (1991) *Out of Hours: A Study of Economic, Social and Cultural Life in Twelve Town Centres in the UK*. London: Comedia.
Coward, M. (2009) 'Network-Centric Violence, Critical Infrastructure and the Urbanization of Security', *Security Dialogue*, 40(4–5): 399–418.
Crang, M. (2010) 'The Death of Great Ships: Photography, Politics, and Waste in the Global Imaginary', *Environment and Planning A*, 42(5): 1084–1102.
Crang, M. and Gregson, N. (2010) 'Materiality and Waste: Inorganic Vitality in a Networked World', *Environment and Planning A*, 42(5): 1026–1032.
Edensor, T. (2005) 'Waste Matter: the Debris of Industrial Ruins and the Disordering of the Material World', *Journal of Material Culture*, 10(3): 311–322.

Eldridge, A. (2010) 'Public Panics: Problematic Bodies in Social Space', *Emotion, Space and Society*, 3(1): 40–44.

Goffman, E. (1959) *Presentation of Self in Everyday Life*, Harmondsworth: Penguin.

Graham, S. and Marvin, S. (2001) *Splintering Urbanism: Networked Infrastructures, Technological Mobilities and the Urban Condition*. London: Routledge.

Graham, S. and Thrift, N. (2007) 'Out of Order: Understanding Repair and Maintenance', *Theory, Culture & Society*, 24(3): 1–25.

Guattari, F. (1993) 'Space and Corporeity', *Columbia Documents of Architecture and Theory*, 2: 139–149.

Guattari, F. (1995) *Chaosmosis: An Ethico-Aesthetic Paradigm*, trans. P. Bains and J. Pefanis, Sydney: Powet.

Guattari, F. (1996a) 'The Place of the Signifier in the Institution', in G. Genosko (ed.) *The Guattari Reader*. Oxford: Blackwell, pp. 148–157.

Guattari, F. (1996b) 'Regimes, Pathways, Subjects', in G. Genosko (ed.) *The Guattari Reader*. Oxford: Blackwell, pp. 95–108.

Guattari, F. (2000) *The Three Ecologies*. New Brunswick, NJ: Athlone Press.

Hadfield, P. (2006) *Bar Wars: Contesting the Night in Contemporary British Cities*. Oxford: Oxford University Press.

Hadfield, P., Lister, S., Hobbs, D. and Winlow, S. (2001) 'The "24-Hour City": Condition Critical', *Town and Country Planning*, 70(11): 300–302.

Hawkins, G. (2011) 'Plastic Materialities', in B. Braun and S. J. Whatmore (eds) *Political Matter: Technoscience, Democracy, and Public Life*. Minneapolis, MN: University of Minnesota Press, pp. 119–138.

Herod, A. and Aguiar, L. L. M. (2006) 'Introduction: Cleaners and the Dirty Work of Neoliberalism', *Antipode*, 38(3): 425–434.

Hobbs, D., Hadfield, P., Lister, S. and Winlow, S. (2003) *Bouncers: Violence and Governance in the Night-Time Economy*. Oxford: Oxford University Press.

Hollands, R. (1995) *Friday Night, Saturday Night*. Newcastle-upon-Tyne: Department of Social Policy, Newcastle University. Available at: http://research.ncl.ac.uk/youthnightlife/HOLLANDS.PDF (accessed 18 Oct. 2011).

Holloway, S. L., Valentine, G. and Jayne, M. (2009) 'Masculinities, Femininities and the Geographies of Public and Private Drinking Landscapes', *Geoforum*, 40(5): 821–831.

Jayne, M., Valentine, G. and Holloway, S. L. (2008) 'Geographies of Alcohol, Drinking and Drunkenness: A Review of Progress', *Progress in Human Geography*, 32(2): 247–263.

Jayne, M., Valentine, G. and Holloway, S. L. (2011) *Alcohol, Drinking, Drunkenness: (Dis)Orderly Spaces*. Aldershot: Ashgate.

Kooy, M. and Bakker, K. (2008) 'Technologies of Government: Constituting Subjectivities, Spaces, and Infrastructures in Colonial and Contemporary Jakarta', *International Journal of Urban and Regional Research*, 32(2): 375–391.

Kubacki, K., Skinner, H., Parfitt, S. and Moss, G. (2007) 'Comparing Nightclub Customers' Preferences in Existing and Emerging Markets', *International Journal of Hospitality Management*, 26(4): 957–973.

Landry, C. and Bianchini, F. (1995) *The Creative City*. London: Demos.

Leyshon, M. (2008) '"We're Stuck in the Corner": Young Women, Embodiment and Drinking in the Countryside', *Drugs: Education, Prevention, Policy*, 15(3): 267–289.

Lovatt, A. (ed.) (1993) *The 24-Hour City: Selected Papers from the First National Conference on the Night-Time Economy*. Manchester: Manchester Institute for Popular Culture.

Malbon, B. (1999) *Clubbing: Dancing, Ecstasy and Vitality*. London: Routledge.

McFarlane, C. (2009) 'Translocal Assemblages: Space, Power and Social Movements', *Geoforum*, 40(4): 561–567.

Melbin, M. (1987) *Night as Frontier: Colonizing the World After Dark*. New York: The Free Press.

Newcastle City Council (2007) *Newcastle in 2021*. Available at: www2.newcastle.gov.uk/wwwfileroot/regen/ppi/RegenStratExec0207.pdf (accessed 18 Oct. 2011).

Orwell, G. (1946) 'The Moon under Water', *The Evening Standard*, 9 February 1946. Available at: www.whitebeertravels.co.uk/orwell.html (accessed 18 Oct. 2011).

Pieterse, E. (2008) *City Futures: Confronting the Cisis of Urban Development*. London: Zed Books.

Pike, A. (2011) 'Placing Brands and Branding: A Socio-Spatial Biography of Newcastle Brown Ale', *Transactions of the Institute of British Geographers*, 36(2): 206–222.

Roberts, M. (2006) 'From "Creative City" to "No-Go Areas": the Expansion of the Night-Time Economy in British Town and City Centres', *Cities*, 23(5): 331–338.

Roberts, M. and Eldridge, A. (2009) *Planning the Night-Time City*. London: Routledge.

Rowbotham, S. (2006) 'Cleaners' Organizing in Britain from the 1970s: A Personal Account', *Antipode*, 38(3): 608–625.

Szmigin, I., Griffin, C., Mistral, W., Bengry-Howell, A., Weale, L. and Hackley, C. (2008) 'Re-Framing "Binge Drinking" as Calculated Hedonism: Empirical Evidence from the U.K.', *International Journal of Drug Policy*, 19(5): 359–366.

Tomic, P., Trumper, R. and Dattwyler, R. H. (2006) 'Manufacturing Modernity: Cleaning, Dirt, and Neoliberalism in Chile', *Antipode*, 38(3): 508–529.

Valentine, G. (1989) 'The Geography of Women's Fear', *Area*, 21(4): 385–390.

Vall, N. (2007) *Cities in Decline? A Comparative History of Malmö and Newcastle after 1945*. Malmö: Högskola.

Whitzman, C. (2007) 'Stuck at the Front Door: Gender, Fear of Crime and the Challenge of Creating Safer Space', *Environment and Planning A*, 39(11): 2715–2732.

# Part IV

# Adjustment and experimentation

# Chapter 9

# Maintaining experiments and the material agency of the urban

*Vanesa Castán Broto and Harriet Bulkeley*

## Introduction

Over the last decade, there has been a growing sense of urgency about the need to develop responses to climate change. Climate change debates are inevitably linked to questions of justice across the world, within countries and even within cities. Climate change debates are also – perhaps not so inevitably – linked to frustration because of perceived inaction and loud claims about humanity running out of time. UN Special Rapporteur Oliver de Schutter likens global climate change talks with the scene of a traffic accident in which 'multiple voices shout each other down in a bid to tell their own version of events' (De Schutter, 2012).

It is not surprising, therefore, that, as scepticism about international negotiations and synchronised action led by national governments grows, a varied range of actors – public and private; at local, regional or national scales – are taking different initiatives within the city, in terms of providing services or just self-regulating, which aim at reconfiguring the socio-technical networks which sustain the city to achieve low carbon and resilient cities. We have called these purposive interventions 'climate change experiments' to emphasise that they are not merely interventions which seek to achieve a named objective, but rather, that in doing so they play on ambiguity and uncertainty and challenge existing regimes for energy and service provision through social and technical innovation, in turn creating the possibilities for opening up those objectives to redefinition. Experimentation is ultimately a way in which urban networked infrastructure comes to be both re-asserted, on the one hand, and re-defined and challenged on the other (Bulkeley and Castán Broto, 2013).

Our research suggests that there are three key movements in the constitution and development of urban climate change experiments (Bulkeley and Castán Broto, 2012). The first is the process whereby an experiment is made, that is, when multiple actors come together in assembling multiple knowledges, financial and material resources for the experiment. However, *making* the experiment alone does not guarantee its continuity. A sustained process of *maintaining* will establish the experiment within the urban fabric. Finally, an experiment reaches a stage in which *living* redefines it within the existing practices of those for whom the experiment becomes part of the everyday life. In terms of the relationship between everyday urban life and infrastructure, maintaining is the moment in which infrastructure becomes both normalised and integrated into broader urban infrastructure configurations.

Maintaining is thus a process whereby urban climate change experiments are brought into the 'everyday production, negotiation, improvisation, contestation and life of urban infrastructures' (Graham et al., 2013). One crucial aspect is that in shaping the urban fabric, maintenance is related to 'the power of things' (Graham and Thrift, 2007). In the case of experiments, attempts to reconfigure existing socio-technical relations are confronted with the obduracy conferred by the embeddedness of artefacts into socio-technical assemblages (Hommels, 2005, 2008). The power of things is revealed by the disruptive (and generative) potential of the experiments. Thus, maintenance emerges associated with these disruptions, not so much as an attempt to tame nature and technology but as a means to redefine new infrastructure configurations of the urban.

Borrowing from the literature on urban political ecology, together with insights from the studies on repair, maintenance and obduracy mentioned above, this chapter advances an argument about the generative power of maintenance through its relationship with the power of things by exploring three vignettes of material histories in a case study of a climate change experiment in housing in Bangalore, India. The case study shows that repeated attempts to deal with unexpected material and nature's agencies resulted in challenges to existing social and political arrangements, thus deviating the generative power of the experiment from its intended outcome to pose a direct challenge to dominant urban socio-technical relations.

## Maintenance and the production of socio-natures

Discussions within urban political ecology have paid attention to the historical construction of highly uneven urban environments through the production of nature in the city (Swyngedouw and Heynen, 2003; Heynen et al., 2006). In particular, there is a realization of the fundamental role that infrastructures play in mediating different processes of urban circulation of resources, people, ideas and power (Swyngedouw, 2006). The specific assemblages of material and discursive components, brought together through the ongoing interaction between different elements, constitute relatively stable configurations, which sustain specific power arrangements within the city, producing landscapes of environmental and social injustices (Keil, 2005; Heynen et al., 2006; Monstadt, 2009; Cooke and Lewis, 2010). Proponents of a transition towards sustainability emphasise the need to overcome the obduracy of the system to catalyse a rapid change of the regime (Geels and Schot, 2007; Angel and Rock, 2009; Bai et al., 2009; Smith et al., 2010). From an urban political ecology perspective, however, such a transition requires a reconfiguration of the specific power and material relations, which generate uneven urban environments, so that sustainability is closely linked to considerations of justice and responsibility. In examining urban circulations all that is material – nature – is revealed as uncanny, as manifest in unexpected events and exhibiting properties beyond anticipated urban routines and normality. This is crucial because:

> Exploring the uncanny materiality of 'the other' in the form of the invisible metabolized nature or technology networks points at the social construction of the separation between the natural and the social, the private and the public. It reveals the individual, the social, and the natural, as a socio-natural continuum that disrupts the boundaries between the above socially constructed categories.
>
> (Kaika, 2005, p. 75)

Indeed, understanding the urban as embedded in a socio-natural or socio-technical continuum goes a certain way in explaining obduracy in urban infrastructure systems. Hommels' (2008) notion of obduracy as embeddedness conceptualises urban systems' resistance to change as emerging from seamless interactions between multiple elements in socio-technical assemblages, glued not only by different discursive sets of norms, conventions and understandings but also by multiple forms of agency raised by its multiple components. In this account of obduracy – which, according to Hommels (2008), shifts attention away from power struggles beyond specific socio-technical assemblages – the material emerges not only as uncanny but also as an actant whose capacity to influence the system should not be overlooked.

This point of view has much in common with Actor Network Theory (ANT) and related perspectives that have grown from an affirmative rejection of the foundational dualisms of modernity such as nature/society; local/global; science/culture; expert/lay knowledge; and human/non-human (Callon, 1986; Haraway, 1991; Latour, 1993; Burgess et al., 2000; Murdoch, 2001). To overcome the nature/society dualism ANT proposes the representation of nature as an actant together with human beings and institutions. This implies that agency (i.e. the capacity to influence their surroundings) is extended to both humans and non-humans (Murdoch, 2001). This does not imply the reification of nature, but a recognition of the capacity of natural actors to cause change and generate responses.

While urban political ecology is imbued with a concern to redefine the significance of nature and the material within urban assemblages, ANT has often been regarded with suspicion because it appears to overlook inequalities, differences and power relations in shifting the analysis to detailed practices of everyday life rather than theoretical explanations (Holifield, 2009). However, Holifield proposes that ANT is 'a useful supplement to an already rich Marxist literature on uneven environments and the production of "social nature"' (ibid., p. 643). He develops this argument through a re-examination of recent ANT work

(Latour, 2004, 2005), arguing that ANT reveals 'competing accounts of what generates inequalities, hierarchies, and relations of domination' (Holifield, 2009, p. 645). Thus:

> The task of an actor-network analysis is not to resolve this uncertainty by explaining which kind of agency – free will, causal necessity, or something in between – belongs to humans and which to nonhumans, or by declaring human and nonhuman agency to be equals. Again, it is to examine controversies and uncertainties about how agency is distributed, and to trace how such controversies come to be resolved.
>
> (ibid., p. 645)

This is crucial to understanding the processes involved in urban maintenance. Graham and Thrift (2007) have related maintenance with Heidegger's notion of the world as a 'ready-to-hand', as involved in practices in which humans become involved with objects and instruments. Maintenance is thus the bridge between the unexpected and the 'ready-to-hand' world and as such, it is an essential process sustaining everyday urban life. This is especially significant in urban infrastructure management, in which maintenance is a crucial process whereby infrastructure becomes 'invisible' (Star, 1999), at least for those whose lives are integrated in the dynamics of urban environments (but not for those who are excluded from urban circulations, occupying static and insecure spaces for whom infrastructure is, rather, too visible, as McFarlane (2010) has shown). Thus defined, maintenance becomes a manifestation of 'the power of things' because

> It is in this space between breakdown and restoration of the practical equilibrium – between the visible (that is, 'broken') tool and the concealed tool – that repair and maintenance makes its bid for significance. For without that capacity, the world cannot go on, cannot become ready-to-hand again.
>
> (Graham and Thrift, 2007, p. 3)

Thus, maintenance:

> relies on the power of things and these things cannot be reduced to the sum of a set of social forces: 'what a thing does, the way in which a thing is present as a thing, cannot be reduced to something non-thingly and must be conceived from the thing itself' (Verbeek, 2004: 89). Things are not just formed matter, they are transductions with many conditions of possibility and their own forms of intentionality.
>
> (Graham and Thrift, 2007, p. 3)

Returning to climate change experimentation within the city and the maintenance of experiments, it seems that the inherent uncertainty associated with the introduction of social and technical innovations within urban infrastructure systems may be associated with changing spaces of possibility for material agencies. These emerging uncertainties will constitute an important issue, which will define the development and impact of the experiment within its particular urban context. If we are going to regard the power of things as constituting part of the power relations of the city, then urban infrastructure systems can be regarded as constituted through the ongoing repair and maintenance interventions which seek to handle the uncanny nature of material interventions. The question here is whether these maintenance interventions seek to reproduce existing power configurations, or if they are able to challenge existing conventions by engaging directly with the power of things in constituting everyday normalities.

## Material chronicles in a low carbon housing development in Bangalore, India

T-Zed (towards zero carbon development) is a pioneering gated community development in the peri-urban area in the east of Bangalore, led by Biodiversity Conservation India Limited (BCIL), a private developer (Figure 9.1). The central idea in T-Zed was to build a near-zero carbon development without compromising the habits and lifestyles of the people living there. To meet this expectation, T-Zed attempts to provide high-standard housing while using exclusively green technologies and keeping the costs in check. The emphasis on self-sufficiency within the development not only helped to find a market niche among green-minded professionals in terms of its sustainability but also in terms of securing the provision of resources. The first residents moved into one of the 91 homes in T-Zed in 2007, and today the whole development is occupied.

T-ZED was the first multi-dwelling residential project to achieve the Platinum Green Homes rating in India. BCIL inaugurated a great amount of innovation in T-Zed, from adapting existing technological fixes to incorporating tailor-made technologies and designs. BCIL also underwent significant social innovation not only in terms of fostering new ways of understanding the home but also in redefining the relationship between the customer and the residential compound.

Initiatives such as T-Zed in Bangalore follow the idea that the privileged classes have a moral duty to reduce their carbon emissions. Residents' motivations are often expressed as a sense of responsibility closely interlinked with their own quality of life: 'We want to be like this, we want to save the trees, we want to teach our children, we want our children to know that [this] is how our quality of life has improved' (Interview R1). This echoes BCIL's representation of the ideal customer, who not only buys a property but also understands its transcendental importance:

> They [residents] are all eco-friendly people ... who have it in their heart that they need to do something for this community; and there are people from all backgrounds, the cream of the society. From software engineers to doctors to

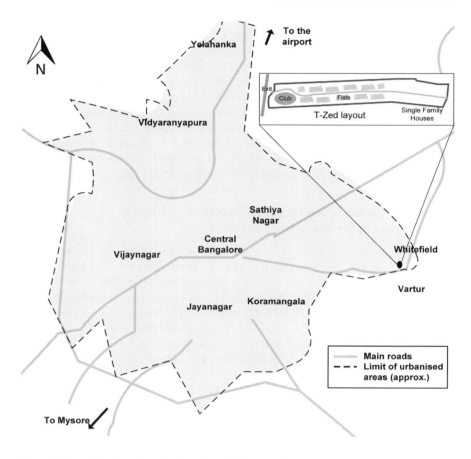

*Figure 9.1* Sketch of the localization of T-Zed in Bangalore

people of retiring age … there is a community as a whole … They figure they
will benefit from it … not only them but the generations ahead of them as
well. It's just not the people who are living here, it's generations of people
who are going to live in, their kids, their grandchildren … [This] makes an
impact on the country and the surrounding world.

(Interview D2)

As this quote suggests, the goodness of the customer is found not only in their
willingness to make something for the world, but also in making the purchase, to
buy into sustainable living designs and technologies to meet such moral duty.

BCIL emphasises that this moral duty can be 'bought' or 'consumed' because a tangible reduction of carbon emissions can be achieved without compromising the lifestyles of the accommodated classes. The role of the developer is, thus, to provide the solutions that would simultaneously meet the demands of lifestyle and the moral duty of customers:

> We build gated communities. There are people who are [working] in various ... professions. They appreciate people like us doing [green developments] but they cannot contribute ... but they want to be a part of those kinds of developments. So then we [give] them an opportunity ... to come ... and be part of it ... be members of this particular project, be owners of this particular project. So, they buy into these campuses ... We are completely Green in this particular place and we are building X homes for select people ... we are building homes for each individual and trying [to] give them that experience of Green homes.
>
> (Interview D1)

The green house is presented as a convenient product that meets customers' lifestyles and moral concerns.

BCIL prided themselves on design rather than technological innovation. In talking about what was innovative in T-Zed, a BCIL director said: 'Nothing! ... We use what is known as "CKCS" software ... common knowledge, common sense!' (Interview D3).[1] Talking about T-Zed, a local architect explained:

> In a sense, there are a lot of small design elements that are really innovative. But by large, most of the elements have been taken from ... what is already in the market which is researched and used, we have not developed anything.
>
> (Interview C1)

In this case, rather than the specific technologies enabled, what makes T-Zed truly innovative is the combination of technologies and design because, as residents highlight, in Bangalore, nothing had been done 'at this scale' (Interview R3).

To accomplish T-Zed, BCIL sought to find local materials with low embodied energy, reducing low transportation costs. While BCIL relied on traditional knowledge to facilitate the implementation of this idea, the use of unconventional materials meant that the developers had to cope with unexpected performances, not only during the construction phase but also once the residents moved in. A greater degree of experimentation was associated with interventions that would simultaneously address the reduction of energy consumption while maintaining the expectations of high-end consumers to have a given standard of energy services. In these cases new technologies had to be developed from scratch. For example, a hybrid LED and CFL system was designed for street illumination. Several models were tested to satisfy the lighting demands of local residents. The most complicated systems within the energy system were the air conditioning (AC) system and the in-house design customised refrigerators. A complete new design was necessary, according to BCIL, 'to avoid the long-term risk of at least half the residents going for energy-guzzling ACs or refrigerators that push up the Demand Load for projects of this kind for upmarket residential homes' (BCIL, 2009). The AC system, in particular, established innovation at three levels through an ammonia-based central chiller-plant for the whole compound (primary cooling), accompanied by cooling towers (secondary cooling) and individual chillers (tertiary cooling) (see vignette 3 on the centralised cooling network, on pp. 211–214). These three examples – the use of materials, the development of LED external lighting, and the development of integrated cooling systems – provide three vignettes to understand how the agency of the material is an obstacle towards the integration of the experiment in the socio-technical landscape, and why maintenance is a key process to achieve this integration.

Managing T-Zed is not only about managing residents' expectations but also about managing the material and technical systems that operate in the compound. Experimental maintenance requires progressive adjustments to fit the technologies to local contexts. Some of these technologies have simply not worked, as it is the case of the custom-made refrigerators and the AC system. Part of the management process has consisted of looking for additional solutions, and thus, the process of design and innovation lives on. This distinguishes T-Zed from other conventional apartment blocks that are delivered as finished and then the developers disappear from the scene. In contrast, T-Zed is an ongoing living project.

## Vignette 1: materials, walls, leakages

As explained above, one of the pillars of T-Zed design is the use of materials with low embodied energy. Quite specific design issues, however, emerged regarding the materials used. For example, polished local materials were used to waterproof the pool; however, now the appearance of the water changes because the light reflects differently on this material from conventional pools. According to the designers, it fitted the overall earthy design in the compound. Although some residents commented in passing that the pool 'looked dirty', plenty of children use it regularly and the pool is a welcome addition to the compound.

Construction methods followed a design to show exposed bricks and were designed to both reduce the amount of materials and to provide an alternative to concrete:

> The thing that was being attempted was … to see if … one could reduce all material consumption in your building; … the second thing was: let's see if we can build using materials right here at the site … let's try and see if we

can build a construction system which is like the conventional but the main structuring system ... uses less concrete.

(Interview C4)

With this aim there was a strong emphasis on local materials that generally are discarded in conventional construction: 'We use local materials like soil-stabilised blocks, mud blocks, dirt blocks ... "earth-oriented" material ... [T-Zed] is the first development where they went particularly using these materials' (Interview D1). Also, there was an emphasis on the 'natural' or 'ecological' nature of materials and whether or not they were reclaimed or recycled: 'We have used a mix of materials... which definitely are all natural materials ... This is all reclaimed material, what we have used' (Interview D2).

The use of materials was difficult in practice. For example, the original ideas about local materials for the exposed brick walls had to be abandoned. Eventually, blocks were imported from Kerala, because they 'found that even if you were to import blocks ... import meaning bringing it from faraway areas ... your landed embodied energy of this building block will be less than that of a concrete block. Or a clay brick' (Interview C4). Moreover, it was difficult to find the right contractors to work with those materials because working with them required specialised knowledge. Often, contractors were wary of abandoning conventional construction methods using concrete, from which they already got good benefits with low risk.

BCIL assumed that the technology of constructing with compressed blocks was well known but the lack of skills among the workforce (accustomed to ready-made materials used in conventional developments) made it difficult to deliver the development in the projected time. Local materials (such as BCIL's preferred local material called *laterite*) were difficult to cut. Initially, careful experimentation led to the completion of beautifully polished laterite walls in the 'community club' (at the entrance of the compound), but, as delays accumulated and influenced the relationship between BCIL and its customers, the building process had to be accelerated. Less careful cuts resulted in rough laterite blocks, which often had to be covered with cement or aided with additional materials to install windows and other features. Mistakes are attributed to execution: 'when it came to the execution, they [the constructors] didn't follow what had been planned' (Interview C6). Other times, problems emerged from the delivery of specific materials, demonstrating a certain resistance among providers to abandon their conventional practices:

> The guy who is actually doing it ... [Would say:] 'Hey, hey, hey ... don't even tell me about this carbon thing ... I don't know what this is about! I need to make my business succeed!'... which means he is not actually willing to invest in the innovation that it takes to bring this figure [the price] down!
>
> (Interview D3)

The combination of multiple materials appears to have satisfied local residents aesthetically: 'All the materials they've used are lovely, they work … it is very important to have compressed blocks in outside walls and natural stone floors and have big windows and lots of light, lots of air' (Interview R5). On the other hand, 'Using several different materials in one building causes problems unless you do it really well, because in this place there are all those leaks and issues' (Interview R4). It is not only the functionality of the materials (e.g., they leak) but also their visual appearance, as in the pool, which lacks the familiarity of industrially produced tiles and concrete blocks. Furthermore, lack of experience with the materials led to some 'mistakes' in completing the building:

> The shiny coating on it is also a mistake! One thing about mud blocks is [that they] breathe! So doing this coating, you prevent it from breathing! … if water does get in, which it would at times from outside … it has no way of coming out so you can see some [mess] like … it comes out like it boils … and it doesn't look very nice!
>
> (Interview R5)

Although it appears that originally BCIL intended to deliver a completed project, today they argue that BCIL needs to take care of the maintenance of the project and provide customised care. Because there was a two-year delay in the delivery, some residents had already moved in when the work was going on:

> About four years ago, 2006, it was half finished: I was the first one to move, but we were so desperate that we had to move. It was very difficult with all the dust, noise, people all around, but it is good now.
>
> (Interview R1)

Some of the houses were completed even after residents moved in: 'after I moved they constructed the bathroom, they had scaffolding all over it, and I had small children' (Interview R3). 'Construction was still going on still two months back' (Interview R2), explained one resident in March 2010. Another explained that 'The work is still going on! … Little things like waterproofing and painting and … all of that' (Interview R4). She explains the consequences of this for her family:

> [A]t some point it just got to me that you are staying here and you are continuously hearing the sound of somebody cutting stone … because they are replacing something or they are changing something, right! And, the kids go down to play … because things are not finished … there are like levels and there are rough edges where you can hurt yourself … it seemed to me: 'Okay, you are trying to do all the environmental stuff but you are not really taking care of the people who are here.' Because the kids can't play freely…because this is a construction site … to me the whole point is lost!
>
> (Interview R4)

Two years after the delivery of the houses and apartments to residents, BCIL is still working in some parts of the development. One argument is that maintenance issues in T-Zed are no different from other developments:

> Initially we had dampness. Initially! Because of the rain or so. And also, the walls, the customers they have painted in their own way and then we have found bubbles in the paint, because of the paint was not absorbed properly; then plumbing, then power problems, but normal maintenance issues, there is not anything specific for T-Zed.
>
> (Interview D4)

However, issues like 'bubbles in the paint' relate to specific materials and technologies used only in T-Zed. The experimentation with new materials led to a whole plethora of unexpected consequences and changed the relationships between BCIL workers, contractors, residents and the materials themselves.

## Vignette 2: LED lighting innovations

Most climate change policies in cities pay great attention to lighting as a means of carbon reduction. Light-emitting diode (LED) lighting has been used in aviation, traffic lights, computers, but it is only now that it is being also applied as a technology for everyday illumination, and there is a growing class of LED consultants and manufacturers who are influencing the building industry: '[There] has been a big, big attraction for these products in India … especially LEDs. …There are so many people, not just the suppliers, who don't just come and supply a light [model] and go…' (Interview N2). The main limitation, however, is that 'adaptation needs to happen to local standards' (Interview N4). Indeed, some construction professionals in Bangalore emphasise that LED is the main form of low carbon innovation: 'The only innovation thing which we have done is … an LED light fitting' (Interview C1).

In this context it is not surprising that LED lights have become a central feature of T-Zed, and a symbol of BCIL's capacity for innovation. The LED lights in T-Zed are hailed as a success, though this was not a straightforward story, as two of the consultants that worked on the project explained. The initial problem was the technology, because LED 'was in its rudimentary stages and I remember us going through some disastrous design options' (Interview C4). The CEO of Flexitron (today a very successful lighting company in Bangalore) dates this to 2005: 'I came to know about T-Zed through some of my associates … and a small presentation was given to MR. Hariharan [BCIL's CEO] … on different forms of lighting in terms of LED and CFL and fluorescent tubes … And then the initiative began.' What he describes is mostly a painful process of technical innovation: '[W]e kept making and breaking and making and breaking … maybe about 500 models … I blew up a lot of LEDs! It's a process where … we need to put in all our best efforts to see how the technology works!'

The breakthrough came when the LED lighting systems were adapted to the T-Zed requirements. This took several trial-and-error efforts. First, there was a consideration of whether the LED lights could be used for both outdoors and indoors. However, the LED was deemed unsuitable for interior lighting: 'LED is … a point source! [It is] … very sharp for the eyes to look at it, it's not very comfortable' (interview with Flexitron CEO). Second, they tried to find a design solution with existing LED technologies, trying different models on site. Some of these models were not successful: 'the first bulkhead which we had …which is just with LED lights … which was pathetic!' (Interview C4). The prototypes went through several rounds of adapting to the requirements of the site. In the first models which used LED alone 'the light was not sufficient' (interview with Flexitron CEO). Subsequent models combined LED and CFL in a hybrid system that during the evening would use both lights, but that after 10 p.m. would turn off the CFL and use only LED, thus reducing energy consumption considerably. Here, the challenge was the perceptions of the residents because

> You want your lighting to dim on the outside of our campus, albeit, there's the security angle to it where people believe that, if I am able to see everything in great clarity, then thieves will not come in so easily … it's a mindset thing.
>
> (Interview C4)

However, 'After a period of about 2 years, we came to know that there are some failures and the light quality is not very good, although we'd used the best quality LEDs' (Interview C4).

Finally, the consultant used T-Zed to experiment with technologies he was not even aware of:

> We brought in a new kind of LED … like a sodium-vapour light … it mimics the [conventional] lamp in the same way of light … So that we standardized and started using for the street lighting! Now, that has kind of become a standard in T-Zed!
>
> (Interview with Flexitron CEO)

The challenge at this stage was to design a device to condition the new type of lamp so that it could be employed in the campus. As the consultant explains:

> It took a little bit of learning it for us to know what the best method to operate a LED is … The breakthrough came due to an engineering of our own originality! That's when I put a small little team together to check exactly how the LED behaves and we found some very cheap solutions for this to suit the Indian conditions! So, even today we have a monopoly on that!
>
> (Interview with Flexitron CEO)

Eventually, they not only found a solution for the specific lighting problem in T-Zed, but also, they were able to 'design and develop an emerging technology at T-Zed, which is LED … to kind of demonstrate that [it is a] much more efficient lighting system' (Interview C4). This has led Flexitron not only being recognised within the development industry but also enabling them to access capital to undertake ambitious projects (such as a project of peri-urban electrification of rural and informal settlements using a combination of solar energy and LED bulbs). However, what is represented here as a 'success' can be also described as a succession of unsuccessful experiments. Overall, the attempt was to tame, or to domesticate the object into an element which would respond to the needs of the developers. Yet, rather than domesticating the object, there were a series of adjustments of expectations which responded to material agencies and mobilities. This process of adjustment is, at its core, a process of maintenance, of making that once strange object more familiar not only for those who develop the product but also for those who will be serviced by this product. The success of the lighting system in T-Zed was not due to mastering the technology but rather, it was due to an ongoing process in which both requirements and expectations were redefined – as were the socio-technical relations about what lighting is or should be, and how it should be obtained.

## Vignette 3: the centralised cooling network

In Bangalore, both environmental activists and professional developers question the use of architectural models which they perceive as imported from Western models or urbanism and badly adjusted to the climatic conditions of the city:

> [S]o one of the things we [modern architects] did is completely copy the Western, North American or European, architecture … Nothing is lazier than modern architecture! … In the Indian context, that does not work … you need at least 200% more energy than in the traditional building … [But] the [Indian] people are just crazy about the West!
>
> (Interview C6)

One of the symbols of 'decadence' and 'distasteful living' mentioned is *glass* which shows 'no regard for other forms of living within the city' (Interview N5). A local activist argues:

> [U]nfortunately we have given up that old traditional architecture and have taken up Western models of living where you cover your building with glass and you use air conditioning systems. And in Bangalore you do not need air conditioning systems at all because the temperature doesn't go beyond 32 degrees; it is only two months during the summer it goes a bit up to 38 … But now it is more fashionable for architects to sell Western houses or a Western-looking building.
>
> (Interview N1)

The consumption of energy to cool glass-made buildings represents a shift in building models from traditional architecture to US-inspired models of big glass skyscrapers which is seen as unnecessarily increasing the carbon emissions of the city while spoiling its scarce resources.

In T-Zed, there was, however, no questioning of the need for cooling. Passive solar designs and natural ventilation were developed to reduce the heating and cooling needs of the building. Additional cooling was provided by simple landscaping solutions, house orientation and sky gardens. In every case, well-known technologies already existed and T-Zed intervened by adjusting these technologies to the context. Yet, apart from these design features, BCIL set up the challenge to develop an environmentally-friendly air conditioning (AC) system for the compound.

Arguably, the AC system and an associated in-house-designed customised refrigerator were the most complicated elements in T-Zed. A completely new design was necessary, according to BCIL, 'to avoid the long-term risk of at least half the residents going for energy-guzzling ACs or refrigerators', which would defeat the purpose. The AC system, in particular, established innovation at three levels through an ammonia-based central chiller plant for the whole compound (primary cooling), accompanied by cooling towers (secondary cooling) and individual chillers (tertiary cooling).

Both the fridges and the air conditioning system were conceived as centralised systems that would provide a homogeneous service to the whole compound. The centralised solution was proposed as a way to reduce the overall energy consumption without compromising the resident's lifestyles: 'Because it was a high energy group, a solution had to be brought forward … the T-Zed Air Conditioning System … [should] bring about at least 40 per cent or 30 per cent efficiency on the conventional air conditioning systems at that time' (Interview C4). As usual, BCIL scouted for the best technologies. The aim was to establish a centralised district refrigeration system and air conditioning system using an ammonia-based chilling unit, a 'system … done post-war in 1945!' (Interview D3). 'What made it really innovative was the establishment of a cooling network in which the fridge was supposed to work without a compressor' (Interview D4). The air conditioning system was complemented with '100 per cent fresh air window-mounted fan coil units' and a 'pre-cooling coil-fed roof-mounted cooling tower', so that, as explained above, the in-house temperature depended on three levels of cooling: the centralised system, the cooling towers and the air window fan. This system generated a need for customised refrigerators and air conditioning units.

However, in March 2010, refrigeration units were piled up in the office that BCIL keeps at T-Zed. A chain of material events led to failures in the delivery of the cooling system. The first problem was in the network:

> Sending the central refrigerant through the dual fridges … was not possible because of that −25 degree centigrade solution and it was getting frozen

because [of] the insulation … the water had damaged [the pipes] really badly! … It is a problem … in the execution …when you insulate the pipes.

(Interview C6)

As a consequence, instead of the original idea of using a compressor for 100 refrigerators, the failure in the refrigeration network led to the incorporation of compressors in each custom-made refrigerator. This, however, had consequences in terms of how the fridges could be used, 'primarily because of the fact [that] it was generally designed as a centralised refrigeration system and then ultimately became as big as compressors in a breadbox' (Interview C4). However, for individual units, more efficient (and more user-friendly) designs existed in the market. Although the technology was well known, it did not actually work as expected. Most interviewees agreed that the design was well known, and that it should have worked, but identified multiple reasons why the implementation failed, whether it was in the execution of the piping system (Interview C6), the design of the appliances (Interview C4) or the management (Interview D3).

Residents, however, found their own solutions to this problem by resorting to conventional appliances: 'Actually the fridge didn't work in my house so I bought a new one from the market' (Interview R1). Regarding the air conditioning system, two residents showed me the cooling towers and window fans which did not appear to be operating:

They seem to have spent all the money putting in those units and all the piping and they have the machinery and the utility block but it's not running yet … and [I] also mind that they […] have spent a lot of money on something which may not take off.

(Interview R4)

Ultimately, BCIL provided a guarantee to residents that sustainable innovations would allow them to avoid compromising between their lifestyle and their environmental concerns. The ultimate responsibility for the material failures fell on the developer:

They tried to bring a lot of elements for the building: common air conditioning, common refrigeration … some of the things did not work out, from the developers' point of view, because it was high capital costs and they did not recuperate the money … because it was innovative high costs occurred at the time of execution.

(Interview C1)

However, the experience of maintenance in T-Zed has had practical implications for residents, who explain that moving to the development has changed their understanding of themselves and their life practices:

> [After living in T-Zed] I am more conscious of my carbon footprint. And about … not using plastics; I never take plastics when I go shopping, never accept plastic bags. And being a bit more conscious, using public transportation … I see people not doing it as a big shame.
>
> (Interview R3)

As this quote suggests, the development of a set of green practices not only influences the resident's conception of self, but also how she comes to understand other people's practices. Residents' comments emphasise a practical element embedded in the development of environmental citizenship because 'only when you do them you realise how important the environment is' (Interview R1). However, this effect has not been homogeneous across the development. For those who already considered themselves environmentally conscious, and who moved to T-Zed not because of the space but as a life choice, the experience of T-Zed has had an almost opposite effect in terms of understanding the material and institutional constraints associated with green buildings:

> I used to be more forceful about it than I am now. Now I think I would be … happy if somebody tried to build these [green] things but I wouldn't be so negative about people who didn't try it! I think there is a balance between practicality and experimentation.
>
> (Interview R4)

Unlike in the case of LED lighting, BCIL had not multiple opportunities to re-enact the cooling experiment, and maintenance and adjustment to specific conditions were not possible.

Individuals may attribute responsibilities according to the chain of events – from the design and the execution to the management and daily performance of the system – but the failure could also be explained from a systemic perspective by emphasising the difficulties in changing the socio-technical relations at so many levels. In maintaining the cooling system in T-Zed, multiple materialities were put in place with unexpected results. However, the expectations of the system (both of the developers and the residents) remained constant and the solutions proposed returned to well-known systems for individual cooling units and refrigerators. Unlike in the case of the lighting system – where there were both room for further experimentation and changing expectations – the innovative cooling system, much more embedded in the original design, was confronted with the obduracy of the socio-technical system and eventually resulted in a business-as-usual solution.

## Conclusion

As experiments become central to understanding how urban low carbon transitions are occurring or may occur, it is important to examine the process and consequences of such experiments. This entails not only an explanation of what makes an experiment possible, how it is made or how it relates to the experiences of those who will stay with the experiment for a long time. There is also a crucial moment in the process of experimentation that entails adjusting it to specific social and material contexts where the experiment is enacted. This is what we have called the maintenance of the experiment.

As it relates to the wider context of urban planning, and as it has been emphasised by Graham and Thrift (2007), maintenance is the process that bridges the intrusion of the experiment and its being ready-to-hand, part of the embodied experience of urban space. Material agencies which mediate urban life practices are thus central to understanding the role of the experiment within wider socio-technical networks.

In the case of T-Zed in Bangalore, maintaining the experiment required maintaining the multiplicity of agencies which emerged as a result of the experiment, including managing the interactions between materials, working practices, the weather, residents' expectations and values among other many heterogeneous components which could not be anticipated in the development design. Familiar materials became complicated because they did not respond to specific job markets created by the housing industry in Bangalore or because they colluded with the expectations of residents about what is normal. In any case, different materials triggered observations of anomaly in what is a fascinating account of walls bubbling and materials just failing ('refusing') to respond to the expectations of developers, consultants and residents.

Overall, the experiment itself is an attempt to tame the agency of innovation materials and natural components, which may be successful – as in the case of the LED lighting – but may also prove to be unruly (cf. Kaika, 2006). When the 'taming' succeeds, this is not so much because the technology agency is dominated, but because a series of adjustments have been developed which enable spaces for that agency. In the case of LED lighting, several attempts with different options and a few consultations with residents about what could and could not be delivered, led to a result which apparently managed to satisfy those involved in its development. In the case of the cooling system, however, an array of technicians, consultants and industrialists (who manufactured the product) were not able to anticipate the need for adjustment to unexpected consequences.

Overall, this is only a partial aspect of what maintenance is about. The management of material agencies at the local scale of the development is clearly observable in everyday practices. But multiple adjustments need to happen as well at the neighbouring and city-wide scale, which include adjustments to material spaces, resources and networks but also adjustments to broader social and political expectations. Maintenance depends on processes of alignment and circulation which shape the urban arena (Castán Broto and Bulkeley, 2013). Experiments such as T-Zed symbolise attempts to integrate green discourses within the existing dynamics of urban development, in particular, meeting the aspirations of a growing middle-upper class who are portrayed as sensitive to global environmental change.

Rather than challenging the existing dynamics of power and inequality in the city, we find that the experiment seeks to re-imagine the identities of the privileged in the context of urban development on the fringes of the city. Both the discourses of developers and some residents emphasise that having a superior environmental morality involves not only being concerned about environmental issues, but also performing an appropriate lifestyle. T-Zed offers a space where those lifestyles can be developed, in opposition to mainstream developments that spray DDT or use plastic. What T-Zed demonstrated for other built environment innovators in Bangalore is that this lifestyle can be both commoditised and transformed into a ready-to-sell product. Now, in Bangalore, developers, consultants and authorities have turned to green innovation both as a discourse to justify urban sprawl and as a strategy to obtain additional returns on capital. Moreover, T-Zed also showed that lifestyles can be both regularised (to the extent to which developers can be prescriptive about how such lifestyles need to be performed) and moralised (in terms of establishing a collective low carbon ethics including both residents and developers).

However, the maintenance experiences in T-Zed demonstrate that similar developments are not only an instrument to advance capital reproduction. They are also sites of experimentation, of the generation of new ideas that challenge established models of working. Some of them involve a redefinition of both actors and technologies and their operation within unexpected opportunity terrains. For example, Flexitron used T-Zed as an expensive demonstration lab, to test cheap but effective technologies which they think will provide access to lighting in poorer areas. Some residents have re-examined their motivations and identities following their experiences of maintenance, raising also questions about the potential of technological and design fixes to open up pathways to sustainability, though there is hardly any reflection over the inherent unsustainability of current urbanisation patterns. Overall, while experiment maintenance is needed to keep business as usual within the city, it is also an unruly process whereby materialities may help re-imagine mainstream discourses and practices.

## Acknowledgements

The ideas and material upon which this chapter is based were developed during Harriet Bulkeley's ESRC Climate Change Fellowship, Urban Transitions: climate change, global cities and the transformation of socio-technical networks (Award Number: RES-066-27-0002). The authors wish to thank the numerous people who provided support during fieldwork in Mumbai and Bangalore. The chapter benefited from the comments and guidance of Steve Graham, Colin McFarlane and Renu Desai. For further information see: www.geography.dur.ac.uk/projects/urbantransitions.

## Note

1    In order to understand the dynamics of T-Zed, fieldwork was carried out in Bangalore, in March 2010. The quotes correspond to 24 selected key interviews with individuals who had a close relationship or had been influenced by T-Zed. In the chapter these interviews have been designated by a letter (developers = D; consultants = C; residents = R; and NGOs = N) and a number.

## Bibliography

Angel, D. and Rock, M.T. (2009) 'Environmental rationalities and the development state in East Asia: prospects for a sustainability transition', *Technological Forecasting and Social Change*, 76: 229–240.

Bai, X., Wieczorek, A.J., Kaneko, S., Lisson, S. and Contreras, A. (2009) 'Enabling sustainability transitions in Asia: the importance of vertical and horizontal linkages', *Technological Forecasting and Social Change*, 76: 255–266.

BCIL (2009) *UNEP: Case Study*. Bangalore: Biodiversity Conservation India Limited.

Bulkeley, H. and Castán Broto, V. (2012) 'Urban experiments and the governance of climate change: towards Zero Carbon Development in Bangalore', *Contemporary Social Science*. Advance online publication.

Bulkeley, H. and Castán Broto, V. (2013) 'Government by experiment? Global cities and the governing of climate change', *Transactions of the Institute of British Geographers*, 38(3): 361–365.

Burgess, J., Clark, J. and Harrison, C.M. (2000) 'Knowledges in action: an actor network analysis of a wetland agri-environment scheme', *Ecological Economics*, 35: 119–132.

Callon, M. (1986) 'The sociology of an actor-network: the case of the electric vehicle', in J.L. M. Callon and A. Rip (eds) *Mapping the Dynamics of Science and Technology: Sociology of Science in the Real World*. Basingstoke: Macmillan, pp. 19–34.

Castán Broto, V. and Bulkeley, H. (2013) 'Maintaining climate change experiments: urban political ecology and the everyday reconfiguration of urban infrastructure', *International Journal of Urban and Regional Research*. Advance online publication.

Cooke, J. and Lewis, R. (2010) 'The nature of circulation: the urban political ecology of Chicago's Michigan Avenue Bridge, 1909–1930', *Urban Geography*, 31: 348–368.

De Schutter, O. (2012) 'Climate change is a human rights issue – and that's how we can solve it', *The Guardian*, Tuesday 24 April.

Geels, F.W. and Schot, J. (2007) 'Typology of sociotechnical transition pathways', *Research Policy*, 36: 399–417.

Graham, S., McFarlane, C. and Desai, R. (2013) 'Water wars in Mumbai', *Public Culture*, 25: 115–141.

Graham, S. and Thrift, N.J. (2007) 'Out of order: understanding repair and maintenance', *Theory, Culture & Society*, 24: 1–25.

Haraway, D. (1991) 'A cyborg manifesto: science, technology, and socialist-feminism in the late twentieth century', *Simians, Cyborgs, and Women: The Reinvention of Nature*. New York: Routledge.

Heynen, N.C., Kaika, M. and Swyngedouw, E. (2006) *In the Nature of Cities: Urban Political Ecology and the Politics of Urban Metabolism*. New York: Routledge.

Holifield, R. (2009) 'Actor-Network Theory as a critical approach to environmental justice: a case against synthesis with urban political ecology', *Antipode*. 41: 637–658.

Hommels, A. (2005) 'Studying obduracy in the city: toward a productive fusion between Technology Studies and Urban Studies', *Science, Technology, & Human Values*, 30: 323–351.

Hommels, A. (2008) *Unbuilding Cities: Obduracy in Urban Sociotechnical Change.* Cambridge, MA: MIT Press.

Kaika, M. (2005) *City of Flows: Modernity, Nature, and the City.* London: Routledge.

Kaika, M. (2006) *City of Flows: Modernity, Nature, and the City.* London: Routledge.

Keil, R. (2005) 'Progress report: urban political ecology', *Urban Geography*, 26: 640–651.

Latour, B. (1993) *We Have Never Been Modern.* Brighton: Harvester Wheatsheaf.

Latour, B. (2004) *Politics of Nature: How to Bring the Sciences into Democracy.* Cambridge, MA: Harvard University Press.

Latour, B. (2005) *Reassembling the Social: An Introduction to Actor-Network-Theory.* Oxford: Oxford University Press.

McFarlane, C. (2010) 'The comparative city: knowledge, learning, urbanism', *International Journal of Urban and Regional Research*, 34: 725–742.

Monstadt, J. (2009) 'Conceptualizing the political ecology of urban infrastructures: insights from technology and urban studies', *Environment and Planning A*, 41: 1924–1942.

Murdoch, J. (2001) 'Ecologising sociology: actor-network theory, co-construction and the problem of human exceptionalism', *Sociology: The Journal of the British Sociological Association*, 35: 111–133.

Smith, A., Voß, J.-P. and Grin, J. (2010) 'Innovation studies and sustainability transitions: the allure of the multi-level perspective and its challenges', *Research Policy*, 39: 435–448.

Star, S.L. (1999) 'The ethnography of infrastructure', *American Behavioral Scientist*, 43(3): 377–391.

Swyngedouw, E. (2006) 'Circulations and metabolisms: (hybrid) natures and (cyborg) cities', *Science as Culture*, 15: 105–121.

Swyngedouw, E. and Heynen, N.C. (2003) 'Urban political ecology, justice and the politics of scale', *Antipode*, 35(5): 898–918.

Verbeek, P. (2004) *What Things Do: Philosophical Reflections on Technology, Agency and Design.* University Park, PA: Pennsylvania State University Press.

# Chapter 10

# Low carbon nation

## Making new market opportunities

*Mike Hodson and Simon Marvin*

## Introduction

The transition to a low carbon future is the key challenge of our time. In the policy and strategy documents of international bodies, the UK government, sub-national authorities, business, and in the work of academics, it is recognised that a massive reduction in greenhouse gas emissions is required. The scale of the transition required is fundamental. Frequently, in both policy and popular discourse, it is the market, technological and behavioural change elements of a low carbon future that are privileged. Yet where, how and involving whom low carbon futures will be made and with what consequences are underdeveloped – so too, at a democratic level, is why.

The transition to the carbon-based society we now inhabit in the UK can be traced to developments occurring from the industrialisation of the second half of the nineteenth century. At that time, the aim of politicians, policy-makers and industrialists was to build the infrastructures to support the development of industrial capitalism. Yet in doing so, there was little explicit mention of build-ing an explicitly carbon-based economy and society. But as the tensions and contradictions of carbon-based industrial capitalism become increasingly appar-ent, both policy and political responses are struggling to articulate broad visions of a society (and an economy) that go beyond carbon. Instead contemporary visions usually start from saying what the transition is not! Consequently, responses to multiple economic and ecological crises, in the UK and the wider Western world, increasingly take the form of carbon prefixes and suffixes: low-carbon, post-carbon, zero-carbon, carbon-neutral, etc. The broad positive visions of a post-carbon future are not being forcefully articulated or at least not being widely communicated and received.

This matters, as what is clear from the historical production of carbon-based industrial (and post-industrial) capitalism is that carbon-based resources were both a means of supporting the development of, and a consequence of, the growth of industrial capitalism. But in current debates about low and post-carbon futures there is limited fundamental questioning of modes of economic organisa-tion and their relationship to low and post-carbon resource organisation and flows.

To contribute to the widening of this debate, in this chapter we develop a critical analysis of the dominant pathways through which low carbon Britain is currently emerging. We do this by examining the ways in which economic and ecological crises are mobilised as the basis for low carbon experimentation. This is underpinned by the spatial politics of the re-organisation of the architectures of governing state-space. The material strategies that follow from this are designed to translate into new interrelationships within and external to state-space through: new sources of energy production, particularly offshore wind; new sources of mobility, here mediated through low carbon vehicles and associated infrastructures; reshaping consumption through a programme of the 'retrofitting' of buildings based on the forging of low carbon consumers; and finally the redesign of the electricity transmission grid. This leads us to a consideration of what low carbon transition means for everyday life and the rather limited role – if at all – envisaged for users. We conclude by revisiting how the dominance of the exclusive coalitions of social interests that shape largely techno-economic response to the question of low carbon transition can be enlarged and challenged.

## Crises and experimentation

The UK government is subject to legally binding carbon reduction targets of 80 per cent by 2050 with intermediate targets on the way to 2050 (Climate Change Act, 2008). It is broadly recognised that a massive reduction in greenhouse gas emissions is required. One only needs to consider the range of energy, transport, water and waste infrastructure systems and the ways in which they have developed in the UK to understand that such a transition is radical in its intent and revolutionary in its implications. Yet, the complex interrelationships within and between these systems are historically deeply embedded. Raising the idea of these carbon-based systems as stable is not to say they have been unchanging, as a history of, for example, the electricity system in the UK demonstrates.

Yet taking transition seriously implies a radical transformation in the ways in which relatively stabilised configurations are organised. These configurations and their material manifestation are fundamental to the production of places. Within this there is an important constitutive role for national-sub-national relations, that are mediated through struggles over the balance of relationships between the economy and the environment, production and consumption, and between public and private, and which shape the organisation of resource flows and the socio-technical infrastructure systems through which they flow into, through and out of places. In any transformation there is a process of transition from something and to something else. The complex organisation of a carbon-based UK society, the multiple relationships that constitute it and the concepts through which these interests are mediated and organised are historically generated, and these relationships have 'locked in' the UK to a carbon-based society.

The possibilities not only to fundamentally question but also to potentially radically and effectively transform a carbon-based society is not only extremely challenging but requires the creation of a set of conditions to do so. These necessary but certainly not sufficient conditions arise every three or so decades with the confluence of multiple crises – economic, ecological and political. The confluence of these crises creates spaces for experimentation – in relationships between national and sub-national units, in the organisation of economic life, with the mutual implications this has for ecology, the organisation of infrastructure systems and the governing of society. Such spaces open up for a period of around ten to fifteen years while the struggle over how to respond to multiple crises is played out. Within these wider shifts the critical issue is in the political struggle to shape the parameters of what sort of low carbon Britain is desirable and possible. Periodisations of the kind we make here are helpful in understanding the historical shifts that are taking place but are also often full of struggle and contradictions and are often never as temporally bounded and neat as their characterisations.

The interrelationships of governing state-space, economy, ecology, resource politics and socio-technical infrastructure systems have been organised in different ways across historical periods and have enjoyed relatively stable periods of interrelationship in different 'phases' since the Second World War. That is not to say that there have not been difficulties and specific crises but that the interrelations have been generally obdurate. There have been periods of a confluence of crises, though, where these interrelationships have come under pressures for fundamental transformation. There was such a period from the late 1960s to the early 1980s and, we would argue, we have been experiencing another such phase since around 2007.

These pressures do not of themselves determine the shape of reconfigured interrelationships between the different elements but they challenge the existing organisation. Andrew Gamble (2009) points out that a capitalist crisis 'signals major adjustments for particular powers and regimes' and that the economic, political and ideological crises that underpin it 'take the form of prolonged periods of political, economic and ideological impasse'. This involves a struggle to defend and discredit the status quo. Crises open up obdurate interrelationships to economic, political, ecological and governing challenges – they also involve a wide range of social and institutional interests, often with diverse aims and variable financial resources and knowledge to be able to draw upon. Many of these are inevitably defenders of the current arrangements but others are seeking to establish a new order. What this means, in relation to low carbon futures, is that the possibilities imagined in low carbon strategies are incorporated into existing contexts on the basis of the organisation of the existing sets of interrelationships, the ways in which pressures open those up, and the political struggle to define a low carbon future that moulds possibilities to the realities of existing contexts. This is a profoundly political struggle.

Whether the neoliberal discourse can be re-energised is a central issue. This has critical implications as neoliberalism was conceived in terms of a multilevel governance and new competing state-spaces predicated on permanent 'innovation' in a 'globalised' system. This was organised through a 'shrinking' state, a facilitatory state whose organising principle is one of 'limits to state intervention' – that often, paradoxically, requires huge state intervention in the processes of regulating to de-regulate and re-regulate in pursuit of place-based accumulation strategies. This has led to processes of not only 'rolling back' the state through institutional destruction, adaptation or capture but also a 'rolling out' (Peck and Tickell, 2002) of new institutional and state formations. Neoliberalisms as demand-led and increasingly privatised economic strategies were reliant on large flows of credit and debt leverage and the emergence of newly industrialising economies as producers but not large-scale consumers of goods. The result of this was the re-investment of surplus as cheap consumer credit in Western economies and the inflation of a credit and debt bubble which exploded in 2007.

Yet, for neoliberal advocates this may be seen as a jolt but no reason to turn on the primacy of the market as a 'state of nature' where seeking to ignore this has been likened to being akin to trying to ignore the laws of gravity (Turner, 2008). While the neoliberal free market logic is in crisis, any replacement is not yet formed (Gamble, 2009). This is likely to be the product of political struggle and experimentation. The spaces of experimentation that opened up in the second half of the 2000s ask whether what follows the neoliberal competition state will be something that is fundamentally different or a re-working of the competition role of the national state in prioritising particular places and spaces.

## Re-engineering state architecture

A range of low carbon strategies and the crises of existing dominant discourses of state-space, economy-ecology and infrastructure and resource organisation open up possibilities for their radical reconfiguration and of the configurations that are re-producing them. A dominant discourse since the early 1980s has been the primacy of the market, the desirability of competition and centrality of economic growth. Whether this context forms the basis for the styles of low carbon futures that are currently being formed and, if so, how, are critical issues. As historically generated power relationships are coming under pressure in the current crises, we need to examine how specific governmental understandings of low carbon futures are being produced through specific interrelationships and institutions (Foucault, 2007; Collier, 2009). Consequently in this section we examine the governmental relations and the processes through which a 'national landscape' of low carbon rationalities is being constructed.

The significance of the 2008 UK Climate Change Act was in its positioning of the UK as the first country in the world to have a legally binding framework for cutting carbon emissions. Among the key priorities in the Act is the setting of binding greenhouse gas emissions reduction targets of at least 80 per cent by 2050 with an interim reduction in emissions of at least 34 per cent, from a 1990 baseline, by 2020. This is to be achieved through five-year carbon budgeting systems. These developments create new pressures relating to climate change and carbon regulation (While, 2008). In addition to statutory carbon reduction targets cascaded down from international agreements (Bulkeley and Betsill, 2003), those developed by national government place renewed emphasis on sub-national territorial units, and will then place a premium on the ability of states and territories to better manage energy consumption and accelerate the development of low carbon energy transitions.

## New interventionism and governance fixes

Relationships between national government departments and sub-national territories are helpfully understood through the lens of a political struggle between 'new' forms of state territorial interventions and the state reconfiguration of sub-national governance architectures. This can be illustrated through analysis of national government 'low carbon' priorities. Historically, government priorities around energy have been formulated in a multiplicity of departments which had a range of issues as their core brief – trade and industry, environment, food and rural affairs, etc. The consequence of this is that current UK priorities around energy need to be pieced together from a variety of different departmental positions.

In July 2009, the UK government published its Low Carbon Transition Plan (LCTP) which detailed broadly how the UK would meet the 2020 and 2050 emissions reduction commitments set out in the Climate Change Act (CCA). The Plan is underpinned by five stated principles: first, to protect the UK public from the immediate risks of climate change; second, to anticipate how the consequences of climate change are prepared for, particularly in relation to infrastructure and housing; third, that climate change requires a new international agreement on global emissions reduction; fourth, that the UK can play its part by developing a low carbon country to meet targets set out in the CCA and address vulnerabilities and promote economic opportunities; and, fifth, that addressing climate change requires widespread participation from communities, businesses, individuals, and so on (DECC, 2009). LCTP is not only a transition route map to 2020 for the UK but also operates in prioritising the carbon savings expected across different sectors.

The Low Carbon Industrial Strategy (LCIS) was launched jointly by the Department for Business, Innovation and Skills (BIS) and DECC in July 2009. It aims to position British businesses to secure the economic and job creation opportunities of a low carbon transition and, in doing so, to minimise the economic costs of inaction. The strategy details a range of potential low carbon sectors and technological areas – wind, wave, tidal, low carbon vehicles, carbon capture and storage, etc. – and also a more strategic approach to the development of low carbon economic activity and technologies across the regions of the UK, particularly through designating low carbon economic areas (LCEAs) (BIS/DECC, 2009).

A less directly 'interventionist' national government role in sub-national activities was outlined in 2008 in the UK government's support for the creation of two city-regions in 2009 and, in doing so, the development of new metropolitan governance structures (HM Treasury 2008, 2009). The broad parameters within the city-regions were to operate as statutory forms of sub-regional cooperation between local authorities with the aim of them being significant contributors to sustainable forms of economic growth. Low carbon economic activities were also worked into these proposals as city-regions took a more active role in shaping low carbon transition in their own contexts.

The priorities of the Climate Change Act and its emphasis on emissions reduction are broadly supported across the UK political parties. There have, similarly, been few dissenting political voices in relation to the LCTP. The principal political tension is in the process of *how* the strategic priorities will be achieved – what are the mediating frameworks and institutions, what economic, social and knowledge resources are allocated to them? While there appears, superficially at least to be a broad consensus on the policy priorities – the achievement of large emissions reduction – the central controversy is around the mode of governing and the ways in which 'intermediary' activity is organised.

The tension is between, first, new forms of state industrial interventionism in regions, city-regions and pan-regions and, second, in constructing new forms of national-sub-national governance fixes that see the state less in the direct role of industrial intervener and more re-cast as a 'facilitator' for city-regions and local economic partnerships to create the conditions for market-based and private-sector led activity. This struggle was inherent within the Labour government, which governed until 2010, and cut across its different strategies. The subsequent Coalition government, from May 2010, is comprehensively re-structuring sub-national governance by actively seeking to abolish and re-design institutional mediators between its central departments and places to create the conditions to compete for limited resources and create private and entrepreneurial responses that will 'emerge' and develop place-based low carbon activities. In short, the existing dominant mediators of national-sub-national relations – the Regional Development Agencies – are being abolished and replaced by local economic partnerships (LEP). At the same time a much less well resourced Regional Growth Fund, from 2011, will intensify competition between places for national resources and support. These national policies and priorities encompass a range of economic, environmental, technological and territorial issues. The ways in which different priorities coalesce within the context of regions, cities, communities and places are unclear but are likely to involve the negotiation of these different national priorities with sub-national priorities.

The struggle over time, between government departments, within government departments and through the governmental relationships and networks that shape and re-shape national government priorities, has been one that can be broadly characterised as the struggle between place-based government 'intervention' in shaping the parameters and capacity development for low carbon futures and a governmental role in the stripping out capacity for private opportunity in the name of a new localism. This is not a zero-sum issue but is the subject of struggle.

## What kind of low carbon nation?

The struggles between these multiple and competing priorities materialise in a variety of ways and often have variable geographical consequences. Using the examples of the dominant pathways to low carbon Britain involving offshore wind, low carbon vehicle infrastructure, retrofit of the built environment, and a reconfigured electricity grid, we examine the relational deployment of these priorities and the configurations of existing institutions, re-cast and re-invigorated institutions and those that are marginalised in doing so.

### Offshore wind: the marketised construction of new production systems

The development of UK offshore wind capacity and capability offers a tangible example of the market-making role of the national state in seeing their purpose as creating the framework and conditions to stimulate market opportunities for investors. This has been done through developing the national targets towards which low carbon activity should be directed and broadly designating the zones and places within which offshore wind should be developed. The UK government's approach to offshore wind is framed through carbon reduction targets of 80 per cent by 2050 and also by renewable energy targets by 2020 of 15 per cent.

The approach of both the current and the previous UK governments has been to organise the development of offshore wind through three successive rounds managed by the Crown Estate. The Crown Estate has a statutory duty to manage the UK's coastal waters in a 'sustainable' way. The UK is favourably positioned to develop offshore wind capacity and capability, given the shallow water depth and consistent high wind speeds around a significant area of its coast. Scotland, alone, is estimated to account for around one-quarter of total potential EU wind power (a potential power output of 36GW) which has led to it being characterised as the 'Saudi Arabia of renewables'.[1] The Crown Estate has, in recent years, begun to shift from a relatively benign role in managing the marine estate. In doing this it has moved to playing a more active role which marries together the technological possibilities afforded by the UK's position and a shifting view of its role as a sustainable manager of the marine estate that considers economic possibilities as well as environmental and social considerations. Its development planning is explicitly orientated around meeting UK targets.

In doing this, the Crown Estate, working closely with UK government departments, has designated leases for offshore wind farms in three rounds. In the first round (announced in 2000), of around 1.6GW of capacity, and second round (with competitive tendering from July 2003), of around 7.4GW of capacity, the emphasis was in many ways on the demonstration of the development of offshore wind, the issues this generated and lessons to be learned. A third round of development (announced in December 2007) is estimated at between three and five times the scale of the first two rounds combined and involves the development of nine zones off the coast of the UK (see Figure 10.1). This is part of a national government attempt to position the UK as a 'leader' in this field and to potentially create the world's largest offshore wind *market*. The zones are widely drawn, where the developer, chosen through competition, can develop in the parts of the zone they consider to be most fruitful. The process of development is long-term (up to four years) and requires addressing and developing an effective response to a wide range of issues. These include, in particular, constructing supply chains in relation to skills, infrastructure installation, manufacturing and component supply, and so on. This has particular geographies to it related to those areas of coastline encountering beneficial wind speed and water depth, but also the adjacent, land-based existing R&D capacity and capability.

Dogger Bank, for example, is the largest of these sites and is positioned between 125 and 195 kilometres off the North-east coast of England. It extends over approximately 8,660 km², with water depth that ranges from 18–63 metres. The consortium that won the bid to develop Dogger Bank, Forewind,[2] has agreed with the Crown Estate a target installed capacity of 9GW, with a potential for approximately 13GW. Dogger Bank (and the other sites) require research, development, manufacturing and implementation capacity based in, this case, the North-East of England and for the attraction of inward investment. The decision, for example, to site the Clipper Windpower manufacturing facility – at the old Neptune shipyard on Tyneside – can be seen in this light. The factory will be the manufacturing base for the blades for the prototype 10MW Britannia offshore turbines. This is part of a push by policy-makers to make the North-East attractive to developers of wind turbines, whereby in this instance a £4.4 million grant from the UK government under its Low Carbon Energy Demonstration capital grants scheme was awarded to Clipper. The aim is that not solely blades will be manufactured on Tyneside but that the towers, motors and foundations will all be built in the North-East.

This regional strategy needs to be viewed through the adaptability of existing assets and capacity in the North-East and the development of new capabilities and assets to support the creation of new markets for investors. There are plans to use old industrial sites and pre-existing skills, such as those from the shipyards and their role in offshore construction work, including wind turbines, that go beyond conventional ship repair and conversion work to support investment and 'market opportunities'. At the development stage the Crown Estate is performing a more active role of bearing a significant share of the risk through funding up to 50 per cent of the development costs prior to consent. In this respect that Crown Estate is increasingly becoming an active partner in the creation of offshore wind market opportunities. Similarly, so is the UK government which, in addition to creating a framework of targets to be achieved, has and is developing policy and, through

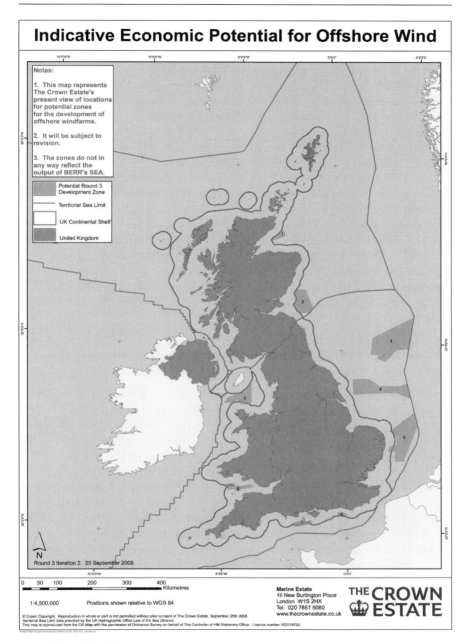

# Indicative Economic Potential for Offshore Wind

Notes:

1. This map represents The Crown Estate's present view of locations for potential zones for the development of offshore windfarms.

2. It will be subject to revision.

3. The zones do not in any way reflect the output of BERR's SEA.

- Potential Round 3 Development Zone
- Territorial Sea Limit
- UK Continental Shelf
- United Kingdom

Round 3 Iteration 2  25 September 2008

0    50    100    200    300    400    Kilometres

1:4,500,000    Positions shown relative to WGS 84

Marine Estate
16 New Burlington Place
London  W1S 2HX
Tel:  020 7851 5080
www.thecrownestate.co.uk

THE CROWN ESTATE

© Crown Copyright. Reproduction in whole or part is not permitted without prior consent of The Crown Estate. September 25th 2008.
Territorial Sea Limit data provided by the UK Hydrographic Office Law of the Sea Division.
This map is reproduced from the OS Map with the permission of Ordnance Survey on behalf of The Controller of HM Stationery Office.  Licence number 100019722.

*Figure 10.1* UK offshore wind zones
Source: Crown Estate.

'arm's-length' regulators, regulatory frameworks to experiment with and build a new offshore wind regulatory regime. This is self-characterised by the regulator, OFGEM, as 'Light handed regulation – a type of regulatory approach that is intended to place a lower administrative burden on the regulated company and the regulator',[3] in the development of a competitive regime. This sets the framework to promote competition to own and operate transmission assets, to attract significant inward investment and to develop supply chains.

The story here is one where there is a primacy of market making with a secondary role for industrial interventionism. The making of offshore wind markets is based on a developing configuration of government targets and zoning, a shifting role for the Crown Estate from benign manager to active market maker, encouraging investors and developers but on the basis of a pre-existing culture of light touch regulation propounded through pre-existing regulatory structures. Industrial interventionism is largely as a means of creating the supply chains required in supporting the making of markets. Here there is a key role for government, with sub-national institutions and actors, in the production of representations of regions and territories as attractive to investors. This has necessitated a more interventionist role in the process of developing supply chains, capacities, research and development and the adapting of existing regional and territorial infrastructures.

## Low carbon vehicles, infrastructure and the prioritisation of places and users

A second leg of the response of the UK government to low carbon transition is focused on the theme of mobility and specifically low carbon vehicles. This section looks at the broad vision and its content, the urban and regional dimensions of the transition, the development of intermediary capacity and the wider consequences of the transition in terms of its socio-material implications.

The UK government's ambitious statutory carbon reduction targets set demanding targets for all sectors, but especially for transport. While the bulk of the improvements required are expected to be gained from improvement to conventional engines and the use of bio-fuels, ultra-low carbon vehicles (ULCV) are expected to have a critical role in the longer term. Consequently in the shorter term, the ambition is to develop an early market and establish a pathway to the mass market development of vehicles and infrastructure. While in the medium term, there is significant potential for decarbonisation, synergies with low carbon electricity objectives and the ambition to realise 'economic benefits' to the UK through the transition. The focus, then, of these activities is primarily around the construction of governmental frameworks to develop capacity to ensure that policies and priorities establish markets for the development of low carbon vehicles (LCVs).

Under both the previous Labour and the current Coalition government there has been significant continuity in the configurations of intermediary governance capacity to develop ULCV markets. For instance, the Office of Low Emission Vehicles (OLEV) was created in 2009 by integrating diverse low carbon initiatives across government, particularly those within the departments of transport and business. The aim of OLEV is to place the UK at the global forefront of ULCV 'development, demonstration, manufacture and use' and, between 2009 and 2014, create a 'flourishing early market with a path to mass market' (OLEV 2009). The view of a civil servant with experience of working in OLEV was that 'the Treasury looked at why the market can't do this on its own', so that, if successful, 'OLEV shouldn't exist forever once the market is up and running …OLEV is here to help create a flourishing market.'[4] The Coalition government has largely reaffirmed these priorities and continued to provide support and funding for OLEV despite the wider cuts in public spending. The focus of OLEV is upon three issues: demand, supply and places. On the demand side, a £230m fund will provide a grant of up to 25 per cent of the cost of an ultra-low carbon car, up to a maximum of £5000. On the supply side a series of research initiatives have been developed including a £140m Low Carbon Innovation Platform and various competitive schemes for funding UK-based research and development on ULCVs.

Alongside these demand and supply side initiatives is 'Plugged in Places', which is designed into two phases to support the early stage of the strategic roll-out of the electric car charging infrastructure in a number of regions. The scheme was launched in late 2009 with two phases and opened to bids from cities and regions with a 'commitment to take the lead in ultra-low carbon transport' (OLEV 2009). The first round of successful bids included London, Milton Keynes and the North-East of England.

There were important connections between the schemes and local priorities in each of these areas. The origin of the North-East scheme was closely linked to the local vehicle production sector where the multinational Nissan and Smiths, a local company, were strategically interested in electric vehicle production. Additional financial support from the Regional Development Agency, One North East, and an early start by Newcastle City Council in developing the expertise and capability to install charging points was meant to demonstrate the potential of electric vehicles application and production for the North-East. London was also strategically interested in electric vehicles as the mayor of London had committed to building the 'Electric Vehicle Capital of Europe'.[5] A stretched target for electric vehicles was adopted in London of 100,000 vehicles by the end of 2020 with incentives built into London's congestion charge. Additionally London's socio-demographic features are seen as particularly amenable as a consumer base for electric cars.

The second phase of Plugged in Places, from November 2010, was also subject to competition but with emphasis on developing more extensive electric vehicle corridors linking the large urban areas selected in the first rounds, to build a longer distance network (Figure 10.2). It is likely that the public sector-led approach – though with private partners and a very bottom-up approach in these

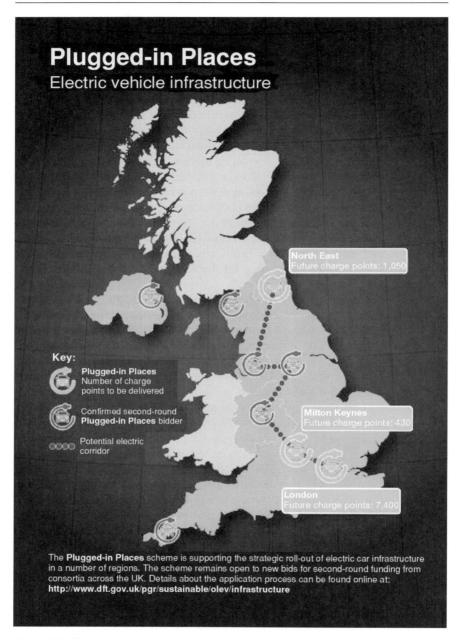

*Figure 10.2* Plugged-in places: electric vehicle infrastructure
Source: OLEV.

early stages – will be replaced by a more private sector and market-led approach
to further development. What we can see here is a competitive and market-led
approach to the development of ULCV where the early role taken by the public
sector in stimulating a response will be increasingly replaced by a more marketised and commercial model particularly with respect to charging infrastructure.
Given the recent stripping out of governance capacity and the sub-regional and
regional intermediaries involved in these schemes, especially in England, the
capacity to present a systemic ULCV response is mainly focused on London
where initiatives are supported by continued governance capacity.

As with offshore wind, the development of low carbon vehicles is framed
primarily in terms of making markets. National government is explicit in its aims
to create a market for ULCV. In doing this, a cross-government department
organisation to facilitate the creation of a market has been established (OLEV).
Schemes to provide the plug-in infrastructure deemed necessary for electric vehicles have been promoted by OLEV where the role of places is seen as competing
with each other to secure the demonstration and development of plug-in infrastructure development and related funds. This has explicitly required the
creation of local and regional networks of local authorities, regional agencies,
automobile manufacturers and potential public sites for plug-in infrastructure,
such as supermarkets. A civil servant with knowledge of OLEV's activities
pointed out that differences between the latter years and of the Labour government and the Coalition government were based on a 'philosophy [that] is
different. [Labour's Business Secretary] Mandleson's [view] was we fund, the
coalition's is we take away barriers and it's about deregulating and encouraging'.[6]
What can be seen here is a degree of asymmetric alignment between these different roles.

## Forging the low carbon consumer through the 'Green Deal'

The 'Green Deal' is the UK Coalition government's response to addressing the
carbon emissions associated with the energy consumed in Britain's poorly insu-
lated buildings. The Green Deal requires new legislation, that is being enacted
through the Energy Security and Green Economy Bill (Energy Bill 2010–11).
The Bill has three principal objectives: (1) tackling barriers to investment in
energy efficiency; (2) enhancing energy security; and (3) enabling investment in
low carbon energy supplies. The ways in which it is envisaged that this is translated through the Green Deal is primarily through new mechanisms for financing
domestic and non-domestic property improvements.

The government is actively trying to construct new market relationships
between private companies and consumers. The basis of the relationship is one
of trying to sell – literally and ideologically – a range of energy efficiency measures. Many of the measures promoted to achieve energy efficiency have
significant upfront costs and long payback periods in terms of recouping investment from energy savings – particularly so in the case of some microgeneration

technologies. There is a critical challenge, in this context, in developing, embedding and creating a view of energy efficiency activity as being not only desirable but 'normal'. A government estimate of the number of jobs created by the Green Deal suggests that up to 250,000 jobs may be created over a 20-year period.[7]

The basis of the Green Deal is one of individuals taking out loans to make their home more energy-efficient and paying that back through additional charges to their energy bill over an up-to-25-year period. The expectation by the Conservative arm of the government was that this would be up to £6,500 depending on the amount of work assessed as being required – although the Liberal Democrats suggested a figure of £10,000. A 'Golden Rule' means that should a homeowner move house, the costs stay attached to the property's energy bill. Levels of repayments will be calculated on the basis that repayments for a given period are less than the resulting energy bill savings, with repayments periods varying. The UK government is discussing with retailers, such as B&Q, Tesco and Marks & Spencer, whether they can provide financing for the loans.

At the centre of the Green Deal is constructing market exchange. This takes place in a time when financial services companies and energy companies are seen by consumers and, thus, there are critical questions of trust. The Green Deal mechanism is based on a series of critical steps. First, the issue of the lack of retrofit activity is conceived through 'customer research' as being a series of practical barriers including cost, payback periods, hassle, lack of awareness of benefits, and so on. Second, the Green Deal is then 'structured around consumer and business needs, because this will ensure widespread update and corresponding provision by the business and finance sectors' (DECC, 2010, p. 8). Finally, in terms of the organisation delivering the Green Deal, the government is 'committed to ensuring competition in all three customer-facing roles in the value chain: advisers, installers and providers' (ibid., p. 19). However, it acknowledges that the Green Deal will only be a success if firms are able to capitalise on consumer interest at 'key trigger points', such as undertaking household projects.

As with offshore wind and ULCV, the Green Deal is concerned with market making. This is even more explicit than in the previous two examples. Yet, in terms of an explicit spatial dimension being built into it, the Green Deal is weak. Instead there is the particular commitment that the economic opportunities of the Green Deal will be 'available across the country, with no regional bias'. In this view the 'national' represents a concern with UK 'needs to become more energy efficient to reduce its greenhouse gas emissions' (ibid., pp. 6–7) while the 'local level' is conceived of as millions of customers, households and businesses seeking to reduce energy consumption and not wasting money. While explicitly there are no levels or scales – regions, sub- or city-regions or local authorities – sitting between national targets and individual 'customers', there is recognition of the role of different forms of 'intermediaries' who may deliver the Green Deal. These intermediaries include local builders, home improvement stores, supermarkets, local councils, and energy companies (ibid., p. 8). While the aim is for customers to receive a 'standardised service', there is recognition that there will be some service variations – and thereby geographical variations – because of the measures that are suitable for different types of property.

Yet, it is clearly evident that the Green Deal agenda is primarily an urban agenda, given that the vast majority of the UK population lives in urban areas and most of the building stock is located in urban areas. Given the critical role of cities in this agenda and the intra-urban differences in the distributions of different types and tenure of buildings and low-income households, greater sensitivity to urban issues might have been expected in the design of the Green Deal. While the spatial dimension of the Green Deal, in terms of its aspirations, is weakly developed, in practice the Green Deal needs to be made manifest somewhere. In this respect, Greater Manchester has been designated a 'pioneering retrofit project' providing 'a model for investors and other social housing providers in demonstrating the vast potential for Green Deal investment in that sector'.[8] The aim is to make 9,000 social homes in Manchester more energy-efficient. Financially the up-front costs will be met by the relevant housing association, with a claimed potential for saving on energy bills of up to £500 per year, potentially the creation of 1,800 jobs and £100 million of activity in the local economy. In this respect Manchester is seen as a test-bed for aspects of the Green Deal. Initially the focus is on 2,500 properties within the Greater Manchester Housing Retrofit Programme – Salix Homes, as part of the Greater Manchester Housing Retrofit Programme, will develop the initiative as part of its current investment programme – as a means of preparing 'the way for Greater Manchester's 260,000 social homes to take up the Green Deal'.[9] This demonstrates that the market-making aspirations of the Green Deal meet in practice a mediating governing framework that is organised at a metropolitan governance level and translated through the examples of social housing. In short, the governmental making and exemplification of market opportunities.

### New interconnections and the grid

The creation of new markets for offshore wind, low carbon vehicles and for energy efficiency and retrofit presents a challenge for the current organisation of the UK's electricity system of production, transmission and consumption. Part of the response, as we have demonstrated, will likely include demand-side management measures. It will also include some on-site generation and localised modes of storage. But the great challenge is in the transformation of the electricity grid that is required to transmit the electricity that is produced from a range of new, often renewable sources, to the main geographical centres of consumption. This may mean a reconfigured grid making new geographical interconnections from, for example, offshore centres of renewable production, the Scottish Highlands and Islands, to large population centres in the South-East of England. It also requires addressing the technical challenge of load balancing that anticipates new forms of consumption (the use of electric vehicles, for example) and dealing with the intermittent generation of renewable energy; and inhibitors such as the development of marine generation when alternating current is of little use for sub-sea transmission over distance, meaning that sub-sea grids have to be direct current.

Without wider change in the grid and its current logic any new production capacity will confront a network that is based on a centralised generating logic (proximate to the coal sources that generated electricity) when the nature of the sources and the geography of future energy generation will be very different. Furthermore, the ageing UK grid is fed by generating capacity where by 2020 significant amounts of the UK's nuclear and coal-based stations will be obsolete, where there are imports of oil and gas from the Middle East and Russia – with the dependencies that creates – and where there will be a commitment to generate around 30 per cent of UK electricity from renewables.

These questions also crucially need to be considered in relation to the relative weight between national priorities – decarbonisation, energy security, job creation, the creation of markets, etc. – and how they translate in relation to the offshore wind, low carbon vehicle and retrofit agendas. So, for example, how is the estimated 32GW of offshore wind development to be organised into circuits of production and consumption? In what ways do concentrations of existing patterns of demand mediate this? How do anticipated future patterns of consumption influence this, for example, through the shift from internal combustion engine vehicles to electric vehicles and their spatial distribution? There are also claims being made that the UK's renewables' potential may mean that the UK can move from being a net importer to a net exporter of energy – and, in times when demand does outstrip supply in the UK, a wider European supergrid is being touted as a means of a Europe-wide balancing of production and consumption. In short, what does this mean for new interconnections of production and consumption and the organisation of this?

There are numerous grid proposals for development at multiple scales, including a re-wired UK grid and also a wider North Sea Grid and European Supergrid. The vision developed by the UK government, through OFGEM to re-wire the UK grid is organised around four principles. First, strengthening the grid is as a means of connecting new forms of renewables generation, both onshore and offshore and new nuclear power stations, often remote from centres of consumption. To do this means a 'radical expansion' of the high voltage transmission network. Second, the assumption that generation from a variety of sources and also consumers being generators means that the generation landscape, its intermittency and its relationship to consumption become more complicated. This requires the development of 'smarter' networks. Third, the development of electric vehicle regimes and other new uses of electrification means that demand for electricity is likely to increase as will patterns and timing of consumption – for example, charging electric cars overnight – where smart meters allow flexibility in consumption patterns. Fourth, much of the existing grid is old and needs replacing (DECC, 2009).

What this might mean is represented in Figure 10.3, with the reinforcement of high voltage grid connections between centres of generation in remote

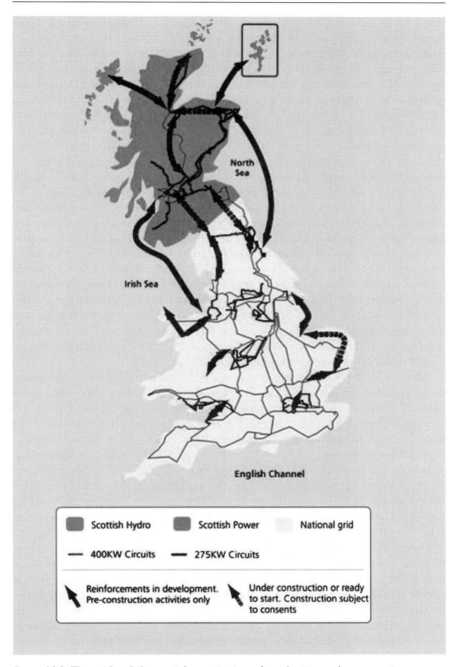

*Figure 10.3* The grid and the spatial organisation of production and consumption
Source: OFGEM/Crown Copyright.

Scotland and centres of consumption in England – through so-called 'boot-straps' connections down the east and west coasts of the UK – and also the reinforcement of connections between England and Wales and within London. The geography of production and consumption is mediated through the development of a newly configured grid but also through the political decisions and priorities, ideology of market-based investment and competition, and technical possibilities.

Proposed developments in the UK grid to make it fit for low carbon purpose are estimated by the regulator OFGEM as requiring £32bn of investment. Given the scale of the investment required, this will mean 'a doubling of the rate of investment but a much more innovative and proactive approach by network companies to meeting the needs of their consumers and network users'.[10] To configure the activities of network companies, OFGEM has developed a RIIO (Revenue = Incentives + Innovation + Outputs) model through which it aims to encourage investment in the financing of new electricity (and gas) transmission and distribution networks and is designed to promote 'innovation and efficiency'. In doing this the RIIO provides a framework that aims to reconfigure the mediation of the role between producers and consumers, between network companies and consumers and network users. This appears to aim to exert greater control over network companies, to promote 'innovation' in the construction of new wires and pipes, to have aspirations for a greater user voice – i.e. an attempt to organise producer–consumer relationships based on consumer preferences – in what those innovations should look like.

This, for example, might mean network companies responding to developers wanting faster connections. The RIIO is designed so that 'fast track price controls' are introduced 'for companies who innovate, deliver good service and produce well-evidenced plans setting out how they will invest efficiently for the future' and 'poorly performing companies will face much more intrusive regulation and lower returns'.[11] It is not entirely clear what the practical implications of this are but it is clear that the RIIO is focused on 'delivery' and performance measurement of the network companies, incorporating consumers and users – i.e. large-scale developers – into the process of what network companies should be delivering, on the basis of a tendering process for large-scale development projects.

Connecting to these debates about the reconfiguration of the grid are efforts to make it 'smarter', that is to say better able to manage the balance of production and consumption. Increasingly the policy response to this in the UK has prioritised the widespread uptake of smart meters – with a target of every home having a smart meter by 2020 – through which real-time energy use data is available to producers and consumers. With the variable and intermittent modes of renewables generation that are currently being developed and also new consumption practices linked to, for example, the electrification of vehicles and the charging of vehicles in off-peak hours, a smarter grid is seen as being necessary to balance production and consumption.

Visions of reconfigured grids are mainly in the planning stages or the early stages of their development. The processes through which these are being developed within the UK and also in terms of the connections between the UK and wider European concerns are deeply political. Under assembly and often in concert but sometimes in struggle are government, commercial, regulatory and technical interests. Symbolically this adds up to fundamental attempts to organise and mediate the flows of energy resources from production through to consumption. This is predicated on a view that the sources of energy production may be far removed from their consumption and that this requires the girding of the UK and Europe with new HV DC cables. These are embryonic attempts to embed structurally the material infrastructures through which production and consumption will be mediated with attempts to make this 'smarter'. There are, though, new centres of production (energy generation, the construction, fabrication and installation infrastructure that supports it and the manufacturing of low carbon vehicles) that are emerging (offshore, the Highlands and Islands, the North-East of England). What shape these take is the subject of struggle and experimentation. The (changing) role of national government(s) is critical here. Whether the creation of new private investor frameworks continues or there is a new manifestation of central government planning and intervention is a critical issue. As is the balance between whether the development of the grid is seen as about geographical development, creating market opportunities and the mediation of production, consumption and resource flows. This is critical because it shapes the geographies of new connections within and beyond the UK.

## Low carbon transition and everyday life?

What these dominant state responses illustrate is the disconnection between low carbon transitions and everyday life. In the case of offshore wind and new grid connections there are relatively little changes envisaged in patterns and rhythms of the everyday. With the exception of those directly impacted by the amenity impact of infrastructure developments this is largely about the maintenance of business as usual rather than transformation. In the case of electric vehicles and retrofit, state responses largely frame the issue of the everyday as a consumer issue (see CBI, 2011). Within this view consumers are seen as central agents of change, as consumers of low carbon products but who require 'reliable and consistent information about the consequences of their choices and much wider access …to low-carbon products and services' (ibid., p. 4). The view here is that changing consumer behaviours provides the basis for emissions reductions and for further innovation in low carbon products and technologies that makes the achievement of emissions reduction an economic benefit thus creating a 'win-win' situation for governments and business. In this view it is the 'green economy' that will be both a product of and contribution to emissions reductions. The mechanism for achieving behavioural change is the market or, more accurately, the creation of markets and decarbonisation through consumer choice.

Yet publics may not just be viewed as consumers to be constructed within market frameworks but also as citizens and employees involved in current and future forms of consumption that are not mediated through market frameworks. This implies a transformation in governing beyond seeing publics as consumers within market frameworks to engaging with other and 'alternative' views to shape and inform public engagement with low carbon futures. This means thinking about the 'problem' of and 'response' to climate change and decarbonisation in much broader terms than through efforts to construct 'green' consumers and to rethink and reframe this. As many debates in the social sciences have shown us, decision-making is a socialised activity that often encompasses habits, assumptions and values. There are many other views of the relationship between the environment and society, climate change and society and decarbonisation and society than those implied by market-based individualised responses. The scale of response required to solve the carbon problem frequently set out requires moving beyond market frameworks for individualised choices and the framing of multiple messages of environment, climate change and society that run counter to the dominant view, and that set out views of low carbon societies rather than narrowly constituted low carbon economies.

This means much more sophisticated understandings of behavioural change are required that are inclusive in their constitution, given the scale of transformation required. It also implies more shared visions of these futures that encompass the contextual dynamics of the ways in which people live their everyday lives and where behaviours have effects. This requires forms of behavioural change that are framed not just as about climate change and about decarbonisation but also through questioning relationships between the environment and society, the economy and the environment and the organisation, control and consumption of resources. Going beyond markets to reframe what has been a dominant set of assumptions in Britain and the wider Western world since the 1980s means coordinating different interests, values and views of the nature of the 'problem' and the 'response' in different settings.

## Opening up and re-thinking exclusivity in making low carbonism

The development of low carbon urban and regional infrastructure is dominated by coalitions – or an emergent hegemony – of agents from existing infrastructure systems and national state priorities with limited consideration of place-based priorities. The regulative, normative and cognitive basis of this is one of economic development consistent with a view of national government creating the conditions for cities and regions to remain competitive in the economic race by being entrepreneurial. Yet, the dominant urban or regional view of territorial priorities is one based on fragmented capacity, and thus weak capability, with a disconnection between growth coalitions, including business elites, city and regional authorities, on the one hand, and citizens, on the other.

This exclusivity and the ideology underpinning it provide the basis for the development of a low carbon Britain where the dominant narratives of low carbon futures are ones of green wash and market making – produced through those very same interests institutions and mirrors of them, where the governmentalisation of low carbon prioritises markets and where low carbon fields are not radically reconfigured but dominated by existing economic interests.

The kind of low carbon Britain that is required is fundamentally different from this; it requires the promotion of socially inclusive economic activity that is beneficial to places, that recognises the ecological consequences of carbon-based growth and that views a profound shift in relationships between the economy and ecology as necessary and desirable. In doing this, low carbon Britain requires a fundamentally reconfigured role for socio-technical infrastructure systems in mediating between state and space and economy and ecology.

Dominant articulations of low carbon Britain and the role of the state, cities and regions are likely to be messy and involve fields or configurations of agents that are dynamic over time. One central concern for us here is whether such fields can be radically reconfigured. If not, the likelihood is that low carbon Britain will be made in the image of the neoliberal Britain that has been constructed from the 1970s onwards. This raises the issue about what a reconfigured field would look like that recognises pre-existing power relations and the messiness of attempts to make a low carbon Britain. But that also seeks to rethink the forms of configuration required in a move to integrate public power into the development of low carbon Britain. Such a view seeks to rethink the power relationships between state and sub-national territory and the discourses of competition that they are constituted on. It also requires re-thinking the place-based relationships and capabilities that contribute to the reproduction of such relationships but also provide the possibility for resisting and reconfiguring such relationships.

The constitution and configuration of the fields that articulate low carbon Britain in a way that encapsulates public power would be less exclusive than privatised neoliberal modes of organisation. This would also be more relational in extending views of relationships between the economic and ecological to be less instrumental and more welfarist in the broad sense of the term. Such a symbolic transformation would seek to create radical reconfigurations of fields that are constituted not only by a range of economic, ecological and infrastructure system agents but that are integrated on the basis of a shared understanding that differs significantly from narrow, utilitarian competitiveness.

The constitutive elements of the field we can understand as capacity to act, and their integration into a collective mode of action we can understand as capability to act. Yet capacity and capability are not static and are likely to be constituted dynamically over time. The episodic nature of much market-based economic activity and the constant search for the replicable product have been predicated on the denigration, indeed by-passing, of place-based capabilities and the integration into everyday life of private, consumerist values. The narrow capability that produces this thus results in the marginalisation of broad place-based capability. This narrow capability is not static. Its organisation, frequently in the name of 'innovation', is constantly experimented with to include and exclude but also to define what 'product' is important and how it relates to place without the breadth and richness of place-based knowledge. Thinking about capability and purpose over time means thinking beyond narrowly constituted economic exchange and distribution as valued by GDP.

In this respect, relational carriers and intermediary roles need to be seen as more than instrumental channels of communication that on the surface are used to underpin market epistemologies and to provide the basis for creating more public forms of epistemology. This is necessary as a means of reshaping the nation, its territories and its politics in an image that differs fundamentally from the status quo. In short, this is a call for 'greater democratic control over the production and utilization of the surplus' (Harvey, 2008, p. 37). This requires addressing urban processes, through their hegemonic, multi-level articulations, as 'the urban process is a major channel of surplus use, establishing democratic management over its urban deployment constitutes the right to the city' (ibid., p.37).

## Conclusion

In this chapter we have examined the where, how and involving whom, of the dominant low carbon future currently being made in Britain. We have done this to contribute towards and further stimulate a wider debate about what kind of low carbon Britain is being developed and with what consequences. The brico-lage of material and argument developed in this chapter offers emerging evidence that the rhetoric of transformation to low carbon futures is pervasive – in ambi-tious carbon reduction targets, massive potential markets for low carbon products and services and the challenges of low carbon lifestyles and consumerism. Yet, the vast majority of discussion and action in political and policy terms concerns low carbon economies and technologies to the notable neglect of low carbon societies. The assumed techno-economic benefits of low carbon economies are laid out, celebrated and presented as the dominant 'solutions'. These solutions claim to offer not only 'new', accelerated forms of economic growth but also secure 'clean' resource flows necessary to literally power growth and (so the claim goes) reduce human impact on global ecological change. In short, techno-economic 'low carbon market solutions' underpin and facilitate claims of widespread economic and ecological transformation to society.

The strategies we examined appear to add up to the construction of low carbon Britain as a market opportunity, where the role of the state is to govern the imposition of a low carbon transition through the preparation of sub-national territories for low carbon accumulation, based on a notion of transition largely constituted by political, regulatory and business elites. We believe that it is crit-ical to expose this hidden politics of low carbonism and the new spaces and the eco-technical landscapes of transition that make it as a necessary forerunner to future attempts to develop more inclusive and generative alternatives.

The opportunities and constraints on our lives individually and collectively from now until well into the next century will be shaped by decisions that inform low carbon transition. Evidence clearly indicates that the dominant transition pathway is as an economic strategy designed to provide a context for another wave of growth-orientated development. This is a profoundly conservative and limited approach dressed within a transformational rhetoric of challenging targets, limitless possibility and economic opportunity. Exclusive sets of techno-economic interests are preparing Britain for a narrowly conceived low carbon economic transition. At the same time, low carbon community responses and social experimentation are much less dominant, are marginal, localised and weakly supported, where low carbon communities are seen primarily as being contexts for the creation of consumers for market fixes.

Yet, there is nothing natural about such a state of affairs. It is deeply political. What low carbon futures look like, who shapes the transitions, how they will be achieved in capitalist economies and for whose benefit, will at best have to be negotiated and at worst may be deeply contested. In Britain, 'low carbonism' is being successfully mobilised to promote new forms of 'green' capitalism. Central to this are the emergence and organisation of exclusive coalitions of social interests devising state strategies of response. The dominant low carbon transition that is being constructed is based on techno-economic fetish, objectification and a narrow economic calculus of creating market opportunities for capital. This techno-economic market representation, however, obscures and is reliant on a developing political and institutional edifice that needs to deliver amenable and supportive contexts for the transition. This requires a fundamental role for the state in the creation of territorial economic low carbon competition and a race between cities, regions and communities. Winners are paraded as low carbon exemplars and the losers lack state resources, funding and approval until they become 'more competitive' and follow the lead of exemplary cities, regions and communities through 'adjusting' themselves to the 'low carbon reality'. In this respect, the role of the state is more of an extension of the competition role developed under neoliberal regimes than the redistributive role of a Keynesian state. This is an ideological choice that is being made by state actors and the corporate interests that infuse state institutions. The claims that solutions do or will in the future contribute to radical carbon emissions reductions are made. Yet, rather than engage in the efforts of collective transformation to achieve wide-ranging carbon emissions reductions over decades, the low carbon nation is being constructed as a plethora of market episodes and experiments.

We are interested in how different voices can be brought into what is currently an elite and exclusive debate about low carbon transition. Specifically where the techno-economic logic can be resisted and re-negotiated with opportunities for socio-technical change that is more sensitive to context. At the same time how new issues can be brought into the debate around social justice and equity, issues around ownership and control of technology, questioning the primacy of economic growth and the development of new priorities for indicators of societal progress. These new 'green' strategies of accumulation are driven by ideological choices by national state actors. These strategies create limited room for manoeuvre for those social interests who wish to follow different paths and mobilise other choices. The ambition of a genuinely radical low carbon transition, reducing emissions fundamentally and the type of society, economy and ecology relationships that is required, needs to be based on the development of enlarged socio-technical capability. This means forging generative relationships between policy-makers, citizens, business, NGOs, regulators, utilities, and so on and creating the institutional spaces to do so in relation to the national, regional, city and community scales of transition. Most importantly this provides the possibility for the marketised logic of exclusive capability to be fundamentally challenged not through solely written critique but through generative processes of constituting new dominant practices.

## Notes

1    Scotland hopes to be 'Saudi Arabia' of renewable marine energy. Scottish First Minister Alex Salmond has officially launched the £10 million Saltire Prize challenge to develop a renewable marine technology that could unleash the region's potential. 'Scotland has one quarter of Europe's tidal power potential; the Pentland Firth is our Saudi Arabia of renewable marine energy,' said Salmond. See www.energyefficiencynews.com/i/1668/ (accessed 2 September 2014).
2    The Forewind Consortium is equally owned by SSE Renewables, RWE Npower Renewables, Statoil and Statkraft, Siemens Project Ventures and Mainstream Renewable Power.
3    See www.ofgem.gov.uk/networks/rpix20/consultdocs/Documents1/rec%20glossary.pdf (accessed 2 September 2014).
4    Interview with authors.
5    See www.tfl.gov.uk/corporate/media/newscentre/metro/17319.aspx (accessed 2 September 2014).
6    Interview with authors.
7    See www.decc.gov.uk/en/content/cms/news/pn10_104/pn10_104.aspx (accessed 2 September 2014).
8    See www.communities.gov.uk/news/housing/1859709 (accessed 2 September 2014).
9    Ibid.
10   www.ofgem.gov.uk/Media/PressRel/Documents1/RIIO%20Oct%20Press%20 notice.pdf/ (accessed 2 September 2014).
11   See www.ofgem.gov.uk/Media/PressRel/Documents1/JULY%20RPI%20PRESS %20NOTICE.pdf/ (accessed 2 September 2014).

## Bibliography

BIS/DECC (2009) *Low Carbon Innovation Strategy: A Vision*, London: TSO.
Bulkeley, H. and Betsill, M. (2003) *Cities and Climate Change: Urban Sustainability and Global Environmental Governance*. London: Routledge.

CBI (2011) 'Buying Into It: Making the Consumer Case for Low-Carbon', 28 March, available at www.cbi.org.uk/media/1056778/consumer_report.pdf (accessed 2 September 2014).

Collier, S. (2009) 'Topologies of Power: Foucault's Analysis of Political Government beyond "Governmentality"', *Theory, Culture & Society*, 26(6): 78–108.

DECC (2009) *The UK Low Carbon Transition Plan*. London: TSO.

DECC (2010) *The Green Deal: A Summary of the Government's Proposals*. London:TSO.

Foucault, M. (2007) *Security, Territory, Population: Lectures at the Collège de France, 1977–1978*. Basingstoke: Palgrave Macmillan.

Gamble, A. (2009) *The Spectre at the Feast: Capitalist Crisis and the Politics of Recession*. Basingstoke: Palgrave Macmillan.

Harvey, D. (2008) 'Right to the City', *New Left Review*, vol. 53, Sept/Oct, available at http://newleftreview.org/II/53/david-harvey-the-right-to-the-city (accessed 2 September 2014).

HM Treasury (2008) *Pre-Budget Review 2008*. London: HMSO.

HM Treasury (2009) *Budget 2009*. London: HMSO.

OLEV (2009) *UK Government's Ultra Low Carbon Vehicle Strategy*, Robin Haycock, OLEV. Available at: www.lowemissionstrategies.org/downloads/LES%20Forum%20Meeting/2010%20Feb/04_LEF_Feb_2010_OLEV%20and%20Plugged%20in%20Places%20-%20Robin%20Haycock.pdf (accessed 2 September 2014).

Peck, J. and Tickell, A. (2002) 'Neoliberalising Space', *Antipode*, 34: 380–404.

Turner, R. (2008) *Neo-Liberal Ideology: History, Concepts and Policies*. Edinburgh: Edinburgh University Press.

While, A. (2008) 'Climate Change and Planning: Carbon Control and Spatial Regulation', *Town Planning Review*, 79(1): vii–xiii.

# Index